D1616268

NOVEMBER 22, 1963

A Reference Guide to the
JFK Assassination

Foreword by
Cyril H. Wecht

William E. Scott

University Press of America,® Inc.
Lanham • New York • Oxford

Copyright © 1999 by
University Press of America,® Inc.
4720 Boston Way
Lanham, Maryland 20706

12 Hid's Copse Rd.
Cumnor Hill, Oxford OX2 9JJ

Library of Congress Cataloging-in-Publication Data

Scott, William E. (William Edward)
November 22, 1963 : a reference guide to the JFK assassination /
William E. Scott ; foreword by Cyril H. Wecht.
p.   cm.
Includes index.
1. Kennedy, John F. (John Fitzgerald), 1917-1963—Assassination—
Dictionaries. 2. Kennedy, John F. (John Fitzgerald), 1917-1963—
Assassination—Bibliography. I. Title.
E842.9.S37 1999   364.15'24'0*92—dc21   98-54261 CIP

ISBN 0-7618-1336-5 (cloth: alk. ppr.)

For

Beverly Hadwal
*My Strength * My Inspiration * My Friend*
1927-1998

and

Reverend J. Vincent Taggart, S.J.
*Priest * Teacher * Friend*
1934-1996

Contents

Acknowledgements ix

Foreword xi

Part I: People and Places 1

Part II: Selected Bibliography 1963-1998 75

    1.   Lee Harvey Oswald And "Related" Subjects 77
    2.   Jack Ruby 99
    3.   The Warren Report 109
    4.   The Warren Commission: For And Against 111
    5.   The Evidence 136
    6.   Conspiracy Theories 153
    7.   Jim Garrison And The Clay Shaw Trial 165
    8.   House Select Committee on Assassinations 1976-1979 ... 177
    9.   Hollywood And The JFK Assassination 183
   10.   The JFK Assassination Records Collection Act 193
   11.   Eyewitness Accounts: November 22-24, 1963 196
   12.   Remembering JFK 199
   13.   Fiction Associated With The JFK Assassination 213
   14.   Reference Books 223
   15.   Dissertations and Theses 227
   16.   Audiovisuals 229
   17.   TV News Segments 1968-1997 241
   18.   Journals, Newsletters, And Quarterlies 261

Index 264

ACKNOWLEDGEMENTS

There are many dedicated and gifted people who assisted me in compiling and organizing the material in this book. First and foremost, I would like to thank my wife, Diane for her patience, understanding, and for teaching me how to use our computer. Her assistance was necessary and invaluable.

I am deeply grateful for the expert help provided by several fine librarians and interns including Adrianne Billingham and William Johnson at the John F. Kennedy Library; Rick Stringer at Penn State University; Barbara Addison, Wendy Chmielewski, and Anne Yoder at Swarthmore College; Aslaku Berhanu and Rosa Grier at Temple University; Elena Balashova at the University of California, Berkeley; Susan Williamson at the University of Pennsylvania; and Mary Cornelius, Michael Foight, and Bente Polites at Villanova University.

Thanks also to the exceptional staff at the Philadelphia Free Library for tolerating my many questions and requests. I am particularly indebted to James Dewalt, Gene Esposito, Linda Franchini, Harry Maurer, Walt Stock, and Joseph Wilson.

I was most fortunate to have my manuscript read by Tom Belzer, a loyal friend and colleague at St. Joseph's Prep, Dave Lovett from The President's Box Bookshop, and Andy Winiarczyk from The Last Hurrah Bookshop. Their constructive criticism added significantly to the development of this book.

To Dr. Cyril Wecht, a respected and long-time critic of the Warren Commission and its findings, my thanks for believing in this project and for writing the foreword.

Finally, there are many academics, colleagues, friends, and relatives who have supported and inspired my efforts over the years. They include: Professor James Burgwyn, Betty Carboy, Professor Louis Casciato, Charlotte Clarkson, Larry Czudak, Professor Albert Dorley, Jr., Tom Fitzpatrick, Steve Ghicondes, Professor Thomas Heston, Professor Donald Kelley, Kendall Mattern, Dolores McPoyle, Professor Ben Peters, John Regan, Dan Scott, Professor Richard Webster, Alice Welsh, and most notably, Jerry Taylor. My thanks to you all.

- William E. Scott

FOREWORD

Over the past 35 years since the assassination of President John F. Kennedy on Friday, November 22, 1963, dozens of books and thousands of articles have been written by a variety of critic-researchers who have challenged the Warren Commission Report's conclusion that Lee Harvey Oswald was the sole assassin and that not one other individual had any direct input either in the planning or execution of this tragic murder. Not all the critics agree on what really happened, and consequently, there has developed a great deal of confusion in the minds of many people regarding the most likely scenario.

As with any other complex event of a highly controversial and extremely important historic nature, it is essential that thorough, meticulous research be done in order to ascertain the truth to the fullest extent possible. Such a detailed and organized compilation of background information, from which current and future researchers and academic scholars can draw conclusions in valid fashion, has been sorely lacking in the JFK assassination

William E. Scott, an American history and government teacher at St. Joseph's Preparatory School in Philadelphia, Pennsylvania, has now compiled a excellent compendium- *November 22, 1963: A Reference Guide to the JFK Assassination*- which takes us from the beginning of the saga to the present time, including biographical entries of the major people, places, and events and a selected bibliography covering the period 1963-1998. This compilation also includes publications that have attempted to buttress and support the Warren Commission Report, and therefore, it is fair and objective, as well as thorough and complete.

Mr. Scott, who holds an M.A. in history from Villanova University and who has won several prestigious awards relating to his academic endeavors, has done an outstanding job of organizing the vast amount of assassination literature.

As a research tool for present and future generations of Americans who wish to study the JFK assassination, this reference guide is an absolute must. It is with much pleasure and great enthusiasm that I recommend this reference guide to every serious scholar from high school to post-doctoral levels who are interested in studying the JFK assassination. It should be in all our personal libraries. Indeed, given the passage of 35 years, and the huge number of commentaries that have been presented during this time, it would be impossible for any serious writer and researcher to address this important subject without having knowledge of the research and investigative activities performed by hundreds of other individuals since 1963.

- Cyril H. Wecht, M.D., J.D.

Part I:
People and Places

A

ABRAMS, GUS: Identified in Dallas Police files as one of the Dealey Plaza tramps.

ABT, JOHN J.: New York attorney; Warren Commission witness; Oswald tried to secure his legal services following his arrest.

"ACROBAT": Code name for Andrews Air Force Base.

ADAMCIK, JOHN: Homicide detective, Dallas Police; Warren Commission witness; interrogated Oswald co-worker, Buell Wesley Frazier.

ADAMS, FRANCIS W. H.: New York attorney; police commissioner, New York City (1954-55); senior counsel, Warren Commission; assigned to Area I: The Basic Facts of the Assassination.

ADAMS, VICTORIA: Assassination witness; employee, Scott-Foresman Company; watched JFK's motorcade from the fourth floor of the Texas School Book Depository; told Warren Commission counsel David Belin that the shots came from below and to the right of her position.

AGUILAR, GARY: Professor of ophthalmology, Stanford University; acknowledged authority on JFK medical evidence; board member, Coalition on Political Assassinations and Citizen's for Truth About the Kennedy Assassination.

AIR FORCE ONE: A specially equipped Boeing 707, it transported JFK to and from Dallas on November 22, 1963.

AKIN, GENE C.: Anesthesiologist, Parkland Hospital; Warren Commission witness; member of the medical team that attended President Kennedy; saw what appeared to be an exit wound on the right side of JFK's head.

3

ALCOCK, JAMES: New Orleans prosecutor; with Alvin Oser and Andrew Sciambia, Alcock represented the state of Louisiana in the Clay Shaw trial.

ALCORN, DAVID S.: Washington attorney; assassination researcher; board member, Assassination Archives and Research Center and Coalition on Political Assassinations.

ALEMAN, JOSE: Wealthly Cuban exile; FBI informant; allegedly told by Santos Trafficante that JFK would be killed; died in 1983.

ALEXANDER, WILLIAM F.: Dallas assistant district attorney; prosecuted Jack Ruby for the murder of Lee Harvey Oswald.

ALLEN, WILLIAM: Assassination witness; *Dallas Times Herald* photographer; famous for photographing the Dealey Plaza tramps; photos have appeared in several books including *Coup d' Etat in America* (1975, 1992) and *On The Trail of the Assassins* (1988, 1991).

ALTGENS, JAMES: Assassination witness; photographer, Associated Press; Warren Commission witness; said JFK appeared to be hit from behind.

ANDERSON, JACK: Washington reporter; claimed in the 1970's that JFK was killed in retaliation for CIA plots against Castro.

ANDREWS AIR FORCE BASE: A U. S. air base located southeast of Washington, D. C. President Kennedy's body was flown to Andrews from Dallas on the evening of November 22, 1963.

ANDREWS, DEAN: New Orleans attorney; Warren Commission witness; allegedly sought by Clay Bertrand (Clay Shaw) to represent Oswald; testified at Shaw's trial; indicted for perjury and convicted.

"ANGEL": Code name for Air Force One.

ANSON, ROBERT SAM: Freelance journalist; former public television producer; published assassination articles for such magazines as *New Times* and *Esquire*; author of " *'They've Killed The President!'* " (1975).

ARCE, DANNY: Assassination witness; employee, Texas School Book Depository; Warren Commission witness; said three shots were fired from the vicinity of the railroad yard.

ASCHKENASY, ERNEST: Acoustics expert; with Mark Weiss, analyzed the Dallas Police dictabelt for the House Assassinations Committee; concluded a fourth shot was possible.

ASSASSINATION ARCHIVES AND RESEARCH CENTER: Founded in 1984 by Bernard Fensterwald, Jr. and James Lesar, the AARC maintains an extensive collection of written and audiovisual materials on the John and Robert Kennedy and Martin Luther King assassinations, organized crime figures and U. S. intelligence activities.

ASSASSINATION INFORMATION BUREAU: Commonly known as the AIB, it was established in 1974 in Cambridge, Massachusetts by activists Bob Katz, Carl Oglesby, David Williams, and Harvey Yazijian. Among its many activities, the AIB sponsored assassination seminars and conferences and monitored the work of the House Assassinations Committee. The group disbanded in 1979.

ASSASSINATION RECORDS REVIEW BOARD: A five-member body established by the President John F. Kennedy Records Collection Act of 1992. It was responsible for overseeing the release of Warren and Rockefeller Commission, Church Committee, and House Assassinations Committee documents. It was also given the authority to hold public hearings, as well as subpoena witnesses.

ATKINS, THOMAS: Assassination witness; White House photographer; motorcade passenger; rode in camera car 1, six cars behind JFK's limousine; thought the shots came from ground level.

B

"BABUSHKA LADY": (See Oliver, Beverly).

BADEN, MICHAEL M.: Former New York City medical examiner; currently director of the New York State Police Forensic Sciences Unit; chaired House Assassinations Committee's medical panel; author of *Unnatural Death: Confessions of a Medical Examiner* (1989).

"BADGEMAN": Captured on film by Mary Moorman and Orville Nix, "Badgeman" is the human-like form that can be seen from the chest-up behind the north pergola wall atop the grassy knoll. So named because he appears to be dressed as a police officer, "Badgeman" was suspected by assassination critics of being the second gunman until photographic analysis determined that the image was nothing more than an illusion.

BAKER, MARRION L.: Assassination witness; motorcycle officer, Dallas Police; Warren Commission witness; with Roy Truly, confronted Oswald in the Texas School Book Depository's second floor lunchroom 90 seconds after the assassination.

BAKER, T. L.: Motorcycle officer, Dallas Police; assigned to the motorcade.

BALL, JOSEPH A.: California trial lawyer; senior counsel, Warren Commission; assigned to Area II: The Identity of the Assassin.

BANISTER, GUY W.: Ex-FBI agent; anti-Castro activist; linked to Oswald, David Ferrie, and Clay Shaw; died in 1964.

BARGER, JAMES: Scientist, Bolt, Beranek and Newman; acoustics expert; analyzed Dallas Police dictabelt for House Assassinations Committee.

BARNUM, GEORGE A.: Yeoman, U. S. Coast Guard; escorted JFK's body from Andrews Air Force Base to Bethesda Naval Hospital; served as a casket bearer at the funeral.

BARRETT, BOB: FBI agent; was present at the time of Oswald's arrest.

BARSON, PHILIP: Supervisor, Internal Revenue Service; member, Warren Commission staff.

BASHOUR, FOUAD A.: Professor of cardiology, Parkland Hospital; Warren Commission witness; one of several doctors who worked on JFK; noticed a large defect in the right occipital-parietal region of the President's head.

BASKIN, BOB: Washington bureau chief, *Dallas Morning News*; motorcade passenger; rode in the press pool car, five cars behind JFK's limousine.

BATCHELOR, CHARLES: Assistant chief, Dallas Police; coordinated security for JFK's motorcade.

BATES, JOHN: Firearms examiner, New York State Police Academy; member, ballistics panel, House Select Committee on Assassinations.

BAXTER, CHARLES R.: Surgeon, Parkland Hospital; Warren Commission witness; assisted Drs. Malcolm Perry and Robert McClelland with JFK's tracheotomy.

BEERS, IRA J.: Photographer, *Dallas Morning News*; photographed Jack Ruby shooting Oswald.

BEESON, PETER G.: Assistant deputy chief counsel for the House Select Committee on Assassinations.

BEHN, GERALD: U. S. Secret Service agent; chief of the White House detail; did not accompany the President to Texas.

BELIN, DAVID: Iowa trial lawyer; junior counsel, Warren Commission; assigned to Area II: The Identity of the Assassin; vocal supporter of the Commission and its findings; author of *November 22, 1963: You Are The Jury* (1973) and *Final Disclosure* (1988).

BELL, AUDREY: Nurse, Parkland Hospital; one of the first to see JFK in Trauma Room One; observed a large defect in the right rear portion of his head.

BELL, JACK: Reporter, Associated Press; motorcade passenger; rode in the press pool car, five cars behind JFK's limousine.

BELLAH, S.: Motorcycle officer, Dallas Police; rode in front of the presidential limousine.

BELLI, MELVIN M.: Famed criminal attorney; defended Jack Ruby; author of *Dallas Justice* (1964); died in 1996.

BENAVIDES, DOMINIGO: Tippit murder witness; auto mechanic; Warren Commission witness; told police that he could not identify the assailant.

BENNETT, GLEN A.: Assassination witness; U. S. Secret Service agent; rode in the right rear seat of the presidential follow-up car; saw JFK hit in the right shoulder.

BENTLEY, PAUL: Chief polygraph examiner, Dallas Police; involved in Oswald's arrest.

BERGER, ANDREW: U. S. Secret Service agent; drove the ambulance carrying JFK's body from Parkland Hospital to Love Field.

BERTRAND, CLAY: Possible pseudonym for Clay Shaw.

BETHESDA NAVAL HOSPITAL: Located outside of Washington, D. C., it was the site of President Kennedy's autopsy. Initially, White House officials discussed the possibility of having the President's remains examined at Walter Reed Army Medical Center, but Jacqueline Kennedy decided that the post-mortem should be conducted at Bethesda because her husband had served in the U. S. Navy during World War II.

BETZNER, HUGH: Assassination witness; employee, Railway Express; photographed the motorcade from the corner of Houston and Elm Streets; said the first shot sounded like a firecracker.

BILLINGS, RICHARD N.: Former magazine editor; congressional staffer; editorial director, House Select Committee on Assassinations; chief architect of its final report; co-author, with G. Robert Blakey, of *The Plot To Kill the President* (1981); re-titled *Fatal Hour: The Assassination of President Kennedy by Organized Crime* (1992); links organized crime to the assassination.

BIRD, SAMUEL R.: Lieutenant, U. S. Army; escorted JFK's body from Andrews Air Force Base to Bethesda Naval Hospital; served as a casket bearer at the funeral.

BISHOP, JIM: Columnist and magazine editor; author of *The Day Kennedy Was Shot* (1968), an hour by hour account of the assassination and its aftermath.

"BISHOP, MAURICE": Possible pseudonym for CIA officer David Phillips.

"BLACK DOG MAN": Photographed by Phil Willis, "Black Dog Man" is the figure standing behind the concrete wall on the north side of Elm Street. So named because his shadowy form resembles a dog resting on its haunches, "Black Dog Man" has never been identified.

BLAKEY, G. ROBERT: Former U. S. Justice Department attorney; later law professor, Cornell and Notre Dame Universities; chief counsel and staff director, House Select Committee on Assassinations (1977-79); co-author, with Richard N. Billings, of *The Plot to Kill the President* (1981); re-titled *Fatal Hour: The Assassination of President Kennedy by Organized Crime* (1992).

BOGGS, HALE: U. S. representative (D-LA); majority whip (1962-71); majority leader (1971-72); member, Warren Commission (1963-64); expressed misgivings for having signed the final report; died in 1972.

BOOKHOUT, JAMES: FBI agent; interrogated Oswald following his arrest.

BOONE, EUGENE: Dallas County deputy sheriff; Warren Commission witness; one of three officers who found the assassination weapon on the sixth floor of the Texas School Book Depository.

BORING, FLOYD: U. S. Secret Service agent; assistant chief of the White House detail; helped plan security for the Texas trip.

BOSWELL, J. THORNTON: Commander, U. S. Navy; chief pathologist, Bethesda Naval Medical Center; member, JFK autopsy team; Warren Commission witness.

BOWERS, LEE JR.: Assassination witness; employee Union Terminal Company; observed two men standing near the stockade fence on the grassy knoll at the time of the shooting; allegedly received death threats after testifying before the Warren Commission; died in 1966.

BOWRON, DIANA H.: Nurse, Parkland Hospital; Warren Commission witness; helped wheel JFK into Trauma Room One; told Harrison Livingstone that Kennedy had an enormous exit wound in the back of his head.

BREHM, CHARLES: Assassination witness; stood on the southside of Elm Street; said part of the President's head flew back and to the left; died in 1996.

BRENNAN, HOWARD L.: Assassination witness; Warren Commission witness; steamfitter; said that Oswald was at the sixth floor window of the Book Depository; later failed to identify him at police headquarters.

BREWER, E. D.: Motorcycle officer, Dallas Police; Warren Commission witness; assigned to the motorcade.

BREWER, JOHNNY: Manager, Hardy's Shoe Store; Warren Commission witness; followed Oswald to the Texas Theater; told cashier Julia Postal to contact police.

BRINGUIER, CARLOS: Cuban exile; political activist; Warren Commission witness; debated Oswald on a New Orleans radio show some three months before the assassination; author of *Red Friday: November 22, 1963* (1969).

BRONSON, CHARLES: Assassination witness; chief engineer, Varel Manufacturing Co.; amateur photographer; filmed Dealey Plaza moments before the assassination; said the first shot sounded like a firecracker.

BROWN, JOE B.: Dallas judge; presided at Jack Ruby's trial; died in 1966.

BROWN, MADELEINE: Alleged mistress of Lyndon Johnson; claimed that Johnson knew of JFK assassination plot.

BROWN, WALT: Professor, Ramapo College; assassination researcher; board member, Coalition on Political Assassinations; co-editor of *Dateline: Dallas*, a quarterly newsletter; author of several books including *The People v. Lee Harvey Oswald* (1992) and *Referenced Index Guide To The Warren Commission* (1995).

BUCHANAN, COKE: Former editor, *Dateline: Dallas;* co-author, with Beverly Oliver, of *Nightmare in Dallas* (1994).

BUCHANAN, THOMAS G.: Journalist; author of *Who Killed Kennedy?* (1964); suggests that a right-wing conspiracy, led by a Texas oilman named "Mr. X," murdered JFK.

BUNDY, VERNON: Convicted drug addict; prosecution witness at Clay Shaw's trial.

BURKE, YVONNE B.: U. S. representative (D-CA); member, House Select Committee on Assassinations; served on JFK subcommittee.

BURKLEY, GEORGE: Admiral, U. S. Navy; JFK's personal physician; rode with Evelyn Lincoln near the back of the motorcade; represented Kennedy family at Bethesda autopsy.

BURLESON, PHIL: Defense counsel for Jack Ruby.

BURROUGHS, HENRY: Photographer, Associated Press; motorcade passenger; rode in camera car 2, seven cars behind JFK's limousine.

BURROUGHS, WARREN: Employee, Texas Theater; told the Warren Commission that he did not see Oswald enter the theater; said that after his arrest, Oswald accused police of violating his civil rights.

C

CABELL, EARLE: Assassination witness; Dallas mayor; Warren Commission witness; rode in an open convertible, four cars behind JFK's limousine; testified that the shots came from the vicinity of the Texas School Book Depository; died in 1974.

CAMPBELL, JUDITH: (See Exner, Judith Campbell).

CANADA, ROBERT O.: Captain, U. S. Navy; commanding officer, Bethesda Naval Hospital; attended JFK's autopsy.

CANCELLARE, FRANK: Photographer, United Press International; rode in camera car 2, seven cars behind JFK's limousine.

CANFIELD, MICHAEL: Editor and publisher; co-author, with Alan J. Weberman, of *Coup d' Etat in America: The CIA and the Assassination of John F. Kennedy* (1975, 1992); alleges that Oswald was working for U. S. intelligence at the time of the assassination.

CARNES, WILLIAM H.: Professor of pathology, University of Utah; member, Clark Panel.

CAROUSEL CLUB: Jack Ruby's burlesque club.

CARR, WAGGONER: Attorney general of Texas; Warren Commission witness; alleged Oswald to have been an FBI informant.

CARRICO, CHARLES J.: Resident, Parkland Hospital; Warren Commission witness; first physician to examine JFK; observed a massive hole in the right rear portion of his head.

CARROLL, BOB K.: Detective, Dallas Police; Warren Commission witness; disarmed Oswald in the Texas Theater; later escorted Oswald to police headquarters.

CARTER, B. THOMAS: FBI agent; with Special Agent John Fain, interviewed Oswald following his return from Russia in June 1962.

CARTER, CLIFF: Political adviser to Lyndon Johnson; motorcade passenger; rode in the vice presidential follow-up car.

"CASTLE": Code name for the White House.

CASTRO, FIDEL: Communist revolutionary; Cuban president; target of CIA-Mafia assassination plots in the 1960s; suspected of involvement in JFK's murder.

CHAMPAGNE, DONALD E.: Firearms examiner, Florida Department of Law Enforcement; member, ballistics panel, House Select Committee on Assassinations.

CHANEY, JAMES M.: Assassination witness; motorcycle officer, Dallas Police; rode on the right side of the presidential limousine; died in 1976.

CHEEK, TIMOTHY: Lance corporal, U. S. Marines; escorted JFK's body from Andrew's Air Force Base to Bethesda Naval Hospital; served as a casket bearer at the funeral.

CHERAMIE, ROSE: Drug addict; prostitute; allegedly had knowledge of JFK assassination plot; killed in a hit-and-run accident in 1965.

CHETTA, NICHOLAS: Coroner, New Orleans Parish; performed autopsy on David Ferrie; testifed at Clay Shaw's trial; died in 1968.

CHURCH COMMITTEE: Formed in 1976 and chaired by Senator Frank Church (D-ID), the committee uncovered evidence of CIA-Mafia assassination plots against Fidel Castro.

CIRELLO, JOSEPH: (See Civello, Joseph).

CITIZEN'S COMMISSION OF INQUIRY: A Washington-based interest group founded in 1975 by attorney and author Mark Lane, it lobbied Congress for a reinvestigation of the JFK assassination.

CITIZENS FOR TRUTH ABOUT THE KENNEDY ASSASSINA-TION: CTKA was founded in 1993 by author and researcher James DiEugenio as a political action group. Its goal is to obtain, through lobbying, the release of all documents relevant to JFK's death.

CIVELLO, JOSEPH (aka JOSEPH CIRELLO): Dallas crime figure; allegedly served as a liaison between Jack Ruby and New Orleans mobster Carlos Marcello.

CLARK, BOB: Reporter, ABC News; motorcade passenger; rode in the press pool car, five cars behind JFK's limousine.

CLARK, HUBERT: Seaman, U. S. Navy; escorted JFK's body from Andrew's Air Force Base to Bethesda Naval Hospital; served as a casket bearer at the funeral.

CLARK PANEL: Appointed in 1968 by U. S. Attorney General Ramsey Clark to review the autopsy evidence, this four-member forensic panel upheld the Warren Commission's conclusion that JFK was struck by two bullets fired from behind and above.

CLARK, WILLIAM K.: Chief of neurosurgery, Southwestern Medical School; Warren Commission witness; pronounced President Kennedy dead at 1pm on November 22, 1963; told reporters that JFK suffered a massive wound in the posterior region of the head.

CLEMMONS, ACQUILLA: Tippit murder witness; claimed that two men were involved in the shooting.

CLIFTON, CHESTER: Major general, U.S. Army; JFK's military aide; rode with Brigadier General Godfrey McHugh near the back of the motorcade.

COALITION ON POLITICAL ASSASSINATIONS: Founded on the 30th anniversary of the JFK assassination. This public interest group, which consists of professional investigators, academicians, medicolegal experts, and concerned citizens, seeks, through scholarly research, lobbying, and public discussion, to resolve the many questions surrounding the deaths of President John F. Kennedy, Senator Robert Kennedy, and Martin Luther King, Jr.

COE, JOHN I.: Medical examiner, Hennepin County, Minnesota; member, medical panel, House Select Committee on Assassinations.

COLEMAN, WILLIAM T.: Philadelphia attorney; senior counsel, Warren Commission; assigned to Area IV: Possible Conspiratorial Relationships.

COMMISSION EXHIBIT 399: (See "Magic Bullet").

CONNALLY, IDANELL "NELLIE": Assassination witness; wife of Governor John Connally; Warren Commission witness; sat to the left of her husband in the presidential limousine; believes that he and Kennedy were hit by separate bullets.

CONNALLY, JOHN: Assassination witness; Texas governor; Warren Commission witness; seriously wounded while riding in Dallas motorcade; supported lone-assassin conclusion, but rejected "Magic-Bullet" theory; author of *In History's Shadow* (1993); died in 1993.

CONROY, EDWARD A.: Internal Revenue Service agent; member, Warren Commission staff.

CONZELMAN, JAMES: Staff investigator, House Select Committee on Assassinations.

COOPER, JOHN SHERMAN: U. S. senator (R-KY); member, Warren Commission (1963-64); objected to Commission's conclusion that President Kennedy and Governor Connally were hit by the same bullet; died in 1991.

CORNWELL, GARY.: U. S. Justice Department attorney; replaced Robert Tannenbaum as deputy chief counsel for the House Select Committee on Assassinations; coordinated JFK investigation task force.

COSTNER, KEVIN: Academy Award-winning director; actor; portrayed District Attorney Jim Garrison in Oliver Stone's *JFK* (1991).

COUCH, MALCOLM: Assassination witness; cameraman, WFAA-TV; Warren Commission witness; motorcade passenenger; rode in camera car 3, eight cars behind JFK's limousine; saw what appeared to be a rifle barrel protruding from the alleged sniper's nest on the sixth floor of the Texas School Book Depository.

COURSON, J. W.: Motorcycle officer, Dallas Police; assigned to the motorcade.

CRAIG, ROGER: Dallas County deputy sheriff; Warren Commission witness; one of three officers who found the assassination weapon; prosecution witness at Clay Shaw's trial; committed suicide in 1975.

CRAVEN, THOMAS J.: Cameraman, CBS News; motorcade passenger; rode in camera car 1, six cars behind JFK's limousine.

CRENSHAW, CHARLES A.: Resident, Parkland Hospital; one of 12 physicians who treated JFK; co-author, with Jens Hansen and J. Gary Shaw, of *JFK: Conspiracy of Silence* (1992).

CRONKITE, WALTER: Anchorman, CBS News; first to report the assassination on network television; narrator, *CBS News Inquiry: The Warren Commission Report* (1967) and *NOVA: Who Shot President Kennedy* (1988).

CUNNINGHAM, ELMO L.: Lieutenant, Dallas Police; one of several officers present at the time of Oswald's arrest.

CURRY, JESSE: Assassination witness; Dallas Police chief; Warren Commission witness; drove the lead car; author of *JFK Assassination File* (1969); died in 1980.

CURTIS, DON T.: Intern, Parkland Hospital; Warren Commission witness; assisted Dr. Charles Carrico with JFK's endotracheal tube; did not see any of JFK's wounds.

CUSHING, RICHARD CARDINAL: Archbishop of Boston; conducted JFK's funeral Mass at St. Matthew's Cathedral in Washington, D. C.

CUSTER, JERROL F.: Medical technician, Bethesda Naval Hospital; took the post-mortem x-rays of President Kennedy; said that JFK's head wound indicated a shot from the front.

CUTLER, R. B.: Architect; assassination researcher; founder, *Grassy Knoll Gazette*; author of *The Flight of CE 399* (1969), *Seventy-Six Seconds in Dallas* (1978), and many other books on the assassination.

D

"DAGGER": Code name for Secret Service Agent Rufus Young-blood.

DALE, BOBBY JOE: Motorcycle officer, Dallas Police; assigned to the motorcade.

DALLAS TRADE MART: A wholesale trade center, the Trade Mart was JFK's last scheduled stop before leaving Dallas.

"DANDY": Code name for Secret Service Agent Thomas Johns.

"DARK COMPLECTED MAN": The name given to the unidentified African or Hispanic male who was standing next to the "Umbrella Man" on Elm Street.

DARNELL, JIMMY: Cameraman, WBAP-TV; motorcade passenger; rode in camera car 3, eight cars behind JFK's limousine.

"DASHER": Code name for Secret Service Agent Thomas Wells.

DAVID, DENNIS: Member, Medical Service Corps., Bethesda Naval Hospital; claimed that JFK's body arrived at Bethesda in a decoy ambulance.

DAVIS, JOHN H.: Former U. S. naval officer; author of such books as *Mafia Kingfish* (1988, 1989) and *The Kennedy Contract* (1993); theorizes that underworld chieftains Carlos Marcello and Santos Traffi-cante ordered the assassination of JFK.

DAVIS, JOSEPH H.: Medical examiner, Dade County, Florida; member, medical panel, House Select Committee on Assassinations.

DAVISON, JEAN: Freelance journalist; author of *Oswald's Game* (1983), a psychological study of the accused assassin.

DAY, CARL: Lieutenant, Dallas Police Identification Bureau; Warren Commission witness; collected evidence at the assassination scene; first to examine Oswald's rifle.

"DAYLIGHT": Code name for Secret Service Agent Jerry Kivett.

"DAZZLE": Code name for Secret Service Agent Clint Hill.

"DEACON": Code name for Secret Service Agent Floyd Boring.

DEALEY PLAZA: The site of President Kennedy's assassination, Dealey Plaza is located west of downtown Dallas and was named for George Bannerman Dealey, a prominent Texas businessman and founder of the *Dallas Morning News*. In 1993 it was officially designated as the Dealey Plaza National Historic Landmark District.

DEALEY PLAZA TRAMPS: Gus Abrams, Harold Doyle, and John Gedney were tramps found in a railroad car behind the grassy knoll approximately one hour after the assassination. Taken into police custody, they were charged with vagrancy and released a few days later. Both the Dallas Police and FBI concluded that the men were not involved in the President's murder.

DEAN, RUTH: Assassination witness; bookkeeper, MacMillan Publishing Company; claimed the first shot sounded like a firecracker.

"DEBUT": Code name for Secret Service Agent Paul Landis.

DECKER, BILL: Assassination witness; Dallas County sheriff; Warren Commission witness; rode in the lead car; died in 1970.

DELGADO, NELSON: U. S. Marine; Warren Commission witness; served with Oswald at El Toro Air Station in California; remembers Oswald as a Castro-supporter.

DEL VALLE, ELADIO: Leader of the Free Cuba Movement; alleged associate of Mafia boss Santos Trafficante and assassination suspect David Ferrie; found murdered in a Miami parking lot on the same day Ferrie died, February 22, 1967.

DEMARIS, OVID: Co-author, with Garry Wills, of *Jack Ruby* (1968, 1994); was standing next to Ruby when he shot and killed Oswald.

DEMOHRENSCHILDT, GEORGE: Russian emigre with CIA connections; Warren Commission witness; cultivated relationship with Oswald; committed suicide in 1977.

DEVINE, SAMUEL L.: U. S. representative (R-OH); member, House Select Committee on Assassinations; served on JFK subcommittee.

DiEUGENIO, JAMES: Assassination researcher; founder, Citizens for Truth About the Kennedy Assassination; board member, Coalition on Political Assassinations; author of *Destiny Betrayed: JFK, Cuba, and the Garrison Case* (1992).

"DIGEST": Code name for Secret Service Agent Roy Kellerman.

DILLARD, THOMAS C.: Photographer, *Dallas Morning News*; Warren Commission witness; motorcade passenger; rode in camera car 3, eight cars behind JFK's limousine.

DODD, CHRISTOPHER: U. S. representative (D-CT); member, House Select Committee on Assassinations.

"DOMINO": Code name for Secret Service Chief James Rowley.

DONAHUE, HOWARD C.: Firearms examiner; assassination researcher; subject of Bonar Menninger's bestseller, *Mortal Error: The Shot That Killed JFK* (1992).

DOWNING, THOMAS N.: U. S. representative (D-VA); chairman, House Select Committee on Assassinations (1976); replaced by Representative Henry Gonzalez (D-TX) (1977).

DOX, IDA: Medical illustrator; sketched JFK autopsy photos for House Assassinations Committee.

DOYLE, HAROLD: Identified in Dallas Police files as one of the Dealey Plaza tramps.

"DRESSER": Code name for Secret Service Agent Robert Foster.

"DRUMMER": Code name for Secret Service Agent Lynn Meredith.

DUFFY, JAMES: New York attorney; author of *Who Killed JFK?* (1989); challenges the theory that Oswald was a loner.

DUKE, JAMES: Surgeon, Parkland Hospital; later director of Emergency Services, University of Texas Medical School; operated on Governor Connally.

DULANEY, RICHARD B.: Physician, Parkland Hospital; Warren Commission witness; attended Governor Connally in Trauma Room Two.

DULLES, ALLEN: Director, Central Intelligence Agency (1953-61); member, Warren Commission (1963-64); withheld information from Commission regarding CIA-Mafia plots against Fidel Castro; died in 1969.

"DUPLEX": Code name for Secret Service Agent Gerald Behn.

"DUSTY": Code name for Secret Service Agent Emory Roberts.

E

EBERSOLE, JOHN H.: Commander, U. S. Navy; radiologist, Bethesda Naval Hospital; x-rayed JFK's remains.

EDDOWES, MICHAEL: British lawyer; author of *The Oswald File* (1977, 1978); concluded after a 14-year investigation that the Soviets sent an Oswald look-a-like to kill Kennedy.

EDGAR, ROBERT W.: U. S. representative (D-PA); member, House Select Committee on Assassinations.

EISENBERG, MELVIN A.: New York attorney; junior counsel, Warren Commission.

ELLIS, STARVIS: Motorcycle officer, Dallas Police; assigned to the motorcade.

ELY, JOHN H.: Supreme Court clerk; member, Warren Commission staff; researched Oswald's background.

EPSTEIN, EDWARD JAY: Assassination researcher; author of three books on the JFK case: *Inquest* (1966), *Counterplot* (1969), and *Legend* (1978).

EVICA, GEORGE M.: Professor emeritus, University of Hartford; director, JFK Assassination Task Force; author of *And We Are All Mortal: New Evidence and Analysis in the Assassination of John F. Kennedy* (1978).

EWELL, JIM: Reporter, *Dallas Morning News*; present at the time of Oswald's arrest.

EWING, MICHAEL: Staff member, House Assassinations Committee; co-author, with Bernard Fensterwald, Jr., of *Coincidence or Conspiracy?* (1977).

EXNER, JUDITH CAMPBELL: Romantically linked to JFK and Chicago mobster Sam Giancana, assassination suspect.

F

FAIN, JOHN: FBI agent; with Special Agent B. Thomas Carter, interviewed Oswald following his return from Russia in June 1962.

FAIR PLAY FOR CUBA COMMITTEE: In May of 1963, Lee Harvey Oswald opened a New Orleans branch of the Fair Play for Cuba Committee, a pro-Castro organization. The chapter's sole member, Oswald distributed leaflets, debated anti-Castro supporters on talk radio and was arrested for street fighting. Some investigators suspect the FPCC provided cover for Oswald's work as an FBI informant.

FAULKNER, JACK: Dallas County deputy sheriff; was present when Oswald's rifle was discovered on the sixth floor of the Book Depository.

FAUNTROY, WALTER E.: (D-DC); member, House Select Committee on Assassinations.

FELDER, JAMES L.: Sergeant, U. S. Army; escorted JFK's body from Andrew's Air Force Base to Bethesda Naval Hospital; served as a casket bearer at the funeral.

FENSTERWALD, BERNARD, JR.: Washington attorney and Warren Commission critic; executive director, Committee to Investigate Assassinations; co-founder, Assassination Archives and Research Center; co-author, with Michael Ewing, of *Coincidence or Conspiracy?* (1977); died in 1991.

FENTON, CLIFF: Homicide detective, New York City Police; chief investigator, House Select Committee on Assassinations.

FERRELL, MARY M.: JFK researcher; member, executive committee of the Citizen's Commission of Inquiry; technical consultant on such films and documentaries as *The Trial of Lee Harvey Oswald* (1976) and *The Killing of President Kennedy* (1978).

FERRIE, DAVID W.: Former airline pilot; right-wing extremist; JFK murder suspect; involved with organized crime and the anti-Castro movement; alleged acquaintance of Oswald; died in 1967.

FINCK, PIERRE A.: Lieutenant colonel, U. S. Army; chief of the Wound Ballistics Pathology Branch of the Armed Forces Institute of Pathology; member, JFK autopsy team; Warren Commission witness; testified at Clay Shaw's trial.

FISHER, RUSSELL: Maryland medical examiner; member, Clark Panel

FITHIAN, FLOYD J.: U. S. representative (D-IN); member, House Select Committee on Assassinations.

FLAMMONDE, PARIS: Author of *The Kennedy Conspiracy: An Uncommissioned Report on the Jim Garrison Investigation* (1969).

FONZI, GAETON: Investigative reporter; network news consultant; staff investigator, Schweiker Committee (1975-76) and House Select Committee on Assassinations (1977-78); author of *The Last Investigation* (1993, 1994).

FORD, GERALD R.: U. S. representative (R-MI); later 38th president of the United States; member, Warren Commission (1963-64); ardent supporter of the lone-assassin theory; co-author, with John R. Stiles, of *Portrait of the Assassin* (1965, 1966).

FORD, HAROLD E.: U. S. representative (D-TN); member, House Select Committee on Assassinations.

FOREMAN, PERCY: Houston attorney; defended both Jack Ruby and James Earl Ray, the convicted killer of Martin Luther King, Jr.

FOSTER, ROBERT: U. S. Secret Service agent; assigned to the Caroline and John F. Kennedy, Jr. security detail.

FOX, SYLVAN: Pulitzer Prize-winning journalist; assassination critic; author of *The Unanswered Questions About President Kennedy's Assassination* (1965, 1966); one of the earliest studies of the Warren Report.

FRAZIER, BUELL WESLEY: Assassination witness; Warren Commission witness; neighbor of Ruth Paine; drove Oswald to the Texas School Book Depository on November 22, 1963; said Oswald was carrying a package which supposedly contained curtain rods.

FRAZIER, ROBERT A.: FBI ballistics expert; test fired Oswald's rifle for the Warren Commission.

FREEMAN, H. D.: Motorcycle officer, Dallas Police; assigned to the motorcade.

FRITZ, WILL: Captain, Dallas Police; chief, Homicide and Robbery Bureau; Warren Commission witness; headed JFK murder probe.

FURIATI, CLAUDIA: Brazilian journalist and filmmaker; author of *ZR Rifle: The Plot to Kill Kennedy and Castro* (1994); asserts that the CIA was behind the assassination.

G

GALLOWAY, CALVIN: Admiral, U. S. Navy; commanding officer, National Naval Medical Center; attended JFK post-mortem.

GARRICK, J. B.: Motorcycle officer, Dallas Police; rode in front of the presidential limousine.

GARRISON, JIM: New Orleans district attorney; later circuit court judge; prosecuted Clay Shaw for conspiracy in the murder of President Kennedy; author of *Heritage of Stone* (1970, 1972) and *On The Trail of the Assassins* (1988, 1991); technical consultant to Oliver Stone's *JFK* (1991); died in 1992.

GAUDREAU, RICHARD E.: Sergeant, U. S. Air Force; escorted JFK's body from Andrew's Air Force Base to Bethesda Naval Hospital; served as a casket bearer at the funeral.

GEARHART, IRA D.: Warrant officer, U. S. Army; carried brief case containing nuclear codes; rode in the Signal Corps car near the rear of the motorcade.

GEDNEY, JOHN: Identified in Dallas Police files as one of the Dealey Plaza tramps.

GIANCANA, SAM: Chicago crime boss; coordinated plots against Castro; JFK murder suspect; killed in 1975.

GIESCEKE, ADOLPH H.: Assistant professor of anesthesiology, Southwestern Medical School; Warren Commission witness; involved in the treatment of both JFK and Governor Connally.

GOLDBERG, ALFRED: U. S. Air Force historian; later an administrator with the Office of the Secretary of Defense; staff member, Warren Commission; helped draft the final assassination report; author of *Conspiracy Interpretations of the Assassination of President Kennedy: International and Domestic* (1968).

GONZALEZ, HENRY B.: U.S. representative (D-TX); motorcade passenger; outspoken chairman of the House Assassinations Committee; replaced by Representative Louis Stokes (D-OH) (1977).

GRANT, DAVID B.: U. S. Secret Service agent; assigned to the Dallas Trade Mart.

GRANT, DONALD C.: Photographer, *Dallas Morning News*; motorcade passenger; rode in camera car 2, seven cars behind JFK's limousine.

GRASSY KNOLL: A hilly section of land located west of the Texas School Book Depository (currently the Dallas County Administration Building). Atop the hill is a pergola, colonade, and slightly west of the pergola is a picket fence. It is in this area that some assassination critics believe that a second gunman fired at President Kennedy's motorcade. To date, there is no hard evidence to substantiate their claims.

GRAVES, A. C.: Detective, Dallas Police; Warren Commission witness; was guarding Oswald when he was shot; died in 1995.

GRAY, L. E.: Motorcycle officer, Dallas Police; assigned to the motorcade.

GREER, WILLIAM R.: Assassination witness; U. S. Secret Service agent; Warren Commission witness; drove the presidential limousine.

GREGORY, CHARLES F.: Orthopedic surgeon, Parkland Hospital; treated Governor Connally's wrist wound; questioned the feasibility of the "Magic Bullet" theory; died in 1976.

GRIFFIN, BURT W.: Assistant U. S. attorney; later common pleas court judge; junior counsel, Warren Commission; assigned to Area V: Oswald's Death.

GRODEN, ROBERT J.: Assassination researcher; foremost authority on the photographic evidence in the JFK assassination; testified before the Rockefeller Commission (1975) and Church Committee (1975); served as consultant to the House Assassinations Committee (1976-78); author of dozens of articles and books including *The Killing of a President* (1993) and *The Search for Lee Harvey Oswald* (1995).

GUINYARD, SAM: Tippit murder witness; Warren Commission witness; identified Oswald as the killer.

GUTH, DELLOYD J.: Co-author, with David R. Wrone, of *The Assassination of John F. Kennedy: A Comprehensive Historical and Legal Bibliography, 1963-1979* (1980).

H

HAGGERTY, EDWARD A.: New Orleans judge; presided at Clay Shaw's trial; died in 1990.

"HALFBACK": Code name for the Secret Service follow-up car, a 1956 Cadillac touring sedan. "Halfback" followed JFK's limousine.

HALL, C. RAY: FBI agent; interrogated Jack Ruby following Oswald's murder.

HALL, KERMIT L.: Dean, University of Tulsa; member, Assassination Records Review Board.

HARDIN, MICHAEL: Dallas ambulance driver; transported the wounded Oswald from Dallas Police headquarters to Parkland Hospital.

HARGIS, BOBBY: Assassination witness; motorcycle officer, Dallas Police; Warren Commission witness; rode on the left side of the presidential limousine; struck by JFK's blood and brain tissue.

HARKNESS, D. V.: Assassination witness; Dallas Police officer; Warren Commission witness; encountered Secret Service impostors behind the Texas School Book Depository.

HARPER BONE FRAGMENT: (See Harper, William).

HARPER, WILLIAM "BILLY": College student; discovered skull fragment in Dealey Plaza the day after the assassination; thought to be JFK's.

HARRELSON, CHARLES: Convicted murderer; father of television and motion picture actor Woody Harrelson; claimed to have participated in the assassination; later denied any involvement.

HARRIS, LARRY R.: Assassination researcher; recognized expert on the J. D. Tippit murder; former archives and research director, JFK Assassination Information Center; co-author, with J. Gary Shaw, of *Cover-Up* (1976, 1992).

HARTOGS, RENATUS: New York psychiatrist; Warren Commission witness; examined Oswald in 1953; characterized him as introverted; co-author, with Lucy Freeman, of *The Two Assassins* (1965, 1976).

HAWKINS, RAY: Dallas Police officer; involved in Oswald's arrest.

HAYGOOD, CLYDE: Motorcycle officer, Dallas Police; Warren Commission witness; assigned to the motorcade.

HELMS, RICHARD: Deputy director for plans, CIA (1962-65); director (1966-73); liaison between the CIA and the Warren Commission.

HEMMING, GERRY P.: U. S. Marine; later soldier of fortune; stationed at Atsugi Air Base in Japan before Oswald; believes Oswald was working for U. S. intelligence in the 1950's.

HENCHLIFFE, MARGARET M.: Parkland Hospital nurse; Warren Commission witness; attended JFK in Trauma Room One; saw a massive wound in the occipital area of the President's head and what appeared to be an entrance wound in his throat.

HENDRIX, RUTH: Assassination witness; bookkeeper, Allyn and Bacon Publishers; said that three shots were fired at JFK's motorcade.

HICKEY, GEORGE: Assassination witness; U. S. Secret Service agent; rode in the left rear seat of the presidential follow-up car; accused in Bonar Menninger's book, *Mortal Error* (1992), of accidentally firing the fatal shot at JFK.

HIDELL, ALEK J.: Alias used by Lee Harvey Oswald.

HILL, CLINT: Assassination witness; U. S. Secret Service agent; Warren Commission witness; rode on the left front running board of the presidential follow-up car; shielded JFK and First Lady; received U. S. Treasury Department's Exceptional Service Award for heroism.

HILL, GERALD L.: Sergeant, Dallas Police; Warren Commission witness; one of three officers who discovered the sixth floor sniper's nest; involved in Oswald's arrest.

HILL, JEAN: Dallas school teacher; witnessed assassination from the south side of Elm Street; claimed that a gunman fired from behind the fence on the grassy knoll; technical consultant on the film *JFK* (1991).

HINCKLE, WARREN: Founder of *Ramparts*; co-author, with William W. Turner, of *The Fish Is Red: The Story of the Secret War Against Castro* (1981); re-titled *Deadly Secrets: The CIA-Mafia War Against Castro and the Assassination of JFK* (1992).

HOCH, PAUL L.: Assassination researcher; recognized expert on Lee Harvey Oswald and the U. S. intelligence community; co-editor of *The Assassinations: Dallas and Beyond: A Guide to Cover-ups and Investigations* (1976).

HOEFEN, JOHN: Sound technician, NBC News; motorcade passenger; rode in camera car 1, six cars behind JFK's limousine.

HOFFA, JAMES R.: Teamster president; associated with organized crime figures; JFK murder suspect; disappeared on July 30, 1975; presumed dead.

HOFFMAN, ED: Witnessed the assassination from Stemmons Freeway; reportedly saw a sniper behind the wooden fence atop the grassy knoll; co-author, with Ron Friedrich, of *Eyewitness* (1995, 1996, 1997).

HOLLAND, S. M.: Employee, Union Terminal Company; Warren Commission witness; watched the assassination from atop the triple underpass; reportedly saw a puff of smoke rising above the stockade fence on the grassy knoll.

HOLMES, HARRY D.: U. S. postal inspector; Warren Commission witness; interrogated Oswald shortly before he was murdered by Jack Ruby; died in 1989.

HOLT, CHAUNCIE: Ex-convict; claimed to be one of the Dealey Plaza tramps; allegedly knew both Oswald and Ruby.

HOOVER, J. EDGAR: FBI director (1924-72); Warren Commission witness; arch-enemy of John and Robert Kennedy; criticized for his handling of the JFK murder probe; died in 1972.

HOSTY, JAMES P.: FBI agent; Warren Commission witness; investigated Oswald prior to the assassination; one of the first to question him after his arrest; author of *Assignment Oswald* (1996).

HOUSE SELECT COMMITTEE ON ASSASSINATIONS: Established by House Resolution 1540 on September 17, 1976 to investigate and report on the assassinations of President John F. Kennedy and Martin Luther King, Jr. Chaired by Representative Louis Stokes (D-OH), the eleven-member committee concluded that JFK's death was in all probability the result of a conspiracy. The Committee did not, however, determine the identity of those who may have been involved.

HOWARD, LARRY: Founder, JFK Assassination Information Center; technical consultant on the film *JFK* (1991); died in 1994.

HOWARD, TOM: Jack Ruby's first attorney; later replaced by Melvin Belli.

HUBER, OSCAR: Roman Catholic priest; administered last rites to President Kennedy; observed a large wound over JFK's left eye; died in 1975.

HUBERT, LEON D.: New Orleans attorney; senior counsel, Warren Commission; assigned to Area V: Oswald's Death.

HUGHES, ROBERT: Assassination witness; customs examiner, U. S. Treasury Department; filmed the motorcade from the corner of Houston and Elm Streets; said the gunfire sounded like firecrackers.

HUGHES, SARAH T.: Federal district judge; administered presidential oath to Lyndon Johnson aboard Air Force One; died in 1985.

HUMES, JAMES J.: Commander, U. S. Navy; director of laboratories, Bethesda Naval Medical Center; performed JFK autopsy; Warren Commission witness.

HUNT, E. HOWARD: CIA officer; spy novelist; Watergate burglar; mistakenly identified by assassination critics as one of the Dealey Plaza tramps.

HUNT, JACKIE H.: Anesthesiologist, Parkland Hospital; Warren Commission witness; assisted Dr. Marion Jenkins with JFK's endotracheal tube.

HURT, HENRY: Investigative reporter; author of *Reasonable Doubt: An Investigation into the Assassination of John F. Kennedy* (1986), a pro-conspiracy study.

HUTSON, T. A.: Dallas Police officer; involved in Oswald's arrest.

HUTTON, PATRICIA: Nurse, Parkland Hospital; helped move JFK into Trauma Room One; secured the plastic mattress cover used to line his casket.

I

IVON, LOU: New Orleans Police officer; future Louisiana legislator; served on Jim Garrison's assassination staff; responsible for investigating David Ferrie.

J

JACKS, HURCHEL: Assassination witness; Texas state trooper; drove LBJ's limousine; guarded JFK's limousine at Parkland Hospital.

JACKSON, DOUGLAS L.: Assassination witness; motorcycle officer, Dallas Police; rode on the right side of the presidential limousine.

JACKSON, ROBERT H.: Photographer, *Dallas Times Herald*; Warren Commission witness; motorcade passenger; rode in camera car 3, eight cars behind JFK's limousine; took Pulitzer Prize-winning photo of Jack Ruby shooting Oswald.

JARMAN, JAMES: Witnessed the assassination from the fifth floor of the Texas School Book Depository; testified that the shots came from below, not from the alleged sniper's nest on the sixth floor.

JAWORSKI, LEON: Warren Commission counsel; later Watergate special prosecutor; concluded that Oswald never worked for the CIA or FBI.

JENKINS, JAMES: Laboratory assistant, Bethesda Naval Hospital; prepared JFK's remains for post-mortem examination.

JENKINS, MARION T.: Anesthesiologist, Parkland Hospital; Warren Commission witness; attended both President Kennedy and Lee Harvey Oswald; one of four doctors invited by PBS to review JFK autopsy photos; died in 1993.

JENNER, ALBERT E.: Chicago attorney; senior counsel, Warren Commission; assigned to Area III: Oswald's Background.

JFK: (See Stone, Oliver).

JOESTEN, JOACHIM: German journalist; first to blame JFK's death on a right-wing conspiracy; author of a dozen books on the assassination including *Oswald: Assassin or Fall Guy?* (1964), *Marina Oswald* (1967), and *The Garrison Enquiry: Truth & Consequences* (1967); died in 1976.

JOHNS, THOMAS L.: Assassination witness; U. S. Secret Service agent; rode in the right rear seat of the vice presidential follow-up car.

JOHNSEN, RICHARD E.: U. S. Secret Service agent; assigned to the Dallas Trade Mart.

JOHNSON, CLEMON EARL: Assassination witness; employee, Union Terminal Railroad; said the first shot sounded like a firecracker.

JOHNSON, LYNDON B.: U. S. vice president at the time of the assassination; later 36th president of the United States; passenger in the Dallas motorcade; created Warren Commission (1963); suspected foreign involvement in JFK's death; died in 1973.

JOHNSTON, DAVID L.: Justice of the peace; Warren Commission witness; arraigned Oswald for the murders of Officer J. D. Tippit and President Kennedy.

JONES, PENN, JR.: Texas newspaper editor; early critic of the Warren Report; first researcher to chronicle the deaths of people linked to the assassination; author of *Forgive My Grief I-IV* (1966, 1967, 1969, 1978); died in 1998.

JONES, RONALD C.: Resident, Parkland Hospital and later chief of surgery, Baylor Medical Center; Warren Commission witness; one of several physicians attending JFK in Trauma Room One.

JOYCE, WILLIAM: Librarian, Princeton University; member, Assassination Records Review Board.

JUDGE, JOHN: The driving force behind the Coalition on Political Assassinations, Judge has researched and written on the murders of John and Robert Kennedy, Martin Luther King, Jr., and Malcolm X. He is a founding member of the Committee for an Open Archives.

K

KANTOR, SETH: Washington correspondent; Warren Commission witness; traveled with JFK` to Texas; encountered Jack Ruby at Parkland Hospital some 30 minutes after the President died; author of *Who Was Jack Ruby?* (1978); died in 1993.

KATZ, BOB: Free-lance writer; co-founder and co-director, Assassination Information Bureau; former member of the National Committee to Investigate Assassinations; wrote articles on political violence for the *Boston Phoenix, Harper's Weekly,* and *Real Paper.*

KELLERMAN, ROY: Assassination witness; U. S. Secret Service agent; rode in the right front passenger's seat of the presidential limousine; told the Warren Commission that the President had a large wound on the right rear side of his head; died in 1984.

KENNEDY, JACQUELINE BOUVIER: Assassination witness; First Lady; Warren Commission witness; sat to the left of her husband in the presidential limousine; remembered for her dignity and courage during JFK's funeral; died in 1994.

KENNEDY, JOHN F.: 35th president of the United States; assassinated in Dallas, Texas while riding in an open limousine, November 22, 1963.

KENNEDY, ROBERT F.: Brother of JFK; U. S. attorney general at the time of the assassination; murdered in 1968.

KENNEY, EDWARD: Surgeon general of the Navy; attended JFK's autopsy.

KHRUSHCHEV, NIKITA: Soviet Premier (1958-64); accused by author Michael Eddowes of ordering JFK's assassination; died in 1971.

KILDUFF, MALCOLM: Assassination witness; assistant White House press secretary; motorcade passenger; rode in the press pool car, five cars behind JFK's limousine; announced President's death at Parkland Hospital news conference.

KILGALLEN, DORTHY: Syndicated columnist; television personality; covered Jack Ruby's murder trial; died in 1965, the victim of an apparent suicide.

KINNEY, SAMUEL: Assassination witness; U. S. Secret Service agent; drove the presidential follow-up car.

KIRKWOOD, JAMES: Pulitzer Prize-winning author; wrote *American Grotesque* (1970, 1992), a comprehensive account of the Garrison-Shaw trial; died in 1989.

KIVETT, JERRY D.: Assassination witness; U. S. Secret Service agent; rode in the right front seat of the vice presidential follow-up car; later escorted Johnson from Parkland Hospital to Love Field; arranged Secret Service protection for Johnson's daughters.

KLEIN, KENNETH D.: Assistant deputy chief counsel, House Select Committee on Assassinations.

KURTZ, MICHAEL: History professor, Southeastern Louisiana University; author of *Crime of the Century* (1982, 1983, 1988, 1992, 1996), the first scholarly analysis of the JFK assassination.

L

"LACE": Code name for First Lady Jacqueline Kennedy.

"LANCER": Code name for President John F. Kennedy.

LANDIS, PAUL E.: Assassination witness; U. S. Secret Service agent; rode on the right rear running board of the presidential follow-up car.

LANE, MARK: Attorney; lecturer; filmmaker; Warren Commission critic; Warren Commission witness; Director, Citizen's Commission of Inquiry; author of *Rush To Judgement* (1966, 1967, 1975, 1992), *Citizen's Dissent* (1968, 1969), and *Plausible Denial* (1991).

"LARK": Code name for John F. Kennedy, Jr.

LATTIMER, JOHN K.: Professor emeritus, Columbia University; first non-government physician to examine JFK autopsy materials; author of *Kennedy and Lincoln: Medical and Ballistic Comparisons of Their Assassinations* (1980) and numerous articles.

LAULICHT, MURRAY J.: New York attorney; member, Warren Commission staff.

LAWRENCE, PERDUE W.: Captain, Dallas Police; Warren Commission witness; drove the advance car, the first vehicle in the motorcade.

LAWSON, WINSTON G.: Assassination witness; U. S. Secret Service agent; Warren Commission witness; coordinated security for the Dallas trip; rode in the lead car with Police Chief Jesse Curry, Sheriff Bill Decker, and fellow agent Forrest Sorrels; reported hearing three shots.

LEAVELLE, JAMES R.: Homicide detective, Dallas Police; Warren Commission witness; was handcuffed to Oswald when he was shot.

LEE, O. H.: Alias used by Lee Harvey Oswald.

LESAR, JAMES H.: Washington attorney; used Freedom of Information Act to obtain documents on JFK and Martin Luther King, Jr. murders; co-founder, Assassination Archives and Research Center; board member, Coalition on Political Assassinations.

LEWIS, DAVID F.: Private investigator; claimed to have seen Oswald in the company of David Ferrie and anti-Castro Cubans prior to the assassination.

LEWIS, L. J.: Tippit murder witness; employee, Reynolds Motor Company; could not identify Oswald as the killer.

LEWIS, RON: Drifter; known fugitive; allegedly worked with Oswald and Guy Bannister; claims that Oswald knew of assassination plot against JFK; author of *Flashback: The Untold Story of Lee Harvey Oswald* (1993).

LEWIS, ROY E.: Assassination witness, employee, Texas School Book Depository; remembers hearing three shots.

LIEBELER, WESLEY J.: New York attorney; later law professor, UCLA; junior counsel, Warren Commission; assigned to Area III: Oswald's Background.

LIFTON, DAVID: Assassination researcher; author of the highly controversial *Best Evidence* (1981, 1988, 1992); asserts that a group of conspirators performed pre-autopsy surgery on the body of President Kennedy somewhere between Dallas and Bethesda.

LINCOLN, EVELYN: JFK's personal secretary (1953-63); rode with Admiral George Burkley near the back of the motorcade; author of *My Twelve Years with John F. Kennedy* (1965, 1966); died in 1995.

LIVINGSTONE, HARRISON EDWARD: Novelist; assassination researcher; co-author, with Robert Groden, of *High Treason* (1989, 1998) and author of *High Treason 2* (1992) and *Killing The Truth* (1993); maintains that JFK autopsy materials were forged.

LIVINGSTON, R. W.: Detective, Dallas Police Crime Lab; present during Oswald's arraignment; helped fingerprint and photograph Oswald's remains; subject of Gary Savage's book, *JFK: First Day Evidence* (1993).

LOPEZ, EDWIN: Cornell law student; researcher; co-authored a report for the House Assassinations Committee entitled, *Lee Harvey Oswald, the CIA and Mexico City*; concluded that someone posing as Oswald visited the Cuban and Soviet embassies in Mexico City in September 1963.

LOQUVAM, GEORGE S.: Director, Institute of Forensic Sciences; member, medical panel, House Select Committee on Assassinations.

LOVE FIELD: Located northwest of downtown Dallas, it was the municipal airport where President Kennedy's plane landed on the morning of November 22, 1963.

LOVELADY, WILLIAM NOLAN: Assassination witness; employee, Texas School Book Depository; Warren Commission witness; Oswald look-a-like; said that shots were fired from the grassy knoll; died in 1979.

LUMPKIN, GEORGE L.: Deputy chief, Dallas Police; drove the pilot car, the second vehicle in the motorcade.

LUMPKIN, W. G.: Motorcycle officer, Dallas Police; assigned to the motorcade.

LUTZ, MONTY C.: Firearms examiner, Wisconsin Regional Crime Laboratory; member, ballistics panel, House Select Committee on Assassinations.

"LYRIC": Code name for Caroline Kennedy.

M

MACK, GARY: Assassination researcher; archivist, Sixth Floor Museum; historical consultant for such documentaries as *The Men Who Killed Kennedy* (1988) and *The JFK Assassination: The Jim Garrison Tapes* (1992).

MacNEIL, ROBERT: White House correspondent and later co-host, *MacNeil-Lehrer Report*; motorcade passenger; author of *The Right Place at the Right Time* (1982) and *The Way We Were: 1963, The Year Kennedy Was Shot* (1988).

"MAGIC BULLET": Fired from Oswald's rifle; allegedly inflicted seven separate wounds in JFK and Governor Connally; discovered on Parkland Hospital gurney; also known as Commission Exhibit 399.

MAILER, NORMAN: Pulitzer Prize-winning writer; director; author of *Oswald's Tale: An American Mystery* (1995, 1996).

MANCHESTER, WILLIAM: Acclaimed author of *The Death of a President* (1967, 1985, 1988); an engaging history of the JFK assassination.

MANNLICHER-CARCANO RIFLE: A bolt-action, clip-fed weapon, the Mannlicher-Carcano was manufactured in Italy from 1891-1941. Considered by most gun experts to be cheap and unreliable, it was sarcastically referred to as the "humanitarian weapon" during World War II. A model 31/98 6.5mm Carcano with a four-power telescopic sight was discovered on the sixth floor of the Texas School Book Depository shortly after the assassination. A subsequent check revealed that the Carcano had been mail ordered from Klein's Sporting Goods Co. in Chicago by A. Hidell, an alias used by Lee Harvey Oswald.

MARCELLO, CARLOS: New Orleans crime boss; deported to Guatemala by U. S. Justice Department (1961); associated with Guy Banister and David Ferrie; JFK murder suspect; died in 1993.

MARCHETTI, VICTOR: CIA officer; assistant to Deputy Director Richard Helms; identified Clay Shaw as a CIA operative; co-author, with John Marks, of *The CIA and the Cult of Intelligence* (1974).

"MARKET": Code name for Rear Admiral George Burkley.

MARKHAM, HELEN LOUISE: Tippit murder witness; waitress; Warren Commission witness; failed to identify Oswald in the police lineup.

MARMOR, ARTHUR K.: U. S. Air Force historian; member, Warren Commission staff.

MARRS, JIM: Award-winning journalist; board member, Coalition on Political Assassinations; author of *Crossfire: The Plot That Killed Kennedy* (1989, 1990).

MARTIN, B. J.: Assassination witness; motorcycle officer, Dallas Police; Warren Commission witness; rode on the left side of the presidential limousine.

MARTIN, JACK S.: Private investigator; associate of Guy Banister; implicated Banister and David Ferrie in assassination plot.

MAYFIELD, DOUGLAS: Specialist 4th class, U. S. Army; escorted JFK's body from Andrew's Air Force Base to Bethesda Naval Hospital; served as a casket bearer at the funeral.

McBRIDE, G. C.: Motorcycle officer, Dallas Police; rode in front of the presidential limousine.

McCLAIN, H. B.: Motorcycle officer, Dallas Police; assigned to the motorcade.

McCLELLAND, ROBERT N.: Parkland Hospital surgeon; Warren Commission witness; assisted with JFK's tracheotomy.

McCLOY, JOHN J.: Assistant Secretary of War (1941-45); High Commissioner of Germany (1949- 52); chairman, Chase Manhattan Bank (1953-60); member, Warren Commission (1963-64); supported "Magic Bullet" theory; died in 1989.

McDONALD, HUGH C.: Former U. S. Army intelligence officer; author of *Appointment in Dallas* (1975, 1992), a *New York Times* best-seller about his eight-year search for a second gunman.

McDONALD, M. N.: Patrolman, Dallas Police; apprehended Oswald in the Texas Theater.

McHUGH, GODFREY: Brigadier general, U. S. Air Force; JFK's military aide; rode with Major General Chester Clifton near the back of the motorcade.

McINTYRE, WILLIAM T.: Assassination witness; U. S. Secret Service agent; rode on the left rear running board of the presidential follow-up car; heard three shots as the motorcade travelled down Elm Street; never called before the Warren Commission.

McKINNEY, STEWART B.: U. S. representative (D-CT); member, House Select Committee on Assassinations.

McMILLAN, PRISCILLA JOHNSON: Newspaper correspondent; interviewed Oswald in the Soviet Union; author of *Marina & Lee* (1977); technical advisor, PBS documentary, *Who Was Lee Harvey Oswald?* (1992).

McWATTERS, CECIL J.: Dallas bus driver; Warren Commission witness; picked-up Oswald in the vicinity of Dealey Plaza some ten minutes after the assassination; told police that Oswald got off the bus after a couple of blocks.

McWILLIE, LEWIS: Nightclub manager; gambler; friend of Jack Ruby; linked to Trafficante crime family.

MEAGHER, SYLVIA: "Grand Dame" of JFK investigators; author of many notable assassination books and articles, among them *Subject Index to the Warren Report and Hearings and Exhibits* (1966, 1971) and *Accessories After the Fact: The Warren Commission, the Authorities and the Report* (1967, 1976, 1992).

MELANSON, PHILIP H.: Assassination researcher; director, Robert F. Kennedy Assassination Archives, University of Massachusetts, Dartmouth; board member, Coalition on Political Assassinations; author of *Spy Saga: Lee Harvey Oswald and U. S. Intelligence* (1990).

MENNINGER, BONAR: Award-winning reporter; author of *Mortal Error: The Shot That Killed JFK* (1992); examines the findings of ballistics expert Howard Donahue who concluded that the fatal headshot was accidentally fired by Secret Service Agent George Hickey.

MERCER, JULIA ANN: Pre-assassination witness; observed a man with a guncase on the grassy knoll the morning of November 22, 1963; never appeared before the Warren Commission.

MEREDITH, LYNN: U. S. Secret Service agent; assigned to the Caroline and John F. Kennedy, Jr. security detail.

MIDGETT, WILLIAM: Physician, Parkland Hospital; first doctor to see JFK following the assassination.

MILTEER, JOSEPH A.: Right-wing extremist; involved with the Ku Klux Klan and other hate groups; predicted JFK's assassination, November 1963; died in 1974.

MONTGOMERY, LESLIE D.: Homicide detective, Dallas Police; Warren Commission witness; was standing directly behind Oswald when he was shot.

MOORE, JIM: Consultant, Dallas County Historical Foundation's Sixth Floor project; author of *Conspiracy of One: The Definitive Book on the Kennedy Assassination* (1992).

MOORE, T. E.: Assassination witness; employee, Texas School Book Depository; said that three shots were fired; died in 1994.

MOORMAN, MARY: Assassination witness; filmed the motorcade from the south side of Elm Street; said the gunfire sounded like firecrackers.

MORGAN, RUSSELL: Professor of radiology, John Hopkins University; member, Clark Panel.

MORIARTY, JACK: Former homicide investigator, Washington, D. C. Police; staff member, House Select Committee on Assassinations.

MORROW, ROBERT D.: Former CIA operative; author of *First Hand Knowledge* (1992); claims involvement in CIA-Mafia plot to kill Kennedy.

MORTIZ, ALAN: Professor of pathology, Case Western Reserve University; member, Clark Panel.

MOSK, RICHARD M.: California attorney; member, Warren Commission staff.

MUCHMORE, MARIA: Assassination witness; employee, Justin McCarthy Manufacturing Company; filmed the motorcade from the landscaped area between Houston and Elm Streets; said the first shot sounded like a firecracker.

MURRET, CHARLES "DUTZ": Lee Harvey Oswald's uncle; New Orleans gambler; Warren Commission witness; linked to Carlos Marcello's crime empire.

MURRET, LILLIAN: Lee Harvey Oswald's aunt; Warren Commission witness.

N

NAGELL, RICHARD CASE: Admitted CIA employee; claimed knowledge of JFK assassination plot; subject of Dick Russell's book, *The Man Who Knew Too Much* (1993).

THE NATIONAL COMMISSION ON THE CAUSES AND PREVENTION OF VIOLENCE: This 13-member panel was established in 1968 to study and report on the growing problem of violence in American society. As part of its mandate, the Commission examined the disturbingly high level of political violence in the 1960's, including the assassinations of Medgar Evers, John Kennedy, and Martin Luther King, Jr.

NECHIPORENKO, OLEG MAXIMOVICH: KGB agent; allegedly met with Oswald in September 1963 in the Soviet embassy in Mexico City; author of *Passport To Assassination: The Never-Before-Told Story of Lee Harvey Oswald By The KGB Colonel Who Knew Him* (1993).

NELSON, ANNA KASTEN: History professor, American University; member, Assassination Records Review Board.

NELSON, DORIS MAE: Nurse, Parkland Hospital; Warren Commission witness; screened medical personnel attending President Kennedy.

NEWMAN, ALBERT H.: Former editor, *The Reporter*; correspondent, *Newsweek*; author of *The Assassination of John F. Kennedy: The Reasons Why* (1970); supports the basic conclusions of the Warren Commission.

NEWMAN, JOHN: Honors professor, University of Maryland, College Park; former U. S. Army officer; member, Coalition on Political Assassinations; author of *Oswald and the CIA* (1995).

NEWMAN, WILLIAM J., and GAYLE: Witnessed the assassination from the northside of Dealey Plaza; claimed that the fatal shot came from the grassy knoll.

NEWQUIST, ANDREW M.: Special agent, Iowa Bureau of Criminal Investigation; member, ballistics panel, House Select Committee on Assassinations.

NIX, ORVILLE O.: Assassination witness; air conditioning repairman; filmed assassination from the south infield between Houston and Main Streets; footage shows the fatal head shot, Secret Service Agent Clint Hill running for the presidential limousine, and the "Badgeman" figure behind the concrete wall atop the grassy knoll.

NORMAN, HAROLD: Witnessed the assassination from the fifth floor of the Texas School Book Depository; told the FBI that during the shooting, he heard shell casings striking the floor above him.

NORTH, MARK: Lawyer; assassination researcher; author of *Act of Treason* (1991); concludes that J. Edgar Hoover concealed evidence of a conspiracy.

NOSENKO, YURI: Soviet intelligence officer; defected to the United States in 1964; says Oswald was not working for the KGB when he assassinated JFK.

O

O'BRIEN, JOHN J.: Internal Revenue Service agent; member, Warren Commission staff.

O'BRIEN, LARRY: Assassination witness; JFK special advisor; Warren Commission witness; later served as chairman of the Democratic National Committee; motorcade passenger; died in 1990.

O'CONNOR, PAUL: Laboratory assistant, Bethesda Naval Hospital; prepared JFK's remains for the post-mortem examination.

ODIO, SYLVIA: Cuban exile; political activist; Warren Commission witness; visited by three strangers in September 1963 who sought funding for anti-Castro activities; later identified one of the men as Oswald.

O'DONNELL, KEN: Presidential assistant; witnessed assassination from the Secret Service follow-up car; co-author, with Dave Powers, of *Johnny We Hardly Knew Ye* (1970); died in 1977.

OGLESBY, CARL: Political activist; co-founder, Assassination Information Bureau; author of *The JFK Assassination: The Facts and the Theories* (1992) and *Who Killed Kennedy?* (1992).

O'LEARY, JOHN J.: U. S. Secret Service agent; attended JFK's autopsy.

OLIVER, BEVERLY: Nightclub performer; assassination witness (Babushka Lady?); alleged acquaintance of Jack Ruby and David Ferrie; technical consultant on the film *JFK* (1991); co-author, with Coke Buchanan, of *Nightmare in Dallas* (1994).

ONEAL, VERNON B.: Dallas funeral director; supplied the Britannia casket that was used to transport JFK's remains from Parkland Hospital to Bethesda Naval Hospital.

O'NEILL, FRANCIS X.: FBI agent; attended Bethesda post-mortem with Agent James Sibert; reported that pre-autopsy surgery had been performed on JFK; later said he was mistaken.

OSER, ALVIN: New Orleans prosecutor; cross-examined JFK autopsist Pierre Finck at Clay Shaw's trial.

OSWALD, JUNE: Oldest daughter of Marina and Lee Oswald.

OSWALD, LEE HARVEY: 24 year old employee, Texas School Book Depository; accused of murdering President John F. Kennedy and Dallas Police Officer J. D. Tippit; shot and killed by Jack Ruby, November 24, 1963.

OSWALD, MARGUERITE C.: Mother of the accused assassin; Warren Commission witness; believed her son was a pawn of the CIA; died in 1982.

OSWALD, MARINA: Russian-born wife of Lee Harvey Oswald; Warren Commission witness; linked husband to General Walker shooting and JFK assassination.

OSWALD, RACHEL: Youngest daughter of Marina and Lee Oswald.

OSWALD, ROBERT LEE, JR.: Brother of the alleged assassin; Warren Commission witness; supports the Commission's conclusion that Oswald killed Kennedy; author of *Lee: A Portrait of Lee Harvey Oswald* (1967).

OSWALD, ROBERT LEE, SR.: Father of Lee Harvey Oswald; died in 1939.

O'TOOLE, GEORGE: Former CIA official; author of *The Assassination Tapes: An Electronic Probe into the Murder of John F. Kennedy and the Dallas Cover-Up* (1975, 1977).

OXFORD, J. L.: Assassination witness; Dallas County deputy sheriff; thought that shots were fired from the grassy knoll.

P

PAINE, RUTH H.: Friend of Marina Oswald; Warren Commission witness; it was in her garage that Oswald kept the assassination rifle.

PARKLAND MEMORIAL HOSPITAL: Located north of downtown Dallas, it was the hospital where President Kennedy, Governor Connally, and Lee Harvey Oswald received medical treatment.

PERRY, MALCOLM O.: Surgeon, Parkland Hospital; performed tracheotomy on JFK; first physician to describe Kennedy's throat wound as a wound of entrance.

PETERS, PAUL C.: Professor of urology, Southwestern Medical School; one of JFK's trauma room doctors; claimed that there was extensive damage to the rear of the President's head.

PETTY, CHARLES S.: Medical examiner, Dallas County, Texas; member, medical panel, House Select Committee on Assassinations.

PHILLIPS, DAVID: CIA officer; involved in anti-Castro activities; allegedly met with Oswald in Dallas prior to the assassination; died in 1988.

PIC, JOHN EDWARD, JR.: Half-brother of Lee Harvey Oswald; Warren Commission witness.

PITZER, WILLIAM B.: Lieutenant commander, U. S. Navy; chief of the Educational Television Division, U. S. Naval Medical School; believed to have photographed JFK autopsy; film never found; shot and killed in 1966; death ruled a suicide.

POLLAK, STUART R.: U. S. Justice Department attorney; member, Warren Commission staff; researched Oswald's foreign travels.

POPKIN, RICHARD H.: Philosophy professor, University of California, San Diego; early critic of the Warren Commission; author of *The Second Oswald* (1966, 1967); believes that Oswald was framed by a look-a-like assassin.

POSNER, GERALD: Former corporate attorney; author of *Case Closed* (1993, 1994); purportedly offers irrefutable evidence of Oswald's guilt.

POSTAL, JULIA: Cashier, Texas Theater; Warren Commission witness; placed the phone call that led to Oswald's arrest.

POWERS, DAVE: Presidential assistant; member of JFK's "Irish Mafia"; witnessed the assassination from the Secret Service follow-up car; said first shot sounded like a firecracker; co-author, with Ken O'Donnell, of *Johnny We Hardly Knew Ye* (1970); died in 1998.

PRESIDENT JOHN F. KENNEDY ASSASSINATION RECORDS COLLECTION ACT: Sponsored by Representative Louis Stokes (D-OH) and Senator David Boren (D-OK), it was signed into law by President George Bush on October 26, 1992. This Act required that all classified government documents relating to the 1963 assassination be stored in the National Archives. The Act also established the Assassination Records Review Board.

PRESIDENT'S COMMISSION ON THE ASSASSINATION OF PRESIDENT KENNEDY: (See Warren Commission).

PREYER, RICHARDSON: U. S. representative (D-NC); member, House Select Committee on Assassinations; chaired JFK subcommittee.

PRICE, J. C.: Employee, Union Terminal Company; witnessed the assassination from the roof of the Terminal Annex Building; saw possible assassin behind the grassy knoll.

PROUTY, L. FLETCHER: Retired U. S. Air Force officer; former Yale professor; assassination researcher; technical advisor on the film *JFK* (1991); author of *The Secret Team* (1973, 1974, 1990) and *JFK: The CIA, Vietnam and the Plot to Assassinate John F. Kennedy* (1992, 1996).

PRUSAKOVA, MARINA NIKOLAEVNA: Marina Oswald's maiden name.

PUTERBAUGH, JACK: Patrolman, Dallas Police; rode in the pilot car, the second vehicle in the motorcade.

Q

"QUEEN MARY": Nickname for "Halfback," the Secret Service follow-up car.

QUIGLEY, JOHN: FBI agent; Warren Commission witness; interviewed Oswald following his arrest for street fighting in New Orleans, August 1963.

R

RAGANO, FRANK: Underworld attorney; represented Jimmy Hoffa and Santos Trafficante; author of *Mob Lawyer* (1994); links Mafia bosses to JFK's murder.

RANDLE, LINNIE MAE: Buell Wesley Frazier's sister; Ruth Paine's neighbor; helped Oswald secure employment at the Texas School Book Depository.

RANKIN, J. LEE: Lawyer; former U. S. solicitor general in the Eisenhower administration; general counsel, Warren Commission (1963-64); controlled direction of probe; acted as liaison between Commission and CIA.

READY, JOHN D.: Assassination witness; U. S. Secret Service agent; rode on the right front running board of the presidential follow-up car; coordinated airport security for the return flight to Washington, D. C.

REDLICH, NORMAN: Law professor, New York University; Warren Commission staffer; executive assistant to General Counsel J. Lee Rankin; edited final report.

REED, EDWARD: Medical technician, Bethesda Naval Hospital; x-rayed JFK's remains.

REID, ELIZABETH: Assassination witness; clerical supervisor; Warren Commission witness; saw Oswald on the second floor of the Texas School Book Depository two minutes after the assassination.

REYNOLDS, WARREN: Tippit murder witness; used car dealer; Warren Commission witness; identified Oswald as the assailant; died in 1964.

RICH, JOE HENRY: Texas state trooper; drove the vice presidential follow-up car.

RIEBE, FLOYD: Medical photographer, Bethesda Naval Hospital; photographed JFK's autopsy.

RICKERBY, ARTHUR: Photographer, *Life*; motorcade passenger; rode in camera car 2, seven cars behind JFK's limousine.

RIKE, AUBREY: Driver, Oneal Funeral Home; one of three men who placed JFK's remains in the casket at Parkland Hospital.

RIVERA, GERALDO: Host, ABC's *Goodnight America*; first to show Zapruder film on nationwide television, March 6, 1975.

ROBERTS, CHARLES: White House correspondent; motorcade passenger; author of *The Truth About the Assassination* (1967), a defense of the Warren Commission.

ROBERTS, DELPHINE: Guy Banister's secretary; said that Banister knew both Oswald and David Ferrie.

ROBERTS, EARLENE: Oswald's landlady in Dallas; Warren Commission witness; died in 1966.

ROBERTS, EMORY P.: Assassination witness; U. S. Secret Service agent; rode in the front passenger's seat of the presidential follow-up car; thought that gunfire came from the area to the right of JFK's limousine.

ROCKEFELLER COMMISSION: The Commission was established in 1975 by President Gerald Ford to investigate and report on the domestic activities of the CIA. It also created a medical panel to reexamine the JFK autopsy evidence.

ROFFMAN, HOWARD: Teenage critic of the Warren Commission; author of *Presumed Guilty* (1975, 1976).

ROSE, EARL: Dallas County medical examiner; tried unsuccessfully to impound JFK's body for a Texas post-mortem; later performed autopsies on J. D. Tippit, Lee Harvey Oswald, and Jack Ruby.

ROSE, GUY F.: Homicide detective, Dallas Police; Warren Commission witness; involved in Oswald's interrogation.

ROSE, JERRY: Former sociology professor, SUNY, Fredonia; JFK researcher; editor of *The Fourth Decade*, an assassination journal.

ROSELLI, JOHNNY: Underworld figure; associate of Sam Giancana and Santos Trafficante; alleged mob involvement in JFK's murder; killed in 1976.

ROWLEY, JAMES J.: Chief of the U. S. Secret Service at the time of the assassination; Warren Commission witness.

RUBENSTEIN, JACOB: Jack Ruby's birth name.

RUBY, EARL: Brother of Jack Ruby.

RUBY, JACK L.: Nightclub owner with underworld connections; gambler; FBI informant; Warren Commission witness; murdered Lee Harvey Oswald, November 24, 1963; convicted and sentenced to death (1964); died of cancer awaiting second trial (1967).

RUDNICKI, JAN GAIL: Laboratory technologist; assisted Dr. Boswell during JFK's autopsy.

RUSSELL, DICK: Freelance journalist; author of *The Man Who Knew Too Much* (1992), the study of Richard Case Nagell, a double agent who uncovered a domestic plot to assassinate JFK.

RUSSELL, RICHARD: U. S. senator (D-GA); president pro tempore of the Senate (1969-71); member, Warren Commission (1963-64); had strong misgivings about the Commission's findings; died in 1971.

RUSSO, PERRY R.: Insurance salesman; acquaintance of David Ferrie; testified at Clay Shaw's trial; claimed to have heard Ferrie, Oswald, and Shaw plotting JFK's assassination.

S

SALERNO, RALPH: Organized crime expert; former New York City police officer; special consultant, House Select Committee on Assassinations.

SALYER, KENNETH E.: Resident, Parkland Hospital; attended JFK in Trauma Room One.

SARTI, LUCIEN: Corsican drug trafficker; professional killer; named in the 1988 British documentary *The Men Who Killed Kennedy* as one of three assassins who ambushed JFK; died in 1972.

SAUVAGE, LEO: French journalist; covered assassination investigation for *LeFigaro;* author of *The Oswald Affair* (1966); concluded that Southern white extremists were behind the JFK's murder.

SAWYER, HAROLD S.: U. S. representative (R-MI); member, House Select Committee on Assassinations; served on JFK subcommittee.

SAWYER, J. HERBERT: Inspector, Dallas Police; Warren Commission witness; conducted Oswald murder investigation.

SCHEIM, DAVID E.: Former chief of Management Information Services, National Institutes of Health; board member, Assassination Archives and Research Center and Coalition on Political Assassinations; author of *Contract on America: The Mafia Murders of John and Robert Kennedy* (1988, 1991).

SCHOENMAN, RALPH: Assassination researcher; founding member, Who Killed Kennedy? Committee.

SCHWEIKER COMMITTEE: Formed in 1975 and chaired by Senator Richard Schweiker (R-PA), this subcommittee was created to examine the role played by U. S. intelligence agencies during the Warren Commission's investigation. After a year-long probe, the Committee reported that the CIA and FBI had intentionally withheld information from the Commission and had failed to pursue conspiratorial leads. As a result of the Schweiker inquiry, the House moved in late 1976 to create the Select Committee on Assassinations.

SCOBEY, ALFREDDA: Georgia attorney; member, Warren Commission staff.

SCOGGINS, WILLIAM W.: Dallas taxi driver; Warren Commission witness; saw Oswald leaving the scene of the Tippit shooting; did not see Oswald pull the trigger.

SCOTT, PETER DALE: Former diplomat; professor emeritus, University of California, Berkeley; founding member, Assassination Information Bureau; author of *The Assassinations: Dallas and Beyond- A Guide To Cover-Ups and Assassinations* (1976) and *Deep Politics and the Death of JFK* (1993).

"SHADOW": Code name for Warrant Officer Ira Gearhart.

SHAFFER, CHARLES N., JR.: U. S. Justice Department attorney; member, Warren Commission staff.

SHANEYFELT, LYNDAL L.: FBI photographic expert; Warren Commission witness; analyzed the Muchmore, Nix, and Zapruder assassination films.

SHANKLIN, GORDON: FBI agent-in-charge, Dallas; after the assassination, ordered Agent James Hosty to destroy a threatening note Oswald had written to the FBI.

SHAW, CLAY: New Orleans businessman; associated with CIA; tried and acquitted on conspiracy charges in the murder of President John F. Kennedy (1969); died in 1974.

SHAW, J. GARY: Architect; assassination researcher; former director, JFK Assassination Information Center; board member, Assassination Archives and Research Center; co-author, with Larry R. Harris, of *Cover-Up* (1976, 1992) and *JFK: Conspiracy of Silence* (1992).

SHAW, ROBERT R.: Professor of thoracic surgery, Southwestern Medical School; Warren Commission witness; operated on Governor Connally.

SHIRES, GEORGE T.: Professor of surgery, Southwestern Medical School; Warren Commission witness; operated on both Governor Connally and Lee Harvey Oswald.

SIBERT, JAMES: (See O'Neill, Francis X.).

SINKLE, BILLY: Patrolman, Dallas Police; rode in the pilot car, the second vehicle in the motorcade.

SITZMAN, MARILYN: Assassination witness; Abraham Zapruder's receptionist; stood next to Zapruder as he filmed the assassination; saw the third shot strike the President in the right temple.

SIXTH FLOOR MUSEUM: Opened in 1989, the museum is located on the sixth floor of the Dallas County Administration Building (the old Texas School Book Depository) in downtown Dallas, Texas. The museum contains hundreds of assassination-related photographs, films, artifacts, and exhibits.

SKELTON, ROYCE G.: Assassination witness; mail clerk, Texas-Louisiana Freight Bureau; Warren Commission witness; stood atop the triple underpass; heard a total of three shots; said one bullet hit the sidewalk.

SLAWSON, W. DAVID: Corporate attorney and later professor of law at USC; junior counsel, Warren Commission; assigned to Area IV: Possible Conspiratorial Relationships; concluded that neither the Soviet Union or Cuba were involved in the assassination.

SLOAN, BILL: Newspaper reporter; journalism professor, Southern Methodist University; author of *JFK: The Last Dissenting Witness* (1992) and *JFK: Breaking the Silence* (1993).

SMART, R.: Motorcycle officer, Dallas Police; assigned to the motorcade.

SMITH, MERRIMAN: White House correspondent; motorcade passenger; rode in the press pool car, five cars behind JFK's limousine; author of *The Murder of the Young President* (1964).

SORRELS, FORREST V.: Assassination witness; U. S. Secret Service agent; Warren Commission witness; rode in the lead car directly in front of the presidential limousine; later told friend Orville Nix that the shots came from the area of the grassy knoll.

SPECTER, ARLEN: Philadelphia attorney; later U. S. senator (R-PA); junior counsel, Warren Commission; assigned to Area I: Basic Facts of the Assassination; author of the "Magic Bullet" theory.

SPITZ, WERNER U.: Medical examiner, Wayne County, Michigan; member, medical panel, House Select Committee on Assassinations.

SPRAGUE, RICHARD A.: Philadelphia attorney; chief counsel and staff director, House Select Committee on Assassinations (1976); after political infighting, resigned (1977); replaced by G. Robert Blakey.

SPRAGUE, RICHARD E.: Assassination researcher; one of the early authorities on the photographic evidence in the JFK assassination; founding member, Committee to Investigate Assassinations.

STAFFORD, JEAN: Pulitzer Prize-winning novelist; author of *A Mother In History* (1966, 1992), a character study of Marguerite Oswald; died in 1979.

STERN, SAMUEL A.: Washington attorney; junior counsel, Warren Commission; assigned to Area VI: The Protection of the President.

STILES, JOHN R.: Co-author, with Gerald Ford, of *Portrait of the Assassin* (1965, 1966).

STOKES, LOUIS: U. S. representative (D-OH); replaced Representative Henry Gonzalez (D-TX) as chairman of the House Select Committee on Assassinations (1977).

STOLLEY, RICHARD B.: Los Angeles bureau chief, *Life*; purchased Abraham Zapruder's film for $150,000.

STONE, OLIVER: Academy Award-winning filmmaker; co-produced and directed *JFK* (1991).

STOUGHTON, CECIL W.: Captain, U. S. Army; White House photographer; motorcade passenger; rode in camera car 2, seven cars behind JFK's limousine; photographed Lyndon Johnson's swearing-in aboard Air Force One.

STOUT, STEWART G.: U. S. Secret Service agent; accompanied JFK's body from Parkland Hospital to Love Field.

STOVER, JOHN: Captain, U. S. Navy; commanding officer, U. S. Naval Medical School; selected JFK autopsy team.

STRINGER, JOHN: Medical photographer, Bethesda Naval Hospital; photographed JFK's autopsy.

STUCKEY, WILLIAM: New Orleans radio host; Warren Commission witness; moderated debate between Oswald and Carlos Bringuier, August 1963.

STUDEBAKER, ROBERT LEE: Photographer, Dallas Police; Warren Commission witness; photographed the sixth floor of the Book Depository following the assassination.

STURGIS, FRANK: CIA operative; Watergate burglar; trained anti-Castro Cubans in the 1960's; mistakenly identified as one of the Dealey Plaza tramps; died in 1993.

SUMMERS, ANTHONY: Former BBC correspondent; free-lance writer; author of the award-winning book, *Conspiracy* (1980, 1981, 1989); suggests that anti-Castro Cubans, Mafia kingpins, and the CIA conspired to kill Kennedy.

SWINDAL, JAMES: Colonel, U. S. Air Force; pilot, Air Force One.

T

TAGUE, JAMES: Assassination witness; Dallas car salesman; Warren Commission witness; stood on the median strip near the triple underpass; wounded by a stray bullet fired from either the Texas School Book Depository or the Dal-Tex Building.

TANNENBAUM, ROBERT K.: Former New York City deputy district attorney; deputy chief counsel, House Select Committee on Assassinations (1976-77); author of several books including *Corruption of Blood* (1995), a fictionalized account of the HSCA.

TAYLOR, WARREN: Assassination witness; U. S. Secret Service agent; rode in the left rear seat of the vice presidential follow-up car.

TEXAS SCHOOL BOOK DEPOSITORY: The seven-story building from which Lee Harvey Oswald allegedly fired the shots that killed President Kennedy and wounded Governor Connally. At the time of the assassination, it contained the offices of several publishing companies and served as a textbook distribution center. Acquired by Dallas County in 1977, the structure currently houses administrative offices and the Sixth Floor Museum.

TEXAS THEATER: Located in the Oak Cliff section of Dallas, it was the site of Oswald's arrest.

THOMPSON, JOSIAH: Former philosophy professor, Haverford College; later private investigator; board member, Coalition on Political Assassinations; author of *Six Seconds in Dallas* (1967), a detailed study of the medical and ballistics evidence.

THONE, CHARLES: U. S. representative (R-NE); member, House Select Committee on Assassinations; served on JFK subcommittee.

THORNLEY, KERRY W.: U. S. Marine; served with Oswald at El Toro Air Station in California; author of *Oswald* (1965) and *The Idle Warriors* (1991).

"TIGER": Code name for Colonel James Swindal.

TIPPIT, J. D.: Dallas Police officer; shot and killed in the Oak Cliff section of the city some 45 minutes after the assassination; allegedly murdered by Oswald.

TOMLINSON, DARRELL C.: Maintenance supervisor; Warren Commission witness; found "Magic Bullet" on Parkland Hospital stretcher; later told Warren Commission attorney Arlen Specter that the bullet could have come from Governor Connally's gurney.

TONAHILL, JOE: Texas lawyer; member of Jack Ruby's defense team.

TONEY, JOHN: Detective, Dallas Police; involved in Oswald's arrest.

TOWNER, JAMES M.: Assassination witness; civil engineer; photographed the "Umbrella Man" and "Dark Complected Man" on Elm Street moments after the shooting.

TRAFFICANTE, SANTOS: Florida-based mobster; coordinated assassination plots against Castro; JFK murder suspect; died in 1987.

TRASK, RICHARD B.: Archivist; lecturer; author of *Pictures of the Pain* (1994), a photographic history of the JFK assassination.

TRULY, ROY S.: Assassination witness; superintendent, Texas School Book Depository; Warren Commission witness; with police officer Marrion Baker, encountered Oswald in the second floor lunchroom, approximately 90 seconds after the assassination.

TUNHEIM, JOHN: Chief deputy attorney general of Minnesota; member, Assassination Records Review Board.

TURNER, F. M.: Patrolman, Dallas Police; rode in the pilot car, the second vehicle in the motorcade.

TURNER, NIGEL: Produced and directed the acclaimed British documentary series *The Men Who Killed Kennedy* (1988).

TURNER, WILLIAM W.: Former FBI agent; board member, Coalition on Political Assassinations; co-author, with Warren Hinckle, of *The Fish Is Red: The Story of the Secret War Against Castro* (1981); re-titled *Deadly Secrets: The CIA-Mafia War Against Castro and the Assassination of JFK* (1992).

U

UNDERHILL, GARY: CIA officer; claimed that JFK's death was the result of a conspiracy; shot and killed in 1964; death ruled a suicide.

UNDERWOOD, JAMES R.: Cameraman, KRLD-TV; motorcade passenger; rode in camera car 3, eight cars behind JFK's limousine.

"UMBRELLA MAN": The mysterious figure who raised his umbrella when the shooting began, he was eventually identifed by the House Assassinations Committee as Louis S. Witt, a Dallas insurance salesman. Witt claimed that when he raised the umbrella, he was not acting in a conspiratorial manner, but that his gesture was merely a sign of protest.

V

"VARSITY": Code name for the vice presidential follow-up car, a 1963 Mercury four-door hardtop. "Varsity" was directly behind LBJ's car and three cars behind JFK's limousine.

VAUGHN, ROY E.: Dallas Police officer; Warren Commission witness; allegedly permitted Jack Ruby to enter the basement of the Dallas jail shortly before he killed Oswald.

VECIANA, ANTONIO: Anti-Castro activist; founder of Alpha 66, a Cuban exile group; allegedly saw Oswald with "Maurice Bishop" prior to the assassination.

"VICTORIA": Code name for Lady Bird Johnson, wife of Vice President Lyndon Johnson.

"VOLUNTEER": Code name for Vice President Lyndon Johnson.

W

WADE, HENRY: Dallas district attorney; Warren Commission witness; initially identified the JFK murder weapon as a 7.65 Mauser.

WALKER, C. T.: Dallas Police officer; Warren Commission witness; involved in Oswald's arrest.

WALKER, EDWIN A.: Ex-U. S. Army general; ultra-conservative spokesman; Warren Commission witness; victim of Oswald assassination attempt, April 1963; died in 1993.

WALTHER, CAROLYN: Assassination witness; dress factory cutter; claimed to have seen two men with a rifle in an upper floor window of the Texas School Book Depository moments before the assassination; never called before the Warren Commission.

WALTHERS, EDDY: Assassination witness; Dallas County deputy sheriff; Warren Commission witness; first officer to speak with James Tague following the assassination; shot to death in 1969.

"WAND": Code name for Ken O' Donnell.

WARREN COMMISSION: A seven-member panel created by President Lyndon Johnson in November 1963 to investigate the murder of John F. Kennedy. Chaired by Chief Justice Earl Warren, the Commission's investigation focused on six areas: The Basic Facts of the Assassination, The Identity of the Assassin, Oswald's Background, Possible Conspiratorial Relationships, Oswald's Death, and Presidential Protection. After nearly ten months of research, the Commission concluded that Lee Harvey Oswald alone fired the shots that killed the President. The Commission also determined that Oswald and Jack Ruby were not part of a conspiracy.

WARREN, EARL: Governor, California (1943-53); chief justice, United States Supreme Court (1953-69); appointed chairman, President's Commission on the Assassination of President John F. Kennedy (1963); died in 1974.

"WARRIOR": Code name for Malcolm Kilduff.

"WATCHMAN": Code name for Major General Chester V. Clifton.

WEBERMAN, ALAN J.: Co-author, with Michael Canfield, of *Coup d' Etat in America: The CIA and the Assassination of John F. Kennedy* (1975, 1992).

WECHT, CYRIL H.: Pathologist; lawyer; lecturer; leading critic of the Warren Commission; board member, Assassination Archives and Research Center; chairman, Coalition on Political Assassinations; technical consultant on the film *JFK* (1991); co-author, with Mark Curriden and Benjamin Wecht, of *Cause of Death* (1993) and numerous articles.

WEGMANN, EDWARD: Defense counsel for Clay Shaw.

WEGMANN, WILLIAM: Defense counsel for Clay Shaw.

WEHLE, PHILIP C.: Major general, U. S. Army; commanding officer, Military District of Washington, D. C.; attended JFK's autopsy.

WEINREB, LLOYD L.: U. S. Justice Department attorney; member, Warren Commission staff.

WEISBERG, HAROLD: Assassination researcher; former Senate investigator; author of nine books on the JFK conspiracy including *Whitewash I-IV* (1965, 1966, 1967, and 1974) and *Case Open* (1994), a denunciation of Gerald Posner's *Case Closed* (1993, 1994).

WEISS, MARK: Professor, City University of New York; acoustics expert; analyzed Dallas Police dictabelt for House Assassinations Committee; concluded that a fourth shot was possible.

WEITZMAN, SEYMOUR: Assassination witness; Dallas County constable; Warren Commission witness; one of three officers who discovered Oswald's rifle on the sixth floor of the Texas School Book Depository.

WELLS, THOMAS: U. S. Secret Service agent; assigned to the Caroline and John F. Kennedy, Jr. security detail.

WESTBROOK, W. R.: Captain, Dallas Police; Warren Commission witness; involved in Oswald's arrest; died in 1996.

WESTON, JAMES: Chief medical investigator, University of New Mexico School of Medicine; member, medical panel, House Select Committee on Assassinations.

WHALEY, WILLIAM W.: Dallas cab driver; Warren Commission witness; drove Oswald to his Oak Cliff neighborhood shortly after the assassination; died in 1965.

WHITE, JACK: Photo-analyst; consultant, House Select Committee on Assassinations; discovered so-called "Badgeman" figure in Mary Moorman's photograph.

WHITE, RICKY: Son of Dallas Police Officer Roscoe White; claimed that his father killed both President Kennedy and J. D. Tippit.

WHITE, ROSCOE: (See White, Ricky).

WIEGMAN, DAVID: Cameraman, NBC News; motorcade passenger; rode in camera car 1, six cars behind JFK's limousine.

WILBER, CHARLES G.: Director, Forensic Science Laboratory, Colorado State University; author of *Medicolegal Investigation of the President John F. Kennedy Murder* (1978).

WILLENS, HOWARD P.: U. S. Justice Department attorney; assistant counsel, Warren Commission; organized daily operations of the legal staff; with Norman Redlich and Arthur Goldberg, edited final assassination report.

WILLIAMS, BONNIE RAY: Assassination witness; employee, Texas School Book Depository; Warren Commission witness; thought the first shot sounded like a motorcycle backfire; heard three shots in all.

WILLIAMS, OTIS: Assassination witness; credit manager, Texas School Book Depository; said that three shots were fired.

WILLIS, PHILIP L.: Assassination witness; automobile salesman; ex-U. S. Air Force officer; Warren Commission witness; photographed the mysterious "Umbrella Man" and "Blackdog Man"; died in 1995.

"WILLOW": Code name for Evelyn Lincoln.

WILLS, GARRY: Pulitzer Prize-winning journalist; co-author, with Ovid Demaris, of *Jack Ruby* (1968, 1994).

"WING": Code name for Brigadier General Godfrey McHugh.

WITT, LOUIS S.: (See "Umbrella Man").

WOODWARD, MARY E.: Assassination witness; employee, *Dallas Morning News*; thought the fatal head shot came from the direction of the grassy knoll.

WRIGHT, FRANK: Tippit murder witness; could not identify Oswald as the killer.

WRIGHT, O. P.: Security chief, Parkland Hospital; gave "Magic Bullet" to federal authorities.

WRONE, DAVID R.: Former history professor, University of Wisconsin, Stevens Point; assassination researcher; co-author, with Delloyd Guth J., of *The Assassination of John F. Kennedy: A Comprehensive Historical and Legal Bibliography, 1963-1979* (1980).

X

"X-100": Code name for JFK's parade car, a 1961 Lincoln Continental four-door convertible. "X-100" preceded the presidential follow-up car. Removed from service in 1977, it is on permanent display at the Henry Ford Museum in Dearborn, Michigan.

Y

YARBOROUGH, RALPH W.: Assassination witness; U. S. senator (D-TX); Warren Commission witness; rode in the backseat of Vice President Johnson's convertible, two cars behind JFK's limousine; critical of Secret Service protection; died in 1996.

YAZIJIAN, HARVEY: Political activist; founding member, Grassy Knoll Debating Society; co-founder, Assassination Information Bureau; co-editor, with Sid Blumenthal, of *Government By Gunplay: Assassination Conspiracy Theories from Dallas to Today* (1976).

YOUNGBLOOD, RUFUS W.: Assassination witness; U. S. Secret Service agent; Warren Commission witness; rode with Vice-President Johnson; author of *20 Years in the Secret Service* (1973).

Z

ZAPRUDER, ABRAHAM: Assassination witness; garment manu-
facturer; Warren Commission witness; took controversial home movie
of assassination; died in 1970.

ZAPRUDER FILM: (See Zapruder, Abraham).

ZIRBEL, CRAIG I.: Arizona attorney; author of *The Texas Connection* (1991, 1992); alleges that Vice President Lyndon Johnson master-
minded the assassination of JFK.

Part II:
Selected Bibliography
1963-1998

LEE HARVEY OSWALD AND "RELATED" SUBJECTS

Books:

Associated Professional Services, ed. *The Bizarre and Intimate Life of an Assassin.* Hollywood, California: Associated Professional Services, 1964.

Chapman, Gil, and Ann. *Was Oswald Alone?* San Diego, California: Publishers Export Co., 1967.

Davison, Jean. *Oswald's Game.* New York: W.W. Norton & Co., 1983.

Epstein, Edward Jay. *Legend: The Secret World of Lee Harvey Oswald.* New York: McGraw-Hill, 1978; Ballantine Books, 1978; Reader's Digest Books, 1978; London: Hutchinson, 1978; Arrow, 1978.

Groden, Robert J.. *The Search for Lee Harvey Oswald.* New York: Penguin Studio Books, 1995.

Hartogs, Renatus, and Lucy Freeman. *The Two Assassins.* New York: Thomas Y. Crowell, 1965; Zebra Books, 1976.

Hosty, James P. *Assignment Oswald.* New York: Arcade Publishing, 1996.

Joesten, Joachim. *Marina Oswald.* London: Dawnay, 1967.

_____. *Oswald: The Truth.* London: Dawnay, 1967.

LaFontaine, Ray, and Mary. *Oswald Talked: The New Evidence in the JFK Assassination.* Gretna, Louisiana: Pelican Publishing, 1996.

Lewis, Ron. *Flashback: The Untold Story of Lee Harvey Oswald.* Roseburg, Oregon: Lewcom Productions, 1993.

Mailer, Norman. *Oswald's Tale: An American Mystery.* New York: Random House, 1995; Ballantine Books, 1996.

McBirnie, William Stewart. *What Was Behind Lee Harvey Oswald?* Glendale, California: Acare Publications, n. d.

McMillan, Priscilla Johnson. *Marina and Lee.* New York: Harper & Row, 1977; Bantam, 1978; London: Book Club Associates, 1978.

Melanson, Philip H. *Spy Saga: Lee Harvey Oswald and U.S. Intelligence.* New York: Praeger Publishers, 1990.

Myers, Dale K. *With Malice: Lee Harvey Oswald and the Murder of Officer J. D. Tippit.* Milford, Michigan: Oak Cliff Press, 1998.

Nechiporenko, Oleg M. *Passport To Assassination: The Never-Before-Told Story of Lee Harvey Oswald By The KGB Colonel Who Knew Him.* New York: Birch Lane Press, 1993.

Newman, John. *Oswald And The CIA.* New York: Carroll & Graf Publishers Inc., 1995.

Oswald, Marguerite C.. *Aftermath of an Execution---The Burial and Final Rights of Lee Harvey Oswald as Told by His Mother.* Dallas, Texas: Published by Author, 1964.

Oswald, Robert L., with Myrick and Barbara Land. *Lee: A Portrait of Lee Harvey Oswald by His Brother.* New York: Coward-McCann, 1967.

Popkin, Richard H. *The Second Oswald.* Introduction by Murray Kempton. New York: Avon Books, 1966; London: Sphere Books, Ltd., 1967.

Posner, Gerald. *Case Closed: Lee Harvey Oswald and the Assassination of JFK.* New York: Random House, 1993; Anchor Books, 1994.

Ralston, Ross F. *History's Verdict: The Acquittal of Lee Harvey Oswald.* Published by Author, 1975.

Ringgold, Gene, and Roger La Manna. *Assassin: The Lee Harvey Oswald Biography.* Professional Services, 1964.

Roffman, Howard. *Presumed Guilty: Lee Harvey Oswald in the Assassination of President Kennedy*. Rutherford, New Jersey: Fairleigh Dickinson University, 1975; London: Thomas Yoselaff, 1976; New York: A. S. Barnes & Co., 1976.

Rogra Research. *Oswald in Mexico*. 3 vols. Evanston, Illinois: VMKRAFT Inc., 1993.

Sckolnick, Lewis B., ed. *Lee Harvey Oswald: CIA Pre-Assassination File*. Leverett, Massachusetts: Rector Press Limited, 1993.

Scott, Peter Dale. *Deep Politics II: Essays on Oswald, Mexico, and Cuba*. Skokie, Illinois: Green Archive Publications, 1995.

Sites, Paul. *Lee Harvey Oswald and the American Dream*. New York: Pageant Press, 1967.

Stafford, Jean. *A Mother in History*. New York: Farrar, Straus, and Giroux, 1966; Bantam, 1966; Pharos Books, 1992.

Thornley, Kerry W. *Oswald*. Chicago: New Classics, 1965.

Signed Articles:

Abrahamsen, David. "A Study of Lee Harvey Oswald: Psychological Capability of Murder." *Bulletin of the New York Academy of Medicine* 43 (1967): 861-88.

Aldridge, John W. "Documents as Narrative [*Oswald's Tale*]." *The Atlantic Monthly* 275 (May 1995): 120-25.

Anderson, A. J. "History: *Legend*." *Library Journal* 103 (June 1, 1978): 1172.

Ansbacher, Heinz, Rowena R. Ansbacher, David and Kathleen Shiverick. "Lee Harvey Oswald: An Adlerian Interpretation." *The Psychoanalytical Review* 53 (Fall 1966): 55-68.

Asbell, Bernard. "10 Years Later: A Legacy of Torment Haunts Those Closest to the JFK Assassination." *Todays Health* 51 (October 1973): 56-60, 62-63, 65.

Auchincloss, Kenneth. "Books: Oswald and the Soviets: *Legend . . .* By Edward Jay Epstein." *Newsweek* 91 (April 10, 1978): 90.

Aynesworth, Hugh. "Oswald's Own Story--As Revealed by His Diary." *U. S. News and World Report* 57 (July 13, 1964): 54-60.

Bachmann, Ida. "Hvem Myrdede Praesident Kennedy? Et Defensorat for Oswald Indleveret [Who Murdered President Kennedy? A Defense of Oswald's Identification]." *Frit Danmark* (Copenhagen) 22 (1963-64): 1-3.

Bagdikian, Ben H. "The Assassin." *The Saturday Evening Post* 236 (December 14, 1963): 22-27.

Bannon, Barbara A. "Forecasts of Paperbacks: Nonfiction: *The Second Oswald.*" *Publishers Weekly* 190 (August 29, 1966): 345.

Beck, Melinda, with Melinda Liu. "Lee Harvey Oswald: The Mind of the Assassin." *Newsweek* 122 (November 22 1993): 71-72.

Berman, Paul. "The Mailer Commission [*Oswald's Tale*]." *The New Republic* 213 (July 17-24, 1995): 46-51.

Blake, Patricia. "Books: The Making of an Assassin." *Time* 110 (November 14, 1977): 106, 109.

Blum, Andrew. "Will Book Close Case On JFK?" *The National Law Journal* 16 (October 4, 1993): 29.

Blyth, Myrna. "Marina Oswald: Twenty-Five Years Later." *Ladies' Home Journal* 105 (November 1988): 184-86, 188, 236-37.

Blythe, Will. "Books: The Lone Novelist Theory [*Oswald's Tale*]." *Esquire* 123 (May 1995): 142, 144.

Bodine, Larry. "Lawsuit Seeks to Open Lee Harvey Oswald's Grave." *The National Law Journal* 2 (May 26, 1980): 35.

Bunton, Lucius D. "Texas Judge Offers Perspectives on Presiding at Oswald's 'Trial'." *Texas Bar Journal* 51 (November 1988): 1045-46.

Carlson, Michael. "Return of the Lone Assassin [*Oswald's Tale*]." *The Spectator* (London) No. 8721 (September 2, 1995): 30-31.

Carmichael, Dan. "Legal Battle Over Oswald's Grave." *The Los Angeles Daily Journal* 94 (April 6, 1981): 3, 6.

Casey, Kathryn. "Marina's Story." *Ladies' Home Journal* 110 (May 1993): 156-58.

Castellano, Lillian. "Oswald Censored: From Readers' Letters." *The Minority of One* 7 (March 1965): 30.

Chaplin, J. P. "Commentary on Three Oswald Interpretations." *Journal of Individual Psychology* 23 (May 1967): 48-52.

Clapperton, Jane. "Cosmo Reads The New Books: *Legend.*" *Cosmopolitan* 184 (June 1984): 26.

Cockburn, Alexander. "Mother of the Decade." *Texas Monthly* 1 (November 1973): 78-80.

_____. "A Tale of Two Conspiracies." *New Statesman* (London) 95 (February 24, 1978): 248.

_____. "Beat The Devil: Thirty Years On: Lee and Mom." *The Nation* 257 (November 29, 1993): 647.

Cohen, Jacob. "Books, Arts & Manners: Just the Facts--Please [*Oswald's Tale*]." *National Review* 47 (August 28, 1995): 42-44.

Cohn, Henry S. "Book Review: *Case Closed.*" *Connecticut Bar Journal* 67 (December 1993): 502- 05.

Costello, George. "Book Reviews: The Kennedy Assassination: Case Still Open." *Federal Bar News & Journal* 41 (March/April 1994): 233-39.

Cuff, Sergeant. "Criminal Record: *The Two Assassins.*" *Saturday Review* 49 (February 26, 1966): 40.

Curtis, C. Michael. "Short Reviews: *Marina and Lee*." *The Atlantic Monthly* 241 (February 1978): 92.

Curtis, Gregory. "Behind The Lines: The Fourth Tramp." *Texas Monthly* 24 (April 1996): 9, 12, 14, 20.

Devlin, Patrick. "Was Oswald Guilty?: A Judicial Summing-Up of the Warren Report." *New Statesman* (London) 69 (March 12, 1965): 399-403.

Dole, Grace Fuller. "New Books Appraised: Biography--Personal Narrative: *A Mother in History*." *Library Journal* 91 (April 15, 1966): 2051.

Dunn, Cyril, and Joyce Egginton. "Das armselige Leben des unseligen Lee H. Oswald [The Miserable Life of the Late Lee H. Oswald]." *Die Zeit* (Hamburg) 18 (1963): 3.

Dyson, Paul H. "Autobiography & Biography: *Oswald's Game*." *Best Sellers* 43 (January 1984): 370.

Epstein, Edward Jay. "Reading Oswald's Hand." *Psychology Today* (April 1978): 97-98, 101-02.

Epstein, Edward Jay, with Susana Duncan. "The War of the Moles." *New York* (February 27, 1978): 28-38; (March 6, 1978): 55-59; (March 13, 1978): 12-13.

Evans, M. Stanton. "Cover-Up Proved in JFK Murder Probe." *Human Events* 36 (July 24, 1976): 13- 15.

_____. "Dark Horses: *Marina and Lee*." *National Review* 30 (April 14, 1978): 483.

Fein, Arnold L. "JFK In Dallas: The Warren Report and Its Critics." *Saturday Review* 49 (October 22, 1966): 36-38, 43-47.

Feldman, Harold. "Oswald and the FBI." *The Nation* 198 (January 27, 1964): 86-89.

Ferrell, Thomas H. "Social Sciences: *Spy Saga.*" *Library Journal* 115 (November 1, 1990): 114.

Fetherling, Douglas. "Books: Assessing an Assassin: Norman Mailer Really Says Oswald Did Do It." *Maclean's* 108 (June 5, 1995): 69.

Freedman, Lawrence Z. "Profile of An Assassin." *Police Magazine* 10 (March/April 1966): 26-30.

Gelman, David, and Elaine Shannon. "Marina Oswald's Story." *Newsweek* 92 (September 25, 1978): 45.

Greenfield, Marjorie. "New Books Appraised: Psychology-Psychiatry: *The Two Assassins.*" *Library Journal* 90 (December 1, 1965): 5288.

Griffin, Leland M. "When Dreams Collide: Rhetorical Trajectories in the Assassination of President Kennedy." *Quarterly Journal of Speech* 70 (May 1984): 111-31.

Gun, Nerin E.. "J. F. K.--One Year Later: Mrs. Oswald's Plea: Give My Children a Chance." *Pageant* 20 (December 1964): 24-31.

Hacker, Andrew. "The Great Riddle." *The New York Review of Books* 25 (May 4, 1978): 3-4, 6.

Hamilton, James W. "Some Observations on the Motivations of Lee Harvey Oswald." *Journal of Psychohistory* 14 (Summer 1986): 43-54.

Hansen, Mark. "Jury Deadlocks in Oswald Mock Trial." *ABA Journal* 78 (October 1992): 35.

Harrity, Richard. "The Face of a Century: Face of Hate: Assassin, 1963." *Look* 29 (January 12, 1965): 70.

Heymann, Stefan. "Lee H. Oswald--der amerikanische van der Lubbe [Lee H. Oswald--the American van der Lubbe= Convicted for Treason by Nazi Government for Burning the Reichstag, 1933, as Ex-Communist]." *Deutsche Aussenpolitik* (Berlin) 10 (1965): 53-57.

Hicks, Granville. "Literary Horizons: Mother of the Accused." *Saturday Review* 49 (March 5, 1966): 33-34.

Himmelfarb, Gertrude, et al. "Correspondence: Oswald the Seed of Doubt." *The New Republic* 150 (January 11, 1964): 28-30.

Holzhauer, Jean. "Books: *A Mother in History.*" *Commonweal* 84 (May 13, 1966): 233-34.

Hunt, George P. "Editors' Note: Searching the Cold Trail That Oswald Left Behind." *Life* 56 (February 21, 1964): 3.

Jackson, Donald. "The Evolution of an Assassin." *Life* 56 (February 21, 1964): 68A-80.

Jackson, Katherine Gauss. "Books in Brief: *A Mother in History.*" *Harper's Magazine* 232 (April 1966): 123.

Joesten, Joachim. "Lazni Osvald [Fake Oswald]." *Oslobodenje* (Belgrade) 21 (November 13, 19 1964): 5927-38.

Johnson, James P. "Review Essay: The Assassination In Dallas: A Search for Meaning [*Legend* and *Marina and Lee*]." *Journal of Psychohistory* 7 (Summer 1979): 105-21.

Johnson, Priscilla. "Oswald in Moscow." *Harper's Magazine* 228 (April 1964): 46-50.

Jones, Mervyn. "Wretched in Dallas." *New Statesman* (London) 95 (April 28, 1978): 563.

Kates, Don B., and Valerie J. Klein. "Gerald Posner, *Case Closed.*" *American Journal of Legal History* 37 (January 1995): 95-97.

Kathchik, Keith. "Lee Harvey's Legacy." *Texas Monthly* 23 (March 1995): 104-05, 110-13.

Katz, Joseph. "President Kennedy's Assassination: Freudian Comments." *Journal of Individual Psychology* 23 (May 1967): 20-23.

Kempton, Murray. "Waiting for the Verdict on Oswald." *The Spectator* (London) No. 7085 (April 10, 1964): 472-73.

Kennedy, Robert F. "A Misfit in Society." *U. S. News and World Report* 57 (July 13, 1964): 60.

Kurtz, Michael. "Lee Harvey Oswald in New Orleans: A Reappraisal." *Louisiana History* 21 (Winter 1980): 7-22.

Lane, Mark. "Lane's Defense Brief for Oswald." *National Guardian* 16 (December 19, 1963): 5-9.

_____. "Oswald's Case: Lane in Dallas." *National Guardian* 16 (January 9, 1964): 1, 6-7.

_____. "The Oswald Case: All Europe Skeptical." *National Guardian* 16 (July 18, 1964): 1, 3.

Latham, Aaron. "Books & The Arts: Under Several Hats: *Legend.*" *The Nation* 22 (April 29, 1978): 509-10.

Lauzon, A. "Oswald a-t-il tue Kennedy? [Did Oswald Kill Kennedy?]" *Le magazine Maclean* (Montreal) 4 (March 1964): 1-2.

Lazar, Emily. "Political Booknotes: *Oswald's Game.*" *The Washington Monthly* 16 (February 1984): 60.

Ludwig, Jack. "Here and There: New York: 'Who Killed Kennedy'?" *Partisan Review* 32 (1965): 63- 69.

Macdonald, Dwight. "Correspondence: Our Baby." *The New Republic* 150 (January 25, 1964): 30.

_____. "That Oswald Paternity Case." *The New Republic* 150 (February 29, 1964): 29-31.

Mailer, Norman. "Annals of Surveillance: Oswald In The USSR." *The New Yorker* 71 (April 10, 1995): 56-99.

Mano, D. Keith. "Family Exonerated." *National Review* 36 (April 6, 1984): 50-51.

Marek, Richard. "Editor's Memo [*Oswald's Tale*]." *Kirkus Reviews* 63 (March 15, 1995): 322.

Martin, William C. "Welcome to the Lee Harvey Oswald Memorial Library and Research Institute, Marguerite Oswald, Director." *Esquire* 79 (January 1973): 142-43, 160.

McMillan, Priscilla Johnson. "Marina and Lee: Why Oswald Really Killed Kennedy." *Ladies Home Journal* 94 (October 1977): 175-86; 94 (November 1977): 122-23, 179-96, 200-08, 212-16.

Meagher, Sylvia. "Oswald--A Patsy?: From Readers' Letters." *The Minority of One* 7 (May 1965): 31.

_____. "A Psychiatrist's Retroactive 'Clairvoyance'." *The Minority of One* 8 (June 1966): 25-27.

_____. "How Well Did the Non-Driver Drive." *The Minority of One* 8 (September 1966): 19-21.

_____. "Oswald and the State Department." *The Minority of One* 8 (October 1966): 22-27; 9 (January 1967): 29.

Meyer, Karl E. "The Triumph of Caliban." *The New Leader* 47 (October 12, 1964): 4-6.

Michaud, Charles. "Social Sciences: *Oswald's Tale.*" *Library Journal* 120 (April 15, 1995): 86.

Morrow, Lance. "History: On Oswald's Trail." *Time* 145 (May 1, 1995): 94.

Mosk, Richard M.. "Book Review: Closing the Book on JFK Conspiracies." *The Los Angeles Daily Journal* 106 (September 30, 1993): 7.

Muggeridge, Malcolm. "A New Kennedy Theory." *New Statesman* (London) 72 (November 18, 1966): 735.

Norton, Linda E., and Vincent J. M. DiMaio. "The Exhumation and Identification of Lee Harvey Oswald." *Journal of Forensic Sciences* 29 (January 1984): 19-38.

O'Brien, Conor Cruise. "No One Else But Him." *New Statesman* (London) 72 (30 September 1966): 479-81.

O'Reilly, Kenneth. "Book Reviews: *Spy Saga.*" *The Journal of American History* 78 (December 1991): 1145-46.

[Oswald, Lee Harvey]. "Lee Harvey Oswald's Letters to His Mother: With Footnotes by Mrs. Oswald." *Esquire* 61 (May 1964): 67-73, 75, 162.

Oswald, Robert L., with Myrick and Barbara Land. "Oswald: He Was My Brother." *Look* 31 (October 17, 1967): 62-74.

O'Toole, George, and Paul Hoch. "Dallas: The Cuban Connection." *The Saturday Evening Post* 248 (March 1976): 44-45, 96.

Parshall, Gerald. "The Man With a Deadly Smirk." *U. S. News and World Report* 115 (August 30, 1993): 62-65, 68, 71-72.

Plastrik, Stanley. "The Oswald Case Should Be Reopened." *Dissent Magazine* 13 (September/October 1966): 469-70.

Posner, Gerald. "The Sniper's Nest [Excerpt from *Case Closed*]." *U. S. News and World Report* 115 (August 30, 1993): 74-80, 82-83, 86-87.

_____. "The Magic Bullet [Excerpt from *Case Closed*]." *U. S. News and World Report* 115 (August 30, 1993): 88-92, 94-95, 97-98.

Preston, Gregor A. "Contemporary Scene: *Marina and Lee.*" *Library Journal* 102 (November 1, 1977): 2250.

Progoff, Ira. "The Psychology of Lee Harvey Oswald: A Jungian Approach." *Journal of Individual Psychology* 23 (May 1967): 37-47.

Reston, James, Jr. "Was Connally the Real Target?" *Time* 132 (November 28, 1988): 30-32, 36-37, 40-41.

Richard, Paul. "Books and the Arts: Mother's Day in Fort Worth." *The New Republic* 154 (March 26, 1966): 22-23.

Rifkind, Shepard. "Correspondence: Oswald the Hunter." *The New Republic* 151 (October 24, 1964): 29.

Rodman, Peter. "*Case Closed.*" *National Review* 45 (October 18, 1993): 72.

Rothstein, David A. "Presidential Assassination Syndrome: II. Application to Lee Harvey Oswald." *Archives of General Psychology* 15 (September 1966): 260-66.

Sauvage, Leo. "Oswald in Dallas: A Few Loose Ends." *The Reporter* 30 (January 2, 1964): 24-26; 30 (January 30, 1964): 6-10.

_____. "The Oswald Affair." *Commentary* 37 (March 1964): 55-65; 38 (July 1964): 16-17.

_____. "Afera Oswald," *Vjesnik u srijedai* (Zagreb) 18 (August 25, 1965): 694-695.

Schneider, Joseph. "*The Saturday Evening Post*, Book Shelf: *Legend.*" *The Saturday Evening Post* 250 (December 1978): 86-87.

Shapiro, Jonathan S. "The Compleat Lawyer: Here's a New Theory: Oswald Not Guilty!" *The California Lawyer* 12 (December 1992): 60.

Silver, Isidore. "Social Science: Law & Criminology: *Presumed Guilty.*" *Library Journal* 100 (August 1975): 1435.

Slawson, W. David, and Richard M. Mosk. "Discounting the Critics: . . . the Case Against Oswald Is Still Totally Convincing." *Skeptic* No. 9 (August 1975): 21-23.

Smith, Jack A. "Oswald Puzzle Deepens as New Questions Arise." *National Guardian* 16 (December 12, 1963): 3.

_____. "Did Oswald Fire the Gun?" *National Guardian* 16 (February 20, 1964): 1, 10.

Snyder, LeMoyne. "Lee Oswald's Guilt: How Science Nailed Kennedy's Killer." *Popular Science* 186 (April 1965): 68-73.

Sokolov, Raymond. "Books: Dallas Housewife." *Newsweek* 90 (October 31, 1977): 105.

Specter, Arlen. " 'Overwhelming Evidence Oswald Was Assassin'." *U. S. News and World Report* 61 (October 10, 1966): 48-50, 53-59, 62-63.

Spencer, B. Z. "Assassins! J. W. Booth and L. H. Oswald." *The Saturday Evening Post* 249 (July 1977): 72.

Sprague, Richard E. "Framing Lee Harvey Oswald." *Computers and People* 22 (October 1973): 21- 36.

Stafford, Jean. "The Strange World of Marguerite Oswald." *McCall's Magazine* 93 (October 1965): 112-13, 192-02.

Taylor, Gilbert. "Nonfiction: Social Sciences: *The Search for Lee Harvey Oswald* and *Assignment Oswald*." *Booklist* 92 (January 1, 1996): 758.

Thompson, Thomas. "Assassin: the Man Held--and Killed--for Murder." *Life* 55 (November 29, 1963): 37-39.

_____. "Bio: Marina Oswald: A Casualty of History Recovers." *People Weekly* 1 (March 4, 1974): 24-29.

Todd, Glenda. "Nonfiction: *Lee*." *Library Journal* 92 (December 15, 1967): 4639.

Van Bemmelen, J. M. "Did Lee Harvey Oswald Act Without Help?" *New York University Law Review* 40 (May 1965): 466-76.

Van Buren, Alice. "Books Considered: *Marina and Lee*." *The New Republic* 178 (April 29, 1978): 35-38.

Vinson, Donald E., and Peter B. Freeman. "Oswald Trial Illustrates Hazards of Over-Reliance on Surface Traits of Jurors in Voir Dire." *Inside Litigation* 6 (December 1992): 16-23.

Vollmann, William T. "The Gathering Norm: *Oswald's Tale*." *The Village Voice* 40 (May 16, 1995): 83.

Ward, Geoffrey C. "Matters of Fact: Targets of Opportunity." *American Heritage* 35 (April/May 1984): 14, 16.

West, Jessamyn. "Prelude to Tragedy: The Woman Who Sheltered Lee Oswald's Family Tells Her Story." *Redbook* 123 (July 1964): 53, 84-92.

_____. "Marina Oswald Porter: Seven Years After Dallas." *Redbook* 135 (August 1970): 57-59, 129-35.

Wolk, Robert L., with Arthur Henley. "A Psychologist Probes the Mind of an Assassin." *Pageant* 21 (December 1965): 20-25.

Wrone, David R. "Book Reviews: *Spy Saga.*" *The Journal of Southern History* 57 (November 1991): 769-71.

Zoglin, Richard. "What If Oswald Had Stood Trial?" *Time* 128 (December 1, 1986): 60.

Unsigned Articles:

"Editors' Bookshelf: *A Mother in History.*" *American Heritage* 43 (October 1992): 109.

"Editor's Choice: Beyond Conspiracy: *Case Closed.*" *American Heritage* 45 (February/March 1994): 100.

"Classified Books: Social Sciences: *Lee.*" *Booklist* 64 (February 15, 1968): 659.

"Nonfiction: History: *Marina and Lee.*" *Booklist* 74 (November 15, 1977): 525.

"Nonfiction: Social Sciences: *Legend.*" *Booklist* 74 (May 15, 1978): 1463.

"Upfront: Advance Reviews: Adult Nonfiction: *Oswald's Tale.*" *Booklist* 91 (April 1, 1995): 1354.

"If Oswald Had Lived . . . Could Impartial Jury Have Been Found To Try Him?" *Broadcasting* 66 (January 6, 1964): 52-53.

"Oswald on Trial for Kennedy Assassination in TV Drama." *Chicago Daily Law Bulletin* 132 (November 12, 1986): 3.

"Psychology: *The Two Assassins*." *Choice* 3 (March 1966): 79.

"This Week: *The Two Assassins*." *The Christian Century* 82 (November 17, 1965): 1424.

"Arts, Books and Sport: The Russian Connection [*Oswald's Tale*]." *The Economist* (London) 335 (June 10-16, 1995): 77-78.

"Editorial: 'Accused' or 'Assassin'." *Editor & Publisher* 96 (December 14, 1963): 6.

"Assassination Story Raised Legal Snares." *Editor & Publisher* 96 (December 14, 1963): 12.

"Detroit Reporter Gets Oswald Album Pictures." *Editor & Publisher* 97 (February 22, 1964): 61.

"Oswald Diary Publication Stirs Furor." *Editor & Publisher* 97 (July 4, 1964): 14.

"Nonfiction: *Lee: A Portrait of Lee Harvey Oswald by His Brother*." *Kirkus Reviews* 35 (October 1, 1967): 1249.

"Nonfiction: *Oswald's Tale*." *Kirkus Reviews* 63 (March 15, 1995): 363.

"Nonfiction: *Oswald And The CIA*." *Kirkus Reviews* 63 (June 15, 1995): 841-42.

"Nonfiction: *Assignment Oswald*." *Kirkus Reviews* 63 (December 15, 1995): 1747-48.

"The News: FBI Studies Oswald's Reading at New Orleans Public Library." *Library Journal* 89 (January 1, 1964): 74.

"Cover: Lee Oswald, With the Weapons He Used to Kill President Kennedy and Officer Tippit." *Life* 56 (February 21, 1964): 1.

"Mrs. Lee Harvey Oswald Watches the Baptism of Her Daughter." *Life* 56 (May 1, 1964): 36B.

"Cover: Oswald's Full Russian Diary: He and Marina in Minsk." *Life* 57 (July 10, 1964): 1, 26-31.

"Marina Oswald Becomes a Michigan Coed." *Life* 58 (January 15, 1965): 40C.

"Wedding of the Week: In Fate, Texas." *Life* 58 (June 11, 1965): 42.

"Texas Attorney Urges a Defender for Oswald." *National Guardian* 16 (January 2, 1964): 7.

"Oswald Case: A Lawyer Barred; A 'Show' on TV." *National Guardian* 16 (January 30, 1964): 9.

"The Oswald Case: Who Wants the Truth Kept Down?" *National Guardian* 16 (February 6, 1964): 1- 2.

"Oswald Panel Hears Mother." *National Guardian* 16 (February 13, 1964): 1, 6.

"How NYU Almost Shut Free Speech Out of Town Hall." *National Guardian* 16 (February 20, 1964): 1-2.

"Overflow at Town Hall." *National Guardian* 16 (February 27, 1964): 9.

"Oswald Case: A New Angle." *National Guardian* 16 (May 9, 1964): 1, 12.

"The Face in the Dallas Doorway." *National Guardian* 16 (May 30, 1964): 1, 8.

"Oswald: Startling New Variation." *National Guardian* 16 (6 June 1964): 1, 9.

"On the Left: The Background of the Assassin, Lee Harvey Oswald ..." *National Review* 15 (December 10, 1963): 2-3.

"Cui Bono? . . . How Lone a Loner." *National Review* 15 (December 10, 1963): 4.

"The Week: [Oswald and $5,000 from Mexico]." *National Review* 15 (December 17, 1963): 509.

"Hypothetical Case: A Letter." *National Review* 15 (17 Dec. 1963): 515-16; 16 (January 14, 1964): 36.

"Friends of Lee Oswald, Inc." *National Review* 16 (March 10, 1964): 183-85.

"The Plot to Clear Lee Oswald." *National Review* 16 (April 7, 1964): 265.

"Oswald: Flat Lux." *National Review* 22 (June 16, 1970): 606.

"The Marxist Marine." *Newsweek* 62 (December 2, 1963): 27.

"Oswald and the Weight of the Evidence." *Newsweek* 62 (December 9, 1963): 36-42.

"Medicine: Portrait of a Psychopath." *Newsweek* 62 (December 16, 1963): 83-84.

"Newsmakers: [Marina Oswald's Interview]." *Newsweek* 63 (February 10, 1964): 48.

"National Affairs: Investigation: 'Brave Little Woman'." *Newsweek* 63 (February 17, 1964): 17-18.

"The Assassination: Week in the Sun." *Newsweek* 63 (February 24, 1964): 29.

"Newsmakers: Town Talk . . . Marguerite Oswald." *Newsweek* 63 (March 2, 1964): 47.

"National Affairs: Puzzle Picture." *Newsweek* 63 (June 1, 1964): 19.

"Letters: The Oswald Diary [by] . . . Mrs. Marina Oswald." *Newsweek* 63 (August 10, 1964): 2.

"TV-Radio: 'Wasn't It Fun'?" *Newsweek* 64 (August 17, 1964): 80.

"The Periscope: Inside Story: Dallas." *Newsweek* 64 (September 21, 1964): 23-24.

"The Periscope: Cross-Country Wire: Dallas." *Newsweek* 64 (October 5, 1964): 28; 64 (October 19, 1964): 22; 64 (November 30, 1964): 60.

"Newsmakers: Gift of Gab." *Newsweek* 65 (January 18, 1965): 46; 65 (February 22, 1965): 46.

"Medicine: The Presidential Disease." *Newsweek* 65 (May 17, 1965): 67-68.

"National Affairs: Americana: Love Story." *Newsweek* 65 (June 14, 1965): 43-46.

"The Periscope: Diplomatic Pouch: Oswald on Trial." *Newsweek* 66 (August 30, 1965): 9.

"Newsmakers: Too Much Already." *Newsweek* 66 (August 30, 1965): 48.

"Newsmakers: [Auction of Lee Harvey Oswald's Letters etc.]." *Newsweek* 66 (October 11, 1965): 66.

"Books: Mama Oswald." *Newsweek* 67 (February 28, 1966): 92A-92B, 94.

"Newsmakers: [Marina Oswald Plans Role in Film 'Countdown in Dallas' for $20,000.00 Plus Royalties]." *Newsweek* 70 (September 25, 1967): 40.

"National Affairs: The Assassination: Scene of the Crime." *Newsweek* 70 (December 4, 1967): 31B- 32.

"The Periscope: The Marina Oswald Story." *Newsweek* 75 (January 12, 1970): 11.

"National Affairs: Investigations: Oswald and the U-2." *Newsweek* 77 (March 1, 1971): 31.

"Newsmakers: [Marina Oswald Porter's Attempts to Recover Lee Harvey Oswald's Possessions from the Government]." *Newsweek* 81 (March 12, 1973): 42.

"Update: Oswald's Widow." *Newsweek* 86 (August 11, 1975): 9.

"Periscope: Another Oswald Connection?" *Newsweek* 89 (March 7, 1977): 13.

"Newsmakers: [Marina Oswald Porter Plugging Her Book, *Marina and Lee*]." *Newsweek* 90 (September 26, 1977): 74.

"No Ordinary Secret Agent: Books: Mailer Talks About Lee and the KGB." *Newsweek* 125 (April 24, 1995): 60.

"Briefly Noted: General: *Lee*." *The New Yorker* 43 (December 2, 1967): 242.

"The Assassination Has Shadowed-But Not Defeated-The Family of Lee Harvey Oswald." *People Weekly* 20 (November 28, 1983): 156-58, 160, 164, 166-68, 172.

"PW Forecasts: Nonfiction: *Lee*." *Publishers Weekly* 192 (October 23, 1967): 51.

"PW Forecasts: Nonfiction: *Marina and Lee*." *Publishers Weekly* 212 (August 22, 1977): 56.

"PW Forecasts: Nonfiction: *Legend*." *Publishers Weekly* 213 (February 20, 1978): 116, 118.

"PW Forecasts: Nonfiction: *Oswald's Game*." *Publishers Weekly* 224 (October 7, 1983): 84.

"PW Forecasts: Nonfiction: *Oswald's Tale*." *Publishers Weekly* 242 (March 20, 1995): 48.

"PW Forecasts: Nonfiction: *Oswald And The CIA*." *Publishers Weekly* 242 (June 12, 1995): 54-55.

"PW Forecasts: Nonfiction: *Assignment Oswald.*" *Publishers Weekly* 242 (November 20, 1995): 57.

"PW Forecasts: Nonfiction: *Oswald Talked.*" *Publishers Weekly* 243 (February 19, 1996): 195.

"Hatred Knows No Logic." *The Saturday Evening Post* 237 (January 4, 1964): 80.

"Killing Still Mystery." *Science Newsletter* 86 (October 10, 1964): 230.

"The Man Who Killed Kennedy; the Man Who Killed Oswald." *Time* 82 (December 6, 1963): 33A-35.

"Investigations: Dear Ma." *Time* 82 (December 20, 1963): 13-14.

"Women: Three Widows." *Time* 83 (January 3, 1964): 29.

"Investigations: Between Two Fires." *Time* 83 (February 14, 1964): 16-20.

"Investigations: A Mother Who Wants to Write." *Time* 83 (February 21, 1964): 23-24.

"Investigations: An Attorney for Oswald." *Time* 83 (March 6, 1964): 47.

"Investigations: The Man Who Wanted to Kill Nixon." *Time* 83 (June 19, 1964): 21.

"Historical Notes: A Compendium of Curious Coincidences." *Time* 84 (August 21, 1964): 19.

"The Presidency: The Others." *Time* 84 (November 27, 1964): 32-34.

"People: 'The Eight-Week Crash Course at the University of Michigan's English Language Institute': Marina Oswald." *Time* 85 (January 1, 1965): 38.

"[Marina Oswald Re-marries]." *Time* 85 (June 11, 1965): 48.

"[Marina Oswald Porter Has Husband Arrested for Assault With a Gun]." *Time* 86 (August 27, 1965): 28.

"People: 'Auctioning Off the Documentary Remains of Her Son'." *Time* 86 (October 8, 1965): 53.

"The Sexes: Love The Analyst." *Time* 105 (March 24, 1975): 76.

"FBI: The Oswald Cover-Up." *Time* 106 (September 15, 1975): 19.

"Nation: FBI: Shaken by a Cover-Up That Failed." *Time* 106 (November 3, 1975): 9-10.

"The Capture of a Killer." *U. S. News and World Report* 55 (December 2, 1963): 10.

"The Assassination- as the Plot Unfolds . . . Case Against Oswald . . . How the President Was Shot." *U. S. News and World Report* 55 (December 9, 1963): 68-71.

"Another Assassination Attempt by Lee Oswald?" *U. S. News and World Report* 55 (December 16, 1963): 8.

"Strange World of Lee Oswald: More Light on the Assassination." *U. S. News and World Report* 55 (December 16, 1963): 8.

"A New Clue in Attempt to Shoot General Walker." *U. S. News and World Report* 56 (January 13, 1964): 10.

"Lee Oswald's Widow Tells Her Story." *U. S. News and World Report* 56 (February 17, 1964): 19.

"People of the Week: 'Counsel' For Oswald--A Top Lawyer Takes Job." *U. S. News and World Report* 56 (March 9, 1964): 16.

"The Oswald Mystery Grows Deeper and Deeper." *U. S. News and World Report* 56 (March 30, 1964): 45.

"New Light on 'Second Assassin' Theory." *U. S. News and World Report* 62 (May 29, 1967): 14.

"Why The JFK Case Is Coming Back To Life." *U. S. News and World Report* 82 (January 17, 1977): 28-30.

"Political Booknotes: *Legend.*" *The Washington Monthly* 10 (April 1978): 65.

JACK RUBY

Books:

Adelson, Alan. *The Ruby-Oswald Affair*. Seattle, Washington: Romar Books, Ltd., 1988.

Belli, Melvin M., with Maurice C. Carroll. *Dallas Justice: The Real Story of Jack Ruby and His Trial*. New York: David McKay Co., 1964.

Currie, Gordon. *Inside the Ruby Trial*. Los Angeles, California: Published by Author, 1964.

Denson, R. B. *Destiny in Dallas*. Dallas, Texas: Denco Corporation, 1964.

Gertz, Elmer. *Moment of Madness: The People vs. Jack Ruby*. Chicago, Illinois: The Follett Publishing Co., 1968.

Hunter, Diana, and Alice Anderson. *Jack Ruby's Girls*. Atlanta, Georgia: Hallux, Ind., 1970.

Joesten, Joachim. *La Verite sur le cas Jack Ruby* [Truth in the Jack Ruby Case]. Paris: Casterman, 1967.

Kantor, Seth. *Who Was Jack Ruby?* New York: Everest House, 1978. Re-titled *The Ruby Cover-Up*. Zebra Books, 1978, 1992.

Kaplan, John, and Jon R. Waltz. *The Trial of Jack Ruby: A Classic Study of Courtroom Strategies*. New York: Macmillan, 1965.

Pabst, Ralph M. *Plodding Toward Terror: A Personal Look at the Jack Ruby Case*. New York: Vantage Press, 1974.

Pottecher, Frederic. *Dallas: l'affaire Ruby*. Geneve: Edito-Service, 1971.

_____. *Grands proces, II: Dallas: affaire Ruby* [Great Trials: Dallas]. Paris: Arthaud, 1964, 1965.

_____. *Le proces de Dallas* [The Trial in Dallas]. Paris: Librairie Jules Tallandier, 1965.

Stern, R. *Le proces Ruby--Dallas* [The Trial of Ruby in Dallas]. Kapellen, Belgium: Beckers, 1967.

Wills, Garry, and Ovid Demaris. *Jack Ruby: The Man Who Killed the Man Who Killed Kennedy.* New York: New American Library, 1968; Da Capo Press, 1994.

Signed Articles:

[Arnoni, M. S.]. "Jack Ruby Cheats History." *The Minority of One* 9 (February 1967): 8.

Andrews, Joseph L. "New Books Appraised: Social Science: *Dallas Justice: The Real Story of Jack Ruby and His Trial.*" *Library Journal* 90 (February 1, 1965): 662.

Beck, Melinda, and Anne Underwood. "Jack Ruby: 'I Wanted to be a Hero'." *Newsweek* 122 (November 22, 1993): 94-95.

Bedford, Sybille. "The Ruby Trial: A Chance to Redeem a Tragedy." *Life* 56 (February 28, 1964): 36- 36B.

_____. " 'Violence, Froth, Sob Stuff--Was Justice Done'?" *Life* 56 (March 27, 1964): 32-34B, 70A-74.

Boroson, Warren. "The Bellicose Mr. Belli." *Fact* 1 (July/August 1964): 2-13.

Bromberg, Walter, and Elmer Gertz. "Correspondence: The Last Madness of Jack Ruby." *The New Republic* 156 (February 25, 1967): 42-43.

Buckley, Priscilla L. "Books, Arts, Manners: Shoot-Out in Dallas." *National Review* 20 (April 9, 1968): 349-50.

Callahan, John W. "Did Jack Ruby Kill the Wrong Man?" *Argosy* 365 (September 1967): 29, 96-104.

Cartwright, Gary. "Who Was Jack Ruby?" *Texas Monthly* 3 (November 1975): 82-86, 129-30, 132- 34.

Cartwright, H. L. "Letters: Justice and Oswald." *The Nation* 197 (December 21, 1963): 424.

Chambliss, Sanford. "Who Killed Jack Ruby?" *Real Magazine* 18 (April 1967): 40-42.

Cuff, Sergeant. "Criminal Record: Fact: *Jack Ruby.*" *Saturday Review* 51 (February 24, 1968): 52.

Dugger, Ronnie. "The Last Madness of Jack Ruby." *The New Republic* 156 (February 11, 1967): 19- 23.

Fiddick, Thomas C. "What Ruby Did Not Tell." *The Minority of One* 7 (November 1965): 15-16.

Forslund, Morris A. "Biography & Personal Narrative: *Jack Ruby.*" *Library Journal* 92 (December 1, 1967): 4406.

Gertz, Elmer. "*JFK* Errs on Jack Ruby." *Chicago Daily Law Bulletin* 138 (January 3, 1992): 2.

_____, and Wayne B. Giampietro. "The Trial of 'State Cases': A Postscript on the Jack Ruby Trial." *DePaul Law Review* 16 (1967): 285-308.

Havemann, Ernest. "Defendant Ruby Will Meet the Ghost of a Long Dead Scot." *Life* 56 (February 21, 1964): 30-33.

Hegyi, Karoly. "A Dallasi Itelethirdetes Utan [After Sentence Was Given at Dallas]." *Elore* (Bucharest) 18 (March 17, 1964): 3.

Kelley, Daniel Otis. "Social Science: Law: *The Trial of Jack Ruby.*" *Library Journal* 90 (September 15, 1965): 3619.

Kempton, Murray. "Jack Ruby--Surviving Victim." *The Spectator* (London), No. 7079 (February 28, 1964): 270.

_____. "Boy, Don't You Know I'm on Camera?" *The New Republic* 150 (February 29, 1964): 7.

_____. "Jack Ruby on Trial: 'Leave Me a Little Dignity'." *The New Republic* 150 (March 7, 1964): 17-20.

_____. "Who Killed Jack Ruby?" *The New Republic* 153 (November 27, 1965): 25-28.

_____. "Ruby, Oswald and the State." *The Spectator* (London) No. 7217 (October 21, 1966): 506-07.

_____. "The Disposable Jack Ruby." *The Spectator* (London) No. 7229 (January 13, 1967): 35.

Lane, Mark. "Who Is Jack Ruby?" *The Minority of One* 7 (April 1965): 8-11.

Lewis, Richard Warren. "A Flashy Lawyer for Oswald's Killer." *The Saturday Evening Post* 237 (February 8, 1964): 28-30.

Linn, Edward. "Appointment in Dallas: The Untold Story of Jack Ruby." *The Saturday Evening Post* 237 (July 25/August 1, 1964): 24-26, 28, 33, 36-37, 40, 48-49.

Mailer, Norman. "The Amateur Hit Man." *The New York Review of Books* 42 (May 11, 1995): 52-59.

Mayer, Martin. "Books in Review: Diminished Responsibility: *The Trial of Jack Ruby*." *Commentary* 41 (February 1966): 83-85, 88.

McCue, Howard, and Daniel W. Luther. "Closing The Door On The Estate of Jack Ruby." *Trusts & Estates* 131 (February 1992): 57.

Pietrusza, David. "Books in Brief: *Who Was Jack Ruby?*" *National Review* 31 (August 17, 1979): 1051.

Plummer, William. "Jack Ruby's Family and Lawyer Battle For Possession Of The Gun That Killed Lee Harvey Oswald." *People Weekly* 31 (May 22, 1989): 42-43.

Popa, Stefan. "Dallas: Procesul Ruby [Dallas: Ruby's Trial]." *Lumea* (Bucharest) 8 (February 20, 1964): 10-11; (February 27, 1964): 8-9.

_____. "Dallas 'Paziti-l Bine pe Ruby [Dallas Guarding Ruby's Rights]." *Lumea* (Bucharest) 2 (March 26, 1964): 10-11.

Poznanska, A. "Proces a Dallas [Trial in Dallas]." *Cite libre* (Montreal) 15 (April 1964): 26-28.

Preston, Gregor A. "Political Science & International Affairs: *Who Was Jack Ruby?*" *Library Journal* 103 (September 1, 1978): 1641-42.

Revere, Guy. "Jack Ruby: The Mafia's Guy in Dallas." *Saga* 33 (March 1967): 28-31, 86-90.

Ruby, Jack, with William Read Woodfield. "Why I Killed the Assassin." *New York Journal-American* (January 28, 1964).

Ruby, Jack, with David Welsh. "A Letter From Jail." *Ramparts* 5 (February 1967): 17-21.

Szasz, Thomas S. "Criminal Insanity: Facts or Strategy?" *The New Republic* 151 (November 21, 1964): 19-22.

Tupa, Stefan. "Dallas: Declaratii si Ipoteze." *Lumea* (Bucharest) 11 (March 12, 1964): 9-10.

Tuteur, Werner. "Dialogue in Dallas: Psychiatric Examination of Jack Ruby." *MH* [Mental Hygene] 58 (Spring 1974): 6-10.

Ushakov, G. "Dallas Merry-Go-Round." *New Times* (Moscow) (March 18, 1964): 27-29.

Wainwright, Loudon. "Exit Jack Ruby, a Nobody With One Big Moment." *Life* 62 (January 13, 1967): 18.

Walker, Timothy. "Why Jack Ruby Shot Lee Harvey Oswald." *Law Institute Journal* 61 (June 1987): 544-45.

Wice, Brian. "A Trial to Remember: Appeal Overturned Conviction for Crime Millions Saw." *New Jersey Law Journal* 118 (October 16, 1986): 1, 22-23.

Wills, Garry, and Ovid Demaris. "You All Know Me! I'm Jack Ruby!; The Disposal of Jack Ruby." *Esquire* 67 (May 1967): 79-87, 153-64; 67 (June 1967): 131-35, 172-84.

Worthington, Peter. "The Limelight: Why Jack Ruby's First Trial Couldn't Happen Here." *Maclean's* 77 (April 18, 1964): 3-4.

Unsigned Articles:

"Editorials: The Rights of Men . . . Power and Responsibility." *America* 109 (December 14, 1963): 761.

"Hungarian Cartoonists and Jack Ruby." *Atlas* 7 (February 1964): 113.

"Radio-TV Barred From Ruby Trial." *Broadcasting* 65 (December 23, 1963): 56.

"Radio-TV Newsmen Testify in Ruby Trial." *Broadcasting* 66 (March 16, 1964): 74.

"Murder, Justice and TV; A Newsy Trio." *Broadcasting* 66 (March 23, 1964): 90.

"Filling Out the Jury." *Chemical Week* 94 (March 7, 1964): 24.

"Political Science: *The Trial of Jack Ruby.*" *Choice* 2 (January 1966): 822.

"History, Geography, and Travel: North America: *Who Was Jack Ruby?*" *Choice* 15 (January 1979): 1584.

"This Week: *The Trial of Jack Ruby.*" *The Christian Century* 82 (October 20, 1965): 1291.

"Dallas on Trial." *The Economist* (London) 210 (February 22, 1964): 700-03.

"Dallas in Two Minds." *The Economist* (London) 210 (March 21, 1964): 1107-08.

"PR Firm Sets Press Rules For Judge at Ruby's Trial." *Editor & Publisher* 96 (December 28, 1963): 9.

"Bloom Tells His Public Relations Role in Ruby Case." *Editor & Publisher* 97 (February 1, 1964): 58.

"Jack Ruby's Story." *Editor & Publisher* 97 (February 1, 1964): 58.

"48 Seats at Ruby's Trial For Press; Protest Filed." *Editor & Publisher* 97 (February 15, 1964): 14, 66.

"125 Allowed in Court at Ruby's Trial." *Editor & Publisher* 97 (February 22, 1964): 61.

"9 Artists Sketch Ruby Trial Scenes." *Editor & Publisher* 97 (March 14, 1964): 15.

"Ruby Always Around, Acting Like Reporter." *Editor & Publisher* 97 (March 14, 1964): 15.

"Ruby Death Verdict: A TV 'Spectacular'." *Editor & Publisher* 97 (March 21, 1964): 11, 55.

"Recent Publications: *The Trial of Jack Ruby*." *Harvard Law Review* 79 (January 1966): 684.

"Nonfiction: *The Trial of Jack Ruby*." *Kirkus Reviews* 33 (July 15, 1965): 723.

"Nonfiction: *Jack Ruby*." *Kirkus Reviews* 35 (October 15, 1967): 1306.

"Biography & Personal Narrative: *Jack Ruby's Girls*." *Library Journal* 96 (February 1, 1971): 471.

"Was This Man Sane?" *Life* 56 (February 21, 1964): 26-29.

"Jack Ruby Cheats History." *The Minority of One* 9 (February 1967): 8.

"Editorials: The Jack Ruby Case." *The Nation* 200 (March 29, 1965): 323.

"A Jack Ruby 'Suicide' Is Predicted." *National Guardian* 16 (April 4, 1964): 6.

"Ruby Is Balked in Plea to Meet Warren Board." *National Guardian* 16 (May 2, 1964): 9.

"Belli Charges a Cop Spurred Ruby to 'Lynching' of Oswald." *National Guardian* 16 (August 8, 1964): 5.

"T. R. B. from Washington: The Dallas Story." *The New Republic* 149 (December 21, 1963): 2.

"Police in Dallas." *The New Republic* 150 (January 18, 1964): 8.

"T. R. B. from Washington: Jack Ruby Died in Dallas of Cancer." *The New Republic* 156 (January 14, 1967): 6.

"National Affairs: 'I Got Principles'." *Newsweek* 62 (December 9, 1963): 44-46.

"The Assassination: Day in Court." *Newsweek* 63 (January 6, 1964): 18-19.

"National Affairs: Dallas: Ruby's 'Fugue State'." *Newsweek* 63 (February 3, 1964): 25-26.

"Press: By Jack Ruby." *Newsweek* 63 (10 Feb. 1964): 79-80; 63 (March 2, 1964): 5.

"National Affairs: Trials: War of Nerves." *Newsweek* 63 (March 2, 1964): 19.

"Press: '. . . A Little Dignity'." *Newsweek* 63 (March 2, 1964): 80.

"National Affairs: Trials: On Camera." *Newsweek* 63 (March 16, 1964): 31-32.

"National Affairs: Trials: The Avenger." *Newsweek* 63 (March 23, 1964): 28-31.

"Medicine: The 'Possessed'." *Newsweek* 63 (March 23, 1964): 66.

"National Affairs: Trials: Good-by, Belli." *Newsweek* 63 (March 30, 1964): 19.

"National Affairs: The Assassination: Ruby's Fantasy." *Newsweek* 63 (May 11, 1964): 23.

"Press: What's Your Source?" *Newsweek* 64 (August 31, 1964): 68-69.

"National Affairs: Dallas: Objection Sustained." *Newsweek* 68 (October 17, 1966): 31-32.

"The Assassination: 'Who Can Understand'?" *Newsweek* 69 (January 16, 1967): 28-29.

"PW Forecasts: Nonfiction: *Jack Ruby.*" *Publishers Weekly* 192 (October 23, 1967): 51.

"PW Forecasts: Nonfiction: *Jack Ruby's Girls.*" *Publishers Weekly* 197 (June 29, 1970): 102.

"PW Forecasts: Nonfiction: *Who Was Jack Ruby?*" *Publishers Weekly* 214 (July 31, 1978): 83.

"In Jurul Procesului de la Dallas. Rasfoind Presa Straina [In the Jury Trial at Dallas: Looking through the Foreign Press]." *Scinteia* 33 (March 9, 1964): 4.

"Jack Ruby: 19. II. 1911--3 I. 1967 [Jack Ruby 19 February 1911-3 January 1967]." *Der Spiegel* (Hamburg) 21 (1967): 72.

"The Law: Lawyers: Belli for the Defense: A Flamboyant Advocate." *Time* 82 (December 20, 1963): 48.

"Investigations: For the Defense." *Time* 83 (January 31, 1964): 20-21.

"Investigations: A Defendant Who Wants Attention." *Time* 83 (February 21, 1964): 23.

"The Law: Juries: 'Like Picking a Wife'." *Time* 83 (February 28, 1964): 53-54.

"Trials: Another Day in Dallas; The Ruby Jurors." *Time* 83 (March 13, 1964). 24-25.

"Trials: Death for Ruby." *Time* 83 (March 20, 1964): 27-28.

"The Law: Lawyers: Casus Belli." *Time* 83 (March 27, 1964): 34-36.

"The Law: Lawyers: The Ruby Scorecard." *Time* 83 (April 3, 1964): 68.

"Texas: Trying for the Truth of It." *Time* 83 (May 8, 1964): 26.

"The Law: Lawyers: And So to Court." *Time* 84 (July 31, 1964): 62.

"The Press: Reporters: 50,000 Word Leak." *Time* 84 (August 28, 1964): 40.

"The Law: Trials: The Ruby Circus." *Time* 86 (November 5, 1965): 86.

"Sequels: A Last Wish." *Time* 88 (December 30, 1966): 12.

"The Assassination: A Non-Entity for History." *Time* 89 (January 13, 1967): 16-17.

"The Law: Criminal Justice: What Does a Change of Venue Gain?" *Time* 89 (January 13, 1967): 39- 40.

"Historical Notes: The Infamous Cobra." *Time* 89 (March 31, 1967): 23.

"Jack Ruby's Strange Trial--New Chapter in Assassination Story." *U. S. News and World Report* 56 (March 23, 1964): 70.

"Now, A Chance of Freedom for Jack Ruby." *U. S. News and World Report* 61 (October 17, 1966): 16.

THE WARREN REPORT

Official Printings:

United States. *Investigation of the Assassination of President John F. Kennedy: Hearings Before the President's Commission on the Assassination of President Kennedy.* 26 vols., Washington, D. C.: U. S. Government Printing Office, 1964.

_____. *Report of the President's Commission on the Assassination of President Kennedy.* Washington, D. C.: U. S. Government Printing Office, 1964.

Other Printings:

United States. *A Concise Compendium of the Warren Commission Report on the Assassination of John F. Kennedy.* Foreword by Robert J. Donovan. New York: Popular Library, 1964.

_____. *The Official Warren Commission Report on the Assassination of President John F. Kennedy.* Analysis and Commentary by Louis Nizer, Historical Afterword by Bruce Catton. Garden City, New York: Doubleday, 1964.

_____. *Report of the Warren Commission: The Assassination of President Kennedy.* Introduction by Harrison E. Salisbury. New York: McGraw-Hill, 1964.

_____. *The Warren Commission Report: The Assassination of President Kennedy.* Analysis by Miriam Ottenberg. Washington, D. C.: U. S. Information Agency, 1964.

_____. *The Warren Commission Report: The Official Report of the President's Commission on the Assassination of President John F. Kennedy.* Stamford, Connecticut: Longmeadow Press, 1992.

_____. *The Warren Commission Report: Report of the President's Commission on the Assassination of President John F. Kennedy.* New York: St. Martin's Press, 1992.

_____. *The Warren Report: Report of the President's Commission on the Assassination of President John F. Kennedy.* New York: Associated Press, 1964.

_____. *Warren Report uber die Ermordung des Prasidenten John F. Kennedy.* Herausgegeben und kommentiert von Robert M. W. Kempner. Cologne: Kiepenhever & Witsch, 1964.

_____. *The Witnesses: The Highlights of Hearings Before the Warren Commission on the Assassination of President Kennedy.* Introduction by Anthony Lewis. New York: Bantam Books, 1964; McGraw-Hill, 1965.

THE WARREN COMMISSION: FOR AND AGAINST

Books:

Associated Professional Services, ed. *Highlights of the Warren Report: The Facts and Findings Surrounding the Assassination of John F. Kennedy.* Hollywood, California: Associated Professional Services, Inc., 1964.

Belin, David W. *Final Disclosure.* New York: Charles Scribner's Sons, 1988.

_____. *November 22, 1963: You Are the Jury.* New York: Quadrangle, 1973.

Brown, Walt. *The Warren Omission: A Micro-Study of the Methods and Failures of the Warren Commission.* Wilmington, Delaware: Delmax, 1996.

Crawford, Curtis, ed. *Critical Reactions to the Warren Report.* New York: Marzani and Munsell, 1964.

David, Jay. *The Weight of the Evidence: The Warren Report and Its Critics.* New York: Meredith Press, 1968.

Davis, Marc, and Jim Mathews, eds. *Highlights of the Warren Report.* Covina, California: Collectors Publications, 1967.

Epstein, Edward Jay. *Inquest: The Warren Commission and the Establishment of Truth.* Introduction by Richard H. Rovere. New York: Viking Press, 1966; Bantam, 1966; London: Hutchinson & Co., Ltd., 1966.

_____. *O relatorio de medo: A Comissao Warren e a busca da verdade* [Translation of *Inquest*]. Rio de Janiero: Ed. Inova, 1967.

Ford, Gerald R., with John R. Stiles. *Portrait of the Assassin.* New York: Simon & Schuster, 1965; Ballantine Books, 1966.

Fox, Sylvan. *The Unanswered Questions About President Kennedy's Assassination.* New York: Award Books, 1965, 1975; London: Mayflower-Dell, 1966.

Joesten, Joachim. *The Gaps in the Warren Report.* New York: Marzani and Munsell, 1964.

_____. *Oswald: Assassin or Fall Guy?* London: The Merlin Press, 1964; New York: Marzani and Munsell, 1964.

_____. *Die Wahrheit uber den Kennedy-Mord: Wie und Warum der Warren Report lugt* [The Truth About the Kennedy Murder: How and Why the Warren Report is Lying]. Zurich: Schweizer Verlagshaus, 1966; Utrecht: Bruna & Zoon, 1966.

Jones, Penn, Jr. *Forgive My Grief: A Critical Review of the Warren Commission Report on the Assassination of President John F. Kennedy.* Midlothian, Texas: Midlothian Mirror, 1966.

_____. *Forgive My Grief II: A Further Critical Review of the Warren Commission Report on the Assassination of President John F. Kennedy.* Midlothian, Texas: Midlothian Mirror, 1967.

_____. *Forgive My Grief III.* Midlothian, Texas: Published by Author, 1969; revised ed., 1976.

_____. *Forgive My Grief IV.* Midlothian, Texas: Published by Author, 1974.

Lane, Mark. *A Citizen's Dissent: Mark Lane Replies.* New York: Holt, Rinehart & Winston, 1968; Fawcett Paperbacks, 1969.

_____. *Rush To Judgement: A Critique of the Warren Commission's Inquiry into the Murder of President John F. Kennedy, Officer J. D. Tippit, and Lee Harvey Oswald.* With Introduction by Hugh Trevor-Roper. New York: Holt, Rinehart & Winston, 1966; Fawcett Paperbacks, 1967; Dell Paperback, 1975; Thunder's Mouth Press, 1992.

Lewis, Richard Warren. *The Scavengers and Critics of the Warren Report.* New York: Delacorte Press, 1967; Dell, 1967.

Maclean, Don, ed. *The Illustrated and Abridged Warren Report.* Washington, D. C.: The Tatler Publishing Co., n. d.

Meagher, Sylvia. *Accessories After the Fact: The Warren Commission, the Authorities, and the Report.* With Introduction by Leo Sauvage. Indianapolis, Indiana: Bobbs-Merrill, 1967; New York: Vintage Books, 1976; Random House, 1992.

Meunier, Robert F. *Shadows of Doubt: The Warren Commission Cover-Up.* Hicksville, New York: Exposition Press, 1976.

Michel, Armand. *L'Assassinat de John Kennedy: le Rapport Warren et ses Critiques.* Paris: Trinckvel, 1968.

Moss, Armand. *Disinformation, Misinformation, and the "Conspiracy" to Kill JFK Exposed.* Hamden, Connecticut: Archon Press, 1987.

Nash, Harry C. *Citizen's Arrest: The Dissent of Penn Jones, Jr., in the Assassination of JFK.* Austin, Texas: Latitudes Press, 1977.

Newman, Albert H. *The Assassination of John F. Kennedy: The Reasons Why.* New York: Clarkson N. Potter, 1970.

Roberts, Charles. *The Truth About the Assassination.* New York: Grosset & Dunlap, 1967.

Sauvage, Leo. *L'affaire Oswald: Reponse au Rapport Warren.* Paris: Les Editions de Minuit, 1965.

_____. *The Oswald Affair: An Examination of the Contradictions and Omissions of the Warren Report.* Cleveland, Ohio: World Publishing Co., 1966.

Scott, Peter Dale, Paul L. Hoch, and Russell Stetler, eds. *The Assassinations: Dallas and Beyond: A Guide to Cover-Ups and Investigations.* New York: Random House, 1976.

Sparrow, John Hanbury Angus. *After the Assassination: A Positive Appraisal of the Warren Report.* New York: Chilmark Press, 1967.

Thomson, George C. *The Quest For Truth: Or How Kennedy Was Really Assassinated.* Glendale, California: G.C. Thomson Engineering Co., 1964.

Weisberg, Harold. *Selections From Whitewash.* New York: Carroll & Graf Publishers, Inc., 1994.

_____. *Whitewash: The Report on the Warren Report.* Hyattstown, Maryland: Published by Author, 1965, 1966; New York: Dell, 1966.

_____. *Whitewash II: The FBI-Secret Service Cover-Up.* Hyattstown, Maryland: Published by Author, 1966; New York: Dell, 1967.

_____. *Whitewash IV: Top Secret JFK Assassination Transcript.* Frederick, Maryland: Published by Author, 1974.

West, John R. *Death of the President: The Warren Commission on Trial.* Covina, California: Collectors Publications, 1967.

White, Stephen. *Should We Now Believe the Warren Report?* New York: Macmillan, 1968.

Signed Articles:

A. D. "Sonderkommission untersucht Kennedy-Attentat [Special Commission to Investigate Kennedy's Assassination]." *Polizei-Polizeipraxis. Fachzeitschrift fur das Sicherheits und Ordnungswewen* (Cologne) 55 (1964): 159-60.

[Arnoni, M. S.]. "Mr. Warren's Prerogative?" *The Minority of One* 6 (March 1964): 2.

Arnoni, M. S. "An Open Letter to Chief Justice Earl Warren." *The Minority of One* 6 (April 1964): 1-2.

[Arnoni, M. S.]. "The Investigation." *The Minority of One* 6 (April 1964): 4.

_____. "A Verdict or Propaganda?" *The Minority of One* 6 (May 1964): 4-5.

_____. "Ripe for the [Warren] Report." *The Minority of One* 6 (June 1964): 5.

_____. "Awaiting the Report." *The Minority of One* 6 (July 1964): 4-5.

_____. "The Report." *The Minority of One* 6 (November 1964): 2-3.

_____. "A Commentator Fights a Reporter." *The Minority of One* 6 (November 1964): 5.

_____. "The Relevance of an *Inquest*." *The Minority of One* 8 (July/August 1966): 8-9.

_____. "Between Two Assassinations." *The Minority of One* 8 (September 1966): 6.

_____. "A Dead Brother Is No Brother." *The Minority of One* 9 (January 1967): 6.

Aynesworth, Hugh. "Oswald Book Filled With Inaccuracies." *Editor & Publisher* 97 (August 1, 1964): 40.

Barber, Gary D. "Social Science: Law & Criminology: *Final Disclosure*." *Library Journal* 113 (December 1988): 127.

Belfrage, Cedric. "Books: Assassination Whitewash." *National Guardian* 18 (July 2, 1966): 12.

Belin, David W. "The Warren Commission Was Right." *Skeptic* No. 9 (August 1975): 12-15, 51-53.

Bernt, H. H. "New Books Appraised: Social Science: *Inquest*." *Library Journal* 91 (August 1966): 3752.

_____. "New Books Appraised: Law, Criminal Procedure: *Rush To Judgement*." *Library Journal* 91 (October 1, 1966): 4688.

_____. "Law, Crime & Criminal Procedure: *Accessories After the Fact*." *Library Journal* 92 (November 1, 1967): 4022.

_____. "Social Science: *After the Assassination.*" *Library Journal* 93 (June 1, 1968): 2254.

_____. "Social Science: *Should We Now Believe the Warren Report?*" *Library Journal* 93 (June 15, 1968): 2516-17.

_____. "Social Science: *A Citizen's Dissent.*" *Library Journal* 93 (June 15, 1968): 2518.

Bickel, Alexander. "The Failure of the Warren Report." *Commentary* 42 (October 1966): 31-39.

_____. "Re-Examining the Warren Report." *The New Republic* 156 (January 7, 1967): 25-28.

_____. "Still At It." *The New Republic* 158 (March 23, 1968): 41.

_____. "Back to the Attack." *The New Republic* 158 (June 22, 1968): 28-29.

Bickel, Alexander, with W. Lister. "CBS On The Warren Report: How Many Bullets?" *The New Republic* 157 (July 15, 1967): 29-30; 157 (August 19, 1967): 30-34.

Bonazzi, Robert. "One Man's Grief." *The Texas Observer* 59 (September 29, 1967): 12-13.

Brandon, Henry, with Tetsuo Tamana. "State of Affairs: Questions From Abroad." *Saturday Review* 47 (May 9, 1964): 9; (June 27, 1964): 21.

Butterfield, Roger. "The Assassination: Some Serious Exceptions to the Warren Report." *Harper's Magazine* 233 (October 1966): 122, 124-26.

Campbell, Alex. "Books and the Arts: What Did Happen in Dallas?" *The New Republic* 154 (June 25, 1966): 23-25.

Cato. "From Washington Straight." *National Review* 16 (April 21, 1964): 311.

Cline, R. A. "Postscript To Warren." *The Spectator* (London) No. 7231 (January 27, 1967): 99.

Cockburn, Alexander. "American Diary: Oswald Frame-Up." *New Statesman* (London) 5 (February 28, 1992): 16-17.

_____. "Beat The Devil: In Defense of the Warren Commission." *The Nation* 254 (March 9, 1992): 294-95, 306.

Cohen, Jacob. "What the Warren Report Omits: The Vital Documents." *The Nation* 203 (July 11, 1966): 43-49.

_____. "The Warren Commission Report and Its Critics." *Frontier* 18 (November 1966): 5-20.

Cook, Fred J. "Some Unanswered Questions: The Warren Commission Report." *The Nation* 202 (June 13, 1966): 705-15.

_____. "Testimony of the Eyewitnesses: The Warren Commission Report." *The Nation* 202 (June 20, 1966): 737-46.

_____. "Letters: Cook on Cohen." *The Nation* 203 (August 22, 1966): 138, 156.

Crawford, Kenneth. "The Warren Impeachers." *Newsweek* 64 (October 19, 1964): 40.

Crinkley, R. "Books in Brief: *After the Assassination.*" *National Review* 20 (September 10, 1968): 918.

Cushman, Robert F. "Why the Warren Commission?" *New York University Law Review* 40 (May 1965): 477-503.

Dellinger, Dave. "The Warren Report?: The Death of a President." *Liberation* 9 (January 1965): 11-12.

_____. "Editorials: The Warren Report?" *Liberation* 10 (March 1965): 3-5.

Dempsey, David. "Warren Report in Mass Production." *Saturday Review* 47 (November 7, 1964): 25, 38.

Devlin, Patrick. "Death of a President: The Established Facts." *The Atlantic Monthly* 215 (March 1965): 112-18.

Drinnon, Richard, with John Jamieson. "War on Violence . . . The Warren Report . . ." *Wilson Library Bulletin* 45 (September 1970): 68-77; 45 (November 1970): 236; 45 (February 1971): 545.

Ellis, W. "The Warren Report." *Jubilee* 12 (December 1964): 24-27.

Epstein, Edward Jay. "Who's Afraid of the Warren Report?" *Esquire* 60 (December 1966): 204, 330- 32, 334.

Erlebacher, Albert. "Book Review: *November 22, 1963*." *Perspective* 3 (January/February 1974): 13-14.

Evans, M. Stanton. "A Sober Assessment." *National Review* 18 (January 11, 1966): 34-37.

Fein, Arnold L. "JFK In Dallas: The Warren Report and Its Critics." *Saturday Review* 49 (October 22, 1966): 36-38, 43-47.

Fensterwald, Bernard, Jr. "The Federal Bureau of Investigation and the Assassination of President Kennedy." *Computers and Automation* 20 (September 1971): 26-29.

Fixx, James F. "As Others See Us." *Saturday Review* 47 (November 7, 1964): 35-37.

Fonzi, Gaeton. "The Warren Commission, the Truth, and Arlen Specter." *Greater Philadelphia* 57 (August 1966): 38-45, 79-91.

_____. "Loose Ends: How Many Did the Warren Commission Leave? And Do They Lead Anywhere?" *Greater Philadelphia* 58 (January 1967): 66-69, 88-108.

Ford, Gerald R. "Piecing Together the Evidence." *Life* 57 (October 2, 1964): 42-51.

Fox, Sylvan. " 'Mein Gott, sie bringen uns alle um!' Die Ratsel um Kennedys Tod ['My God, You Bring Everything to Us.' The Riddle of Kennedy's Death]." *Der Spiegel* (Hamburg) 15 (1967): 88-110; 16 (1967): 102-19; 17 (1967): 106-17; 18 (1967): 108-24.

Freese, Paul L. "The Warren Commission and the Fourth Shot: A Reflection on the Fundamentals of Forensic Factfinding." *New York University Law Review* 40 (May 1965): 424-65.

Friedman, Rick. "The Weekly Editor: Assassination Book: [Penn Jones, Jr.]." *Editor & Publisher* 99 (November 12, 1966): 100.

Gest, Ted, and Joseph P. Shapiro. "JFK: The Untold Story of the Warren Commission." *U. S. News and World Report* 113 (August 17, 1992): 28-31, 36-42.

Goodhart, Arthur L. "The Warren Commission from a Procedural Standpoint." *New York University Law Review* 40 (May 1965): 404-23.

_____. "The Warren Commission: The Critics and the Law: 2. Legal Ignorance and False Logic." *The Reporter* 35 (December 15, 1966): 47-50.

Graziani, Gilbert. "Le Mystere Kennedy [The Kennedy Mystery]." *Paris Match* 920 (November 26, 1966): 75-86.

Gross, Alfred A. "Shadows of Doubt." *The Christian Century* 83 (September 28, 1966): 1178.

Habe, Hans. "Die Halfte der Wahrheit. Der Morder gefunden--der Mord ungeklart. Bemerkungen zum Bericht des Warren-Ausschusses [Half of the Truth. The Murderer Identified--the Murder Unexplained. Remarks on the Warren Commission's Report]." *Weltoche* (Zurich) 32 (1964): 13.

Hamsher, J. Herbert. "Interpersonal Trust, Internal-External Control, and the Warren Commission Report." *Journal of Personality and Social Psychology* 9 (July 1968): 210-15.

Handlin, Oscar. "The Warren Commission." *The Atlantic Monthly* 218 (August 1966): 117-18.

_____. "Oswald's Ghost." *The Atlantic Monthly* 218 (October 1966): 144-45.

_____. "Reader's Choice: *Accessories After the Fact.*" *The Atlantic Monthly* 221 (February 1968): 141.

Hermann, Kai. "Wer War Kennedys Morder? [Who Murdered Kennedy?]." *Die Zeit* (Hamburg) 19 (1964): 7.

Holland, Max. "The Key To The Warren Report." *American Heritage* 46 (November 1995): 50-52, 54, 56-58, 60, 62, 64.

Jacobson, Dan. "Mean Street: Warren Commission Report." *New Statesman* (London) 69 (January 15, 1965): 76-77.

Jenkins, Gareth. "Who Shot President Kennedy-or Fact and Fable in History." *Computers and Automation* 21 (February 1972): 43-46.

Joesten, Joachim. "Der falsche Oswald. Was der Warren-Bericht enthult--aber nicht ausspricht [The Fake Oswald, What the Warren Report Reveals--But Does Not State]." *Weltwoche* (Zurich) 32 (1964): 49.

Kaplan, David A. "The JFK Probe-25 Years Later." *The National Law Journal* 11 (November 28, 1988): 1, 24.

Kaplan, John. "The Assassins." *The American Scholar* 36 (Spring 1967): 271-86, 288, 290, 294, 296, 298, 300, 302, 304, 306.

_____. "The Assassin." *Stanford Law Review* 19 (1967): 1110-51.

Karp, Irwin. "Debate Over Dallas." *Saturday Review* 51 (March 9, 1968): 113-14.

Keisler, J. R. "The Warren Report: From Readers' Letters." *The Minority of One* 8 (June 1966): 29.

Kelly, Frank. "Book Reviews: *Inquest.*" *America* 115 (July 30, 1966): 118-20.

_____. "Book Reviews: *Rush To Judgement.*" *America* 115 (September 24, 1966): 350-52.

Kempton, Murray. "Oswald: May We Have Some Facts Please?" *The New Republic* 150 (June 13, 1964): 13-15.

_____. "The Warren Report--Reasonable Doubt." *The Spectator* (London) No. 7110 (October 2, 1964): 428-29.

_____. "Warren Report: Case for the Prosecution." *The New Republic* 151 (October 10, 1964): 13-17.

Kerby, Phil. "This Month: The Critics." *Frontier* 18 (November 1966): 2, 26.

Kitching, Jessie. "Forecasts: Additional Listings: *Rush To Judgement.*" *Publishers Weekly* 190 (July 18, 1966): 76-77.

Knebl, Fletcher. "The Warren Commission Report on the Assassination Is Struck by 'A New Wave of Doubt'." *Look* 30 (July 12, 1966): 66-72.

Krebs, A. V. "Books: *Accessories After the Fact.*" *Commonweal* 88 (September 20, 1968): 637-39.

Kurtz, Michael L. "Book Review: *Disinformation, Misinformation, and the "Conspiracy" to Kill JFK Exposed.*" *Journal of American History* 75 (September 1988): 677-78.

_____. "Book Review: *Final Disclosure.*" *Journal of American History* 76 (December 1989): 993-94.

Lane, Mark. "Lane on Warren Report: The Doubts Remain." *National Guardian* 16 (October 3, 1964): 3-6.

_____. "The Warren Report: A First Glance." *The Minority of One* 6 (November 1964): 6-8.

Macdonald, Dwight. "A Critique of the Warren Report." *Esquire* 63 (March 1965): 59-63, 127-28.

Macdonald, Neil. "Confidential and Secret Documents of the Warren Commission Deposited in the U. S. Archives." *Computers and Automation* 19 (November 1970): 44-47.

Meagher, Sylvia. "On 'Closing Doors, Not Opening Them' or The Limits of the Warren Investigation." *The Minority of One* 8 (July/August 1966): 29-32.

_____. "Four Books on the Warren Report: The Summer of Discontent." *Studies On The Left* 6 (September/October 1966): 72-84.

_____. "Letters: The Warren Commission Report and Its Critics." *Frontier* 18 (January 1967): 23-24.

_____. "Post-Assassination Credibility Chasm." *The Minority of One* 9 (March 1967): 21-22.

_____. ""Wheels Within Deals: How the Kennedy 'Investigation' Was Organized." *The Minority of One* 10 (July/August 1968): 23-27.

_____. "Finishing the Commission's Unfinished Business." *Skeptic* No. 9 (August 1975): 31-38, 61-62.

Meyer, Karl E., and N. MacKenzie. "Spotlight on Warren." *New Statesman* (London) 68 (October 2, 1964): 474-76.

Michalak, Thomas J. "New Books Appraised: History: *Portrait of the Assassin.*" *Library Journal* 90 (June 15, 1965): 2850.

Mills, Andrew. "Who Killed Kennedy? The Warren Report Is Right." *True* 48 (December 1967): 31- 32, 72-77.

Montague, Ivor. "The Warren Report." *Labour Monthly* (London) 46 (November 1964): 449-503.

Mosk, Richard M. "The Warren Commission and the Legal Process." *Case & Comment Magazine* 72 (May/June 1967): 13-20.

_____. "Yes: 'Beyond a Reasonable Doubt'." *ABA Journal* 77 (April 1992): 36.

Muggeridge, Malcolm. "Books: . . . *Inquest* by Edward Jay Epstein." *Esquire* 66 (October 1966): 14- 16.

Muhlen, Norbert. "Mord und Legende. Die Kritiker des Warren-Reports [Murder and Legend. Critics of the Warren Report]." *Der Monat. Internationale Zeitschrift fur Politik und geistiges Leben* (Frankfurt/Main) 199 (January 17, 1965): 14-28.

Nash, George, and Patricia. "The Other Witnesses." *The New Leader* 47 (October 12, 1964): 6-9.

Northcott, Kaye. "Belin Asks Too Much." *The Texas Observer* 63 (August 13, 1971): 23.

O'Brien, Conor Cruise. "Veto by Assassination?" *The Minority of One* 9 (December 1967): 16-18.

Olds, Greg. "The Official Doubters." *The Texas Observer* 61 (February 6, 1970): 9-11.

Osterburg, James W. "The Warren Commission: Report and Hearings." *Journal of Forensic Sciences* 11 (July 1966): 261-71.

Osvald, Frank. "Kan Man Stole pa Warren? [Can One Trust Warren?]" *Verdens Gang* (Copenhagen) 18 (1964): 274-79.

Oswald, Marguerite C. "The Warren Report: From Readers' Letters." *The Minority of One* 8 (June 1966): 29.

Packer, Herbert L. "The Warren Report: A Measure of the Achievement." *The Nation* 199 (November 2, 1964): 295-99.

Podhoretz, Norman. "The Warren Commission: An Editorial." *Commentary* 37 (January 1964): 24.

Policoff, Jerry. "The Belin Connection." *Rolling Stone* No. 185 (August 24, 1975): 31.

Possony, Stefan T. "Clearing the Air." *National Review* 17 (February 9, 1965): 113-14, 116.

Rosen, Sol Z. "Book Reviews: *Rush To Judgement*." *The Journal of American History* 53 (March 1967): 869-70.

Rosenberg, Maurice. "The Warren Commission." *The Nation* 199 (September 14, 1964): 110-12.

Russell, Bertrand. "16 Questions on the Assassintion." *The Minority of One* 6 (September 1964): 6- 8.

Russell, Francis. "Doubts About Dallas." *National Review* 18 (September 6, 1966): 887-88, 890-93.

Sauvage, Leo. "As I Was Saying." *The New Leader* 47 (November 9, 1964): 11-13.

_____. "The Warren Commission's Case Against Oswald." *The New Leader* 48 (November 22, 1965): 16-21.

_____. "Oswald's Case Against the Warren Commission." *The New Leader* 48 (December 20, 1965): 5-10, 30.

_____. "The Case Against Mr. X." *The New Leader* 49 (January 3, 1966): 13-18, 33.

_____. "Professor Bickel and the Warren Commission." *The New Leader* 49 (November 7, 1966): 16-19.

_____. "As I Was Saying." *The New Leader* 49 (November 21, 1966): 21-22.

Schoenmann, Ralph. "Ist der Warren-Bericht uber den Tod Prasident Kennedys glaubwurdig? [Is the Warren Report on President Kennedy's Death Believable?]" *Frankfurter Hefte. Zeitschrift fur Kultur und Politik* (Frankfurt/Main) 20 (January 1965): 15-24.

Schwartz, Jay. "A Legal Demurrer to the Report of the Warren Commission." *Journal of Forensic Sciences* 11 (July 1966): 318-29.

Scobey, Alfredda. "A Lawyer's Notes on the Warren Commission Report." *ABA Journal* 51 (January 1965): 39-43.

Sevilla, Charles M. "Social Science: Law & Criminology: *November 22, 1963.*" *Library Journal* 99 (February 1, 1974): 376, 378.

Shannon, William V. "National Affairs: Enough Is Enough." *Commonweal* 85 (November 18, 1966): 191-92.

Simpson, Alan W. B. "Letters to the Editor: Postscript to Warren." *The Spectator* (London) No. 7232 (February 3, 1967): 133.

Smith, Jack A. "The Questions Before the Warren Commission: The Dallas Murders: Motives? Evidence? Guilt?" *National Guardian* 16 (December 5, 1963): 3.

_____. "Warren Commission Finds the FBI Report Inadequate: News 'Leaks' Don't End Oswald Mystery." *National Guardian* 16 (December 26, 1963): 1, 4.

_____. "Before Warren Commission: Oswald's Mother Asks Lane to Take Up Case." *National Guardian* 16 (January 16, 1964): 4.

_____. "Presidential Commission: The Men and the Job: 'National Security' vs. the Facts About Oswald." *National Guardian* 16 (February 13, 1964): 5.

_____. "Oswald Commission Invites Lane: Inquiry Board Acts as Public Pressure Mounts." *National Guardian* 16 (March 7, 1964): 1, 4.

_____. "President's Panel Turns to Ruby: Were Oswald and His Slayer Linked?" *National Guardian* 16 (March 21, 1964): 1, 8.

_____. "Nagging Doubts on the 'Crime of the Century': Two Major Books on the Kennedy Assassination." *National Guardian* 16 (August 22, 1964): 5.

_____. "A Yardstick for Warren Report: Oswald Case: The Questions." *National Guardian* 16 (September 26, 1964): 1, 8.

_____. "Riddles in the Warren Report: Oswald Case--Still Mystery." *National Guardian* 16 (October 3, 1964): 1, 6.

_____. "3 Critics of the Warren Report Present Views." *National Guardian* 17 (October 17, 1964): 3.

_____. "Findings on Shots Challenged: Warren Report Target Again." *National Guardian* 17 (January 2, 1965): 12.

Steiner, Stan. "Books: The Politics of Assassination." *National Guardian* 20 (August 24, 1968): 30.

Stone, Oliver. "No: 'A Pre-Ordained Conclusion'." *ABA Journal* 78 (April 1992): 37.

Szulc, Tad. "The Warren Commission in Its Own Words: The Documents." *The New Republic* 173 (September 27, 1975): 9-48.

_____. "The Death of JFK: An Eye for an Eye?" *The New Republic* 174 (June 5, 1976): 6-8.

Thompson, Josiah. "Books: *After the Assassination.*" *Commonweal* 88 (May 10, 1968): 244-45.

Tillinger, Eugene, ed. *The Warren Report About President Kennedy's Assassination.* New York: Natlus Publications, 1964.

Trillin, Calvin. "Reporter at Large: The Buffs." *The New Yorker* 43 (June 10, 1967): 41-71.

Tuchler, Maier I. "Psychiatric Observations on the Warren Commission Report." *Journal of Forensic Sciences* 11 (July 1966): 289-99.

Watson, Allan C. "Realism at the Grassy Knoll." *The Christian Century* 84 (December 13, 1967): 1596-97.

Whalen, Richard J. "The Kennedy Assassination." *The Saturday Evening Post* 240 (January 14, 1967): 19-25, 69.

Williamson, Chilton. "Books Arts & Manners: Random Notes: *Final Disclosure.*" *National Review* 40 (October 28, 1988): 45.

Wolanin, Thomas R. "Book Review: *Accessories After the Fact.*" *Perspective* 5 (September 1976): 159.

Unsigned Articles:

"In The Nation's Interest." *America* 109 (December 21, 1963): 789.

"Classified Books: Social Sciences: *Portrait of the Assassin*." *Booklist* 62 (October 1, 1965): 121.

"Classified Books: History: *Inquest*." *Booklist* 63 (September 15, 1966): 92-93.

"Classified Books: Social Sciences: *The Oswald Affair*." *Booklist* 63 (November 15, 1966): 347.

"Upfront: Advance Reviews: Adult Nonfiction: *Final Disclosure*." *Booklist* 85 (September 15, 1988): 99.

"History, Geography and Travel: North America: *Portrait of the Assassin*." *Choice* 2 (December 1965): 729.

"Political Science: *Inquest*." *Choice* 3 (October 1966): 717.

"Political Science: *November 22, 1963*." *Choice* 11 (July/August 1974): 822.

"Letters From Readers: The Warren Report." *Commentary* 43 (April 1967): 7-8, 10, 12, 14, 16, 18, 20, 23-26, 28.

"The Warren Report." *Commonweal* 81 (October 9, 1964): 59-60.

"Johnson Names Commission to Probe Assassination." *Congressional Quarterly Weekly Report* 21 (December 6, 1963): 2122-23.

"Floor Action: Assassination Investigation." *Congressional Quarterly Weekly Report* 21 (December 13, 1963): 2150.

"Warren Commission." *Congressional Quarterly Weekly Report* 22 (May 22, 1964): 1013.

"Warren Commission Report Rules Out Conspiracy." *Congressional Quarterly Weekly Report* 22 (October 2, 1964): 2331, 2340.

"Text of Summary of Warren Commission Report." *Congressional Quarterly Weekly Report* 22 (October 2, 1964): 2332-40.

"Testimony Before Warren Commission Released." *Congressional Quarterly Weekly Report* 22 (November 27, 1964): 2731-32.

"Who Was to Blame?" *The Economist* (London) 209 (December 7, 1963): 1022.

"The End of the Tragedy." *The Economist* (London) 213 (October 3, 1964): 45.

"Books: Dallas Again: *Oswald: Assassin or Fall Guy?*" *The Economist* (London) 214 (March 27, 1965): 1395.

"Was Oswald Alone?" *The Economist* (London) 220 (August 6, 1966): 544.

"Books: Beyond Reasonable Doubt?" *The Economist* (London) 220 (September 24, 1966): 1252.

"Warren Commission Reports Are Routine." *Editor & Publisher* 97 (February 15, 1964): 66.

"Warren Text for All Probable By Sept. 15." *Editor & Publisher* 97 (August 22, 1964): 10.

"AP Is Rushing Book Containing Warren Report." *Editor & Publisher* 97 (September 26, 1964): 11.

"The Lead Was Obvious After Reading Was Done." *Editor & Publisher* 97 (October 3, 1964): 13.

"*New York Times* Runs 48 Pages of Report." *Editor & Publisher* 97 (October 3, 1964): 61.

"*New York Times* Team Probes JFK's Death." *Editor & Publisher* 99 (December 10, 1966): 10.

"A Primer of Assassination Theories." *Esquire* 66 (December 1966): 205-10, 334-35; 67 (May 1967): 104-07.

"Recommendation No. 9." *Journal of the American Medical Association* 191 (January 11, 1965): 131.

"Nonfiction: *Portrait of the Assassin.*" *Kirkus Reviews* 33 (March 1, 1965): 299.

"Nonfiction: *Accessories After the Fact.*" *Kirkus Reviews* 35 (October 1, 1967): 1248.

"Nonfiction: *Should We Now Believe the Warren Report?*" *Kirkus Reviews* 36 (March 15, 1968): 382.

"Nonfiction: *Citizen's Dissent.*" *Kirkus Reviews* 36 (May 15, 1968): 581.

"Nonfiction: *November 22, 1963.*" *Kirkus Reviews* 41 (October 15, 1973): 1183.

"Nonfiction: *Final Disclosure.*" *Kirkus Reviews* 56 (October 1, 1988): 1440.

"Cover: The Warren Report: How the Commission Pieced Together the Evidence: Told By One of Its Members." *Life* 57 (October 2, 1964): 1.

"Assassination: The Trail to a Verdict." *Life* 57 (October 2, 1964): 40-41.

"Warren Report: Bureaucratic Blunders Left J. F. K. A Target." *Life* 57 (October 2, 1964): 50B.

"Porocilo Warrennove Komisije [Report of the Warren Commission]." *Ljubljanski dnevnik* (Ljubljana) 14 (October 8, 1964): 268-75.

"*Assassination,* a New Book (by Sylvan Fox) Poses Some Unanswered Questions." *Maclean's* 79 (April 16, 1966): 18-19.

"Editorials: The Warren Commission." *The Nation* 197 (December 28, 1963): 445.

"Editorials: Task of the Warren Commission." *The Nation* 198 (January 27, 1964): 81.

"Editorials: The Warren Commission . . . Did Its Work Well." *The Nation* 199 (November 2, 1964): 290.

"Warren Group Expected to Duck on Oswald." *National Guardian* 16 (January 23, 1964): 1, 5.

"Attorney Denied Right to Cross-Examine Witnesses: Lane Cities Curb at Oswald Inquiry." *National Guardian* 16 (March 14, 1964): 4.

"Warren Board Will Report: 'Irrational Action By An Individual'." *National Guardian* 16 (April 4, 1964): 6.

"Oswald--Is the Commission in Doubt?: No Final Finding Yet, It Now Says." *National Guardian* 16 (June 13, 1964): 4.

"Mark Lane Challenges Warren to Hear Tape on Disputed Evidence: Oswald Case Testimony." *National Guardian* 16 (July 11, 1964): 4.

"Editorial Report to Readers: Earl Warren's 'Lost Cause'?" *National Guardian* 16 (August 29, 1964): 2.

"Report to Readers: A Chapter Still Not Closed." *National Guardian* 16 (October 3, 1964): 2.

"Warren Report Greeted Skeptically: Doubt Clings Abroad on Oswald." *National Guardian* 17 (October 10, 1964): 1, 8.

"Debate on Warren Report: It's Lane (Doubts) vs. Belli (Faith)." *National Guardian* 17 (October 24, 1964): 16.

"Lane Group Says New Data Do Not Uphold Warren Board Finding: Oswald--Case Details Add to Doubt." *National Guardian* 17 (December 5, 1964): 1, 10.

"Trevor-Roper Says Commission Presented Only 'The Prosecution Case': Historian Calls Warren Report a 'Smokescreen'." *National Guardian* 17 (December 26, 1964): 3.

"Study of Transcript Contradicts the 'Lone Assassin' Theory: Warren Report is Challenged Anew on Bullets." *National Guardian* 17 (March 13, 1965): 7.

"Warren Report Veils Data on Shots: Kennedy Assassination Evidence at Odds With Theory." *National Guardian* 17 (March 20, 1965): 9.

"What's Ahead?: The Warren Commission: Present Questions, Future Answers?" *National Review* 15 (December 24, 1963): 4-5.

"Warren's Secret." *National Review* 16 (April 7, 1964): 265-66; 16 (April 21, 1964): 311.

"How to Read the Warren Report." *National Review* 16 (October 6, 1964): 858-59.

"Confusion Compounded." *National Review* 18 (October 18, 1966): 1032-33.

"Assassination." *National Review* 18 (December 13, 1966): 1253-54.

"Warren Commission." *The New Republic* 150 (February 29, 1964): 4-5.

"National Affairs: The Assassination: History's Jury." *Newsweek* 62 (December 16, 1963): 25-27.

"National Affairs: Anniversaries: Nightmare Revisited." *Newsweek* 63 (June 8, 1964): 48.

"National Affairs: The Assassination: Eye on That Window." *Newsweek* 63 (June 22, 1964): 32-34.

"Press: Jumping the Gun." *Newsweek* 64 (July 13, 1964): 50.

"The Assassination: The Warren Commission Report." *Newsweek* 64 (October 5, 1964): 32-64.

"National Affairs: What They Saw That Dreadful Day in Dallas." *Newsweek* 64 (December 7, 1964): 28-30, 35-36, 38, 40, 42.

"Press: History or Hysteria?" *Newsweek*, 64 (December 28, 1964): 35-36.

"Education: Instant History." *Newsweek* 65 (February 1, 1965): 47.

"National Affairs: *Inquest*: How Many Assassins?" *Newsweek* 67 (June 13, 1966): 36-38.

"National Affairs: Again, The Assassination." *Newsweek* 68 (August 15, 1966): 30-33.

"International: Soviet Union: Banned in Moscow." *Newsweek* 68 (September 12, 1966): 40.

"National Affairs: The Assassination: Deep and Growing Doubts." *Newsweek* 68 (October 10, 1966): 36, 41.

"National Affairs: Assassination: Any Number Can Play." *Newsweek* 68 (November 7, 1966): 37-38.

"The Periscope: Inside Story: Warren on the Warren Commission Report." *Newsweek* 68 (November 28, 1966): 19.

"JFK: The Death and the Doubts." *Newsweek* 68 (December 5, 1966): 25-26.

"Newsmakers: [Discusses Albert H. Newman's *The Assassination of John F. Kennedy: The Reason's Why*]." *Newsweek* 75 (June 8, 1970): 49.

"Books: General: *Portrait of the Assassin*." *The New Yorker* 41 (July 3, 1965): 74.

"Briefly Noted: General: *After the Assassination*." *The New Yorker* 44 (May 4, 1968): 186-87.

"Five Publishers Issue Warren Panel's Report." *Publishers Weekly* 186 (October 5, 1964): 43-44.

"Warren Report: Paperback Edition Were Produced at Record-Breaking Pace." *Publishers Weekly* 186 (October 5, 1964): 80-82; (October 12, 1964): 39-40.

"Currents: Warren Report in Italian." *Publishers Weekly* 186 (October 19, 1964): 23.

"Lane Says JFK Death is Still Unsolved Murder." *Publishers Weekly* 190 (August 22, 1966): 58.

"Currents: How Persuasive Are Anti-Warren Books?" *Publishers Weekly* 191 (March 13, 1967): 30.

"PW Forecasts: Nonfiction: *Accessories After the Fact.*" *Publishers Weekly* 192 (October 23, 1967): 51.

"PW Forecasts: Nonfiction: *A Citizen's Dissent.*" *Publishers Weekly* 193 (May 27, 1968): 57.

"PW Forecasts: Nonfiction: *The Weight of the Evidence.*" *Publishers Weekly* 193 (May 27, 1968): 57.

"PW Forecasts: Nonfiction: *November 22, 1963.*" *Publishers Weekly* 204 (October 15, 1973): 54.

"PW Forecasts: Nonfiction: *Final Disclosure.*" *Publishers Weekly* 234 (September 16, 1988): 74-75.

"Editorial: November 22, 1966." *Ramparts* 5 (November 1966): 3.

"A New Warren Commission?" *The Saturday Evening Post* 240 (January 14, 1967): 74.

"Kennedy Assassination: Something Rotten . . . ." *The Saturday Evening Post* 240 (December 2, 1967): 88.

"Questions That Won't Go Away." *The Saturday Evening Post* 247 (December 1975): 38-39.

"Warren Commission Report: Verdict: One Man Alone." *Senior Scholastic* 85 (October 7, 1964): 9- 10.

"Comment: Reaction to the Warren Commission Report." *Senior Scholastic* 85 (October 14, 1964): 17.

"The Warren Commission and the Death of John F. Kennedy." *Senior Scholastic* 89 (November 18, 1966): 14-20.

"The Debate on Who Killed John Kennedy?" *Senior Scholastic* 89 (November 18, 1966): 21-22, 35.

"Zeitgeschichte: Kennedy-Mord: Finstere Machte [Contemporary History: Kennedy-Murder: Powers of Darkness]." *Der Spiegel* (Hamburg) 15 (1967): 82-86.

"Investigations: A Sad and Solemn Duty." *Time* 82 (December 13, 1963): 26-27.

"The Warren Commission Report." *Time* 84 (October 2, 1964): 45-50, 55.

" The Nation: The Secret Service: Trying to Protect the Unprotectable." *Time* 84 (October 9, 1964): 28.

"The Warren Commission: The Witnesses." *Time* 84 (December 4, 1964): 25-27.

"Food for the Suspicious." *Time* 88 (July 8, 1966): 86, E3.

"Time Essay: Autopsy on the Warren Commission." *Time* 88 (September 16, 1966): 54-55.

"The Assassination: The Mystery Makers." *Time* 90 (December 22, 1967): 21.

"In the JFK Murder Case--Chief Investigator Lee Rankin." *U. S. News and World Report* 55 (December 30, 1963): 10.

"As Warren Inquiry Starts: Latest on the Assassination." *U. S. News and World Report* 55 (December 30, 1963): 28-30.

"Assassination Inquiry: Slow, Careful." *U. S. News and World Report* 56 (January 27, 1964): 49.

"Back of the Secrecy in the Assassination Probe." *U. S. News and World Report* 56 (February 24, 1964): 52-55.

"Latest on Murder of Kennedy: A Preview of the Warren Report." *U. S. News and World Report* 56 (June 1, 1964): 43-44.

"Warren Findings: Some New Facts." *U. S. News and World Report* 57 (July 6, 1964): 44.

"Here's What the Warren Commission Will Show." *U. S. News and World Report* 57 (September 14, 1964): 42-43.

"Unraveling the Mystery Of The Assassination Of John F. Kennedy: The Official Story." *U. S. News and World Report* 57 (October 5, 1964): 35-42, 70-71, 96-97.

"Rush To Buy The Report On Kennedy Assassination." *U. S. News and World Report* 57 (October 12, 1964): 20.

"The Untold Stories--Aftermath of the Assassination; Abroad: Praise-- and Doubt." *U. S. News and World Report* 57 (October 12, 1964): 58- 62.

"Overwhelming Evidence Oswald Was Assassin." *U. S. News and World Report* 61 (October 10, 1966): 48-50, 53-59, 62-63.

"New Conflict Over the Assassination." *U. S. News and World Report* 61 (December 5, 1966): 6-8.

"Allen Dulles Answers Warren Report Critics." *U. S. News and World Report* 61 (December 19, 1966): 20.

"JFK Assassination: British Expert's View." *U. S. News and World Report* 62 (January 23, 1967): 11.

"Joseph A. Ball: An Oral History." *Western Legal History* 5 (Sum- mer/Fall 1992): 167-85.

THE EVIDENCE

Books:

Bartholomew, Richard. *Possible Discovery of an Automobile Used in the JFK Conspiracy*. Published by Author, 1993.

Bloomgarden, Henry S. *The Gun: A "Biography" of the Gun That Killed John F. Kennedy*. New York: Grossman Publishers, 1975; Bantam, 1976.

Bonner, Judy Whitson. *Investigation of a Homicide: The Murder of John F. Kennedy*. New York: Grosset & Dunlap, 1969.

Cutler, Robert Bradley. *Crossfire: Evidence of Conspiracy*. Manchester, Massachusetts: Cutler Designs, 1975.

_____. *The Flight of CE399: Evidence of Conspiracy*. Manchester, Massachusetts: R.B. Cutler, 1969.

_____. *Mr. Chairman: Evidence of Conspiracy*. Manchester, Massachusetts: Cutler Designs, 1979.

_____. *Two Flightpaths: Evidence of Conspiracy*. Manchester, Massachusetts: R.B. Cutler, 1969.

_____. *The Umbrella Man: Evidence of Conspiracy*. Manchester, Massachusetts: Cutler Designs, 1975.

DeLoria, Robin T. *Mirror of Doubt*. Pittsburgh, Pennsylvania: Dorrance Publishing, 1993.

Dunshee, Tom, and Richard Duncan. *Motorcade--November 22, 1963*. Trenton, New Jersey: Published by Author, 1975.

Fetzer, James H. *Assassination Science: Experts Speak Out on the Death of JFK*. Chicago, Illinois: Catfeet Press, 1998

Galanor, Stewart. *Cover-Up*. New York: Kestrel Books, 1998.

Groden, Robert J. , and Harrison Edward Livingstone. *High Treason.* Baltimore, Maryland: The Conservatory Press, 1989; New York: Carroll & Graf Publishers, Inc., 1998.

_____. *The Killing of A President.* New York: Viking Studio Books, 1993.

Hanson, William H. *The Shooting of John F. Kennedy: One Assassin, Three Shots, Three Hits--No Misses.* San Antonio, Texas: Naylor Co., 1969.

Hobbs, Richard. *The Carcano: Italy's Military Rifle.* California: Published by Author, 1997, 1998.

Houts, Marshall. *Where Death Delights: The Story of Dr. Milton Helpern and Forensic Medicine.* New York: Coward-McCann, 1967; Dell, 1968.

Hoyle, Jeffrey P. *Wound Analysis.* Swansea, Massachusetts: Published by Author, 1978.

Joesten, Joachim. *Panel Review.* Munich: Published by Author, 1968.

Kurtz, Michael. *Crime of the Century.* Knoxville, Tennessee: University of Tennessee Press, 1982, 1983, 1988, 1992, 1996.

Lattimer, Dr. John K. *Kennedy and Lincoln: Medical and Ballistic Comparisons Of Their Assassinations.* New York: Harcourt, Brace, Jovanovich, 1980.

Lifton, David. *Best Evidence: Disguise and Deception In The Assassination of John F. Kennedy.* New York: Macmillan, 1981; Carroll & Graf Publishers Inc., 1988; Signet, 1992.

Livingstone, Harrison Edward. *High Treason 2: The Great Cover-Up.* New York: Carroll & Graf Publishers Inc., 1992.

_____. *Killing Kennedy: And the Hoax of the Century.* New York: Carroll & Graf Publishers Inc., 1995.

_____. *Killing The Truth*. New York: Carroll & Graf Publishers Inc., 1993.

Marcus, Raymond. *The Bastard Bullet: A Search for Legitimacy for Commission Exhibit 399*. Los Angeles, California: Rendell Publications, 1966; Los Angeles, California: Published by Author, 1990.

_____. *The HSCA, The Zapruder Film, and the Single Bullet Theory*. Los Angeles, California: Published by Author, 1992.

_____. *The HSCA, The Zapruder Film, and the Single Bullet Theory*. Los Angeles, California: Published by Author, 1995.

_____. *#5 Man: November 22, 1963*. Los Angeles, California: Published by Author, 1997.

Menninger, Bonar. *Mortal Error: The Shot That Killed JFK*. New York: St. Martin's Press, 1992.

Moore, Jim. *Conspiracy of One: The Definitive Book on the Kennedy Assassination*. Fort Worth, Texas: The Summit Group, 1991, 1992.

Nivaggi, Gary. *The Marketing Of A Weapon*. Published by Author, 1994.

O'Toole, George. *The Assassination Tapes: An Electronic Probe into the Murder of John F. Kennedy and the Dallas Cover-Up*. New York: Penthouse Press, 1975; Zebra, 1977.

Russell, Brian, and Charles Sellier. *Conspiracy To Kill A President*. New York: Bantam, 1982.

Savage, Gary. *JFK: First Day Evidence*. Monroe, Louisiana: The Shoppe Press, 1993.

Shaw, J. Gary, and Larry R. Harris. *Cover-Up*. Austin, Texas: Thomas Publications, Inc., 1976, 1992.

Thomas, Ralph D. *Missing Links In The JFK Assassination Conspiracy*. Austin, Texas: Thomas Investigative Publications, Inc., 1992.

_____. *Photo Computer Image Processing and The Crime of The Century*. Austin, Texas: Thomas Investigative Publications, Inc., 1992.

Thompson, Josiah. *Six Seconds in Dallas: A Micro-Study of the Kennedy Assassination*. New York: Bernard Geis Associates, 1967; Berkeley, 1976.

Trask, Richard B. *Pictures of the Pain*. Danvers, Massachusetts: Yeoman Press, 1994.

_____. *That Day In Dallas*. Danvers, Massachusetts: Yeoman Press, 1998.

Wecht, Cyril, with Mark Curriden, and Benjamin Wecht. *Cause of Death*. New York: Onyx, 1994.

Weisberg, Harold. *Post Mortem: Assassination Cover-Up Smashed*. Frederick, Maryland: H. Weisberg, 1975.

Wilber, Charles G. *Medicolegal Investigation of the President John F. Kennedy Murder*. Springfield, Illinois: Charles C. Thomas Publisher, 1978.

Signed Articles:

Aguilar, Gary. "The Injuries to JFK." *Journal of the American Medical Association* 268 (October 7, 1992): 1681-82.

_____. "Letters: That JAMA Verdict." *Columbia Journalism Review* 32 (November/December 1993): 6.

Alexander, John. "The Assassination Tapes." *The Saturday Evening Post* 247 (May/June 1975): 6, 120.

Annin, Peter. "National Affairs: The Shootout Over Ruby's Gun." *Newsweek* 116 (October 22, 1990): 33.

Artwohl, Robert R. "JFK's Assassination: Conspiracy, Forensic Science, and Common Sense." *Journal of the American Medical Association* 269 (March 24/31 1993): 1540-43.

Baker, John F. "St. Martin's Book Offers New JFK Shooting Theory." *Publishers Weekly* 239 (February 24, 1992): 7, 10.

Barringer, Floyd S. "Book Review: *Kennedy and Lincoln.*" *Journal of the Illinois State Historical Society* 77 (Summer 1984): 148-49.

Berkeley, Edmund C. "Response: [Schwartz vs Sprague]." *Computers and Automation* 20 (March 1971): 40-43.

Bernt, H. H. "History: *Six Seconds in Dallas.*" *Library Journal* 93 (January 15, 1968): 187.

Bickel, Alexander M. "Return To Dallas." *The New Republic* 157 (December 23, 1967): 34.

Boeth, Richard. "JFK: What the FBI Found." *Newsweek* 90 (December 19, 1977): 28-33.

Bonventre, Peter. "Opening the JFK Files." *Newsweek* 90 (December 12, 1977): 34-35.

Braverman, Shelley. "Backfire! The Assassination of J. F. K." *Guns* 13 (May 1967): 18-21, 56-57.

Breo, Dennis L. "JFK's Death-The Plain Truth From The MDs Who Did The Autopsy." *Journal of the American Medical Association* 267 (May 27, 1992): 2794-803.

_____. "JFK's Death, Part II- Dallas MDs Recall Their Memories." *Journal of the American Medical Association* 267 (May 27, 1992): 2804-07.

_____. "The Injuries to JFK." *Journal of the American Medical Association* 268 (October 7, 1992): 1684-85.

_____. "JFK's Death, Part III-Dr. Finck Speaks Out: 'Two Bullets, From the Rear'." *Journal of the American Medical Association* 268 (October 7, 1992): 1748-54.

Breslin, Jimmy. "A Death in Emergency Room No. One." *The Saturday Evening Post* 236 (December 14, 1963): 30-31.

Cohen, Jacob. "Conspiracy Fever." *Commentary* 60 (October 1975): 33-42.

_____. "Yes, Oswald Alone Killed Kennedy." *Commentary* 93 (June 1992): 32-40; 94 (November 1992): 10-12, 14-15, 17-21.

Cole, Alwyn. "Assassin Forger." *Journal of Forensic Sciences* 2 (July 1966): 272-88.

Cook, Fred J. "Books: & the Arts: The Warren Report and the Irreconcilables." *The Nation* 206 (February 26, 1968): 277-81.

Crenshaw, Charles A. "Commentary on JFK Autopsy Articles." *Journal of the American Medical Association* 273 (May 24, 1995): 1632.

Donahue, Howard C. "JFK/Connally Shooting Reexamined: Was The 'Magic Bullet' Really Magic?" *Maryland State Medical Journal* 27 (February 1978): 83-85.

Emerson, William A. "From the Editor [About Josiah Thompson]." *The Saturday Evening Post* 240 (December 2, 1967): 3.

Forman, Robert. "The Wounds of President JFK." *People and the Pursuit of Truth* (March 1976).

Graham, Hugh Davis. "Book Review: *Kennedy and Lincoln*." *Register of the Kentucky Historical Society* 80 (Summer 1982): 359-61.

Graves, Florence. "The Mysterious Kennedy Out-Takes." *Washington Journalism Review* (September/October 1978): 24-28.

Grichot, Jack. "Cyril Wecht: Coroner and Skeptic." *Medical Dimensions* (March 1975): 19-21.

Groden, Robert J. "The Killing of a President." *Arena*, 42 (November 1993): 120-35.

Handlin, Oscar. "Reader's Choice: *Six Seconds in Dallas*." *The Atlantic Monthly* 221 (February 1968): 141.

Houts, Marshall. "Dr. Milton Helpern, World's Greatest Expert on Gunshot Wounds, Speaks Out: 1. Warren Commission Botched the Kennedy Autopsy; 2. Warren Commission One-Bullet Theory Exploded." *Argosy* 365 (July 1967): 21-22, 108-16.

Howard, Clyde W. "The Injuries to JFK." *Journal of the American Medical Association* 268 (October 7, 1992): 1682-83.

Humes, James J., and J. Thornton Boswell. "The Injuries to JFK." *Journal of the American Medical Association* 268 (October 7, 1992): 1685.

James, Patricia L. "The Injuries to JFK." *Journal of the American Medical Association* 268 (October 7, 1992): 1682.

Joesten, Joachim. "Lee Harvey Oswalds Gewehr [Oswald's Gun]." *Frankfurter Hefte. Zeitschrift fur Kultur und Politik* (Frankfurt/Main) 20 (September 1965): 596-99.

Joling, Robert J. "The JFK Assassination: Still An Unsolved Murder Mystery, Part III." *The Saturday Evening Post* 247 (December 1975): 44-46, 120.

Kartsonis, Louis P. "JFK: What Really Happened in Dallas." *San Diego Magazine* 44 (September 1992): 74-77, 100, 102-04.

Krebs, A. V. "Books: *Six Seconds in Dallas.*" *Commonweal* 88 (September 20, 1968): 637-39.

Lattimer, Gary, John K. Lattimer, and Jon Lattimer. "The Kennedy-Connally One Bullet Theory: Further Circumstantial and Experimental Evidence." *Medical Times* 102 (November 1974): 33-56.

Lattimer, John K. "Similarities in Fatal Woundings of John Wilkes Booth and Lee Harvey Oswald." *New York State Journal of Medicine* 66 (July 1, 1966): 1782-94.

_____. "Factors in the Death of President Kennedy." *Journal of the American Medical Association* 198 (October 24, 1966): 327, 332-33.

_____. "Observations Based on a Review of the Autopsy Photographs, X-Rays, and Related Materials of the Late President John F. Kennedy." *Resident and Staff Physician* (May 1972): 33-64.

_____. "Additional Data on the Shooting of President Kennedy." *Journal of the American Medical Association* 269 (March 24/31, 1993): 1544-47.

_____. "Experimental Duplication of the Important Physical Evidence of the Lapel Bulge of the Jacket Worn by Governor Connally When Bullet 399 Went Through Him." *Journal of the American College of Surgeons* 178 (May 1994): 517-22.

Lattimer, John K., and Jon Lattimer. "The Kennedy-Connally Single Bullet Theory: A Feasibility Study." *International Surgery* 50 (December 1968): 524-32.

Lattimer, John K., Jon Lattimer, and Gary Lattimer. "Could Oswald Have Shot President Kennedy: Further Ballistic Studies." *Bulletin of the New York Academy of Medicine* 48 (April 1972): 513-24.

_____. "An Experimental Study of the Backward Movement of President Kennedy's Head." *Surgery, Gynecology and Obstetrics* 142 (February 1976): 246-54.

Lattimer, John K., Edward B. Schlesinger, and H. Houston Merritt. "President Kennedy's Spine Hit By First Bullet." *Bulletin of the New York Academy of Medicine* 53 (April 1977): 280-90.

Levi, Barbara G. "NAS Panel Says Sounds on JFK Tapes Are Not Shots." *Physics Today* 35 (September 1982): 49-51.

Lundberg, George D. "Closing the Case in *JAMA* on the John F. Kennedy Autopsy." *Journal of the American Medical Association* 268 (October 7, 1992): 1736-38.

Magnuson, Ed. "Nation: Now, a 'Two Casket' Argument." *Time* 117 (January 19, 1981): 22-23.

Mantik, D. W. "The Injuries to JFK." *Journal of the American Medical Association* 268 (October 7, 1992): 1683.

McReynolds, R. Michael. "Archivist's Perspective: Records on the Assassination of John F. Kennedy." *Prologue* 24 (Winter 1992): 384-88.

McWilliams, Carey. "Book Marks: *The Assassination Tapes.*" *The Nation* 221 (August 30, 1975): 153.

Meagher, Sylvia. "The Case of the Urologist Apologist." *The Texas Observer* 64 (May 26, 1972): 22-24.

Micozzi, Marc S. "Lincoln, Kennedy, and the Autopsy." *Journal of the American Medical Association* 267 (May 27, 1992): 2791.

_____. "The Injuries to JFK." *Journal of the American Medical Association* 268 (October 7, 1992): 1684.

Miller, William Thomas. "Book Review: History: *Crime of the Century.*" *Library Journal* 107 (March 15, 1982): 636.

Minnis, Jack, and Staughton Lynd. "Seeds of Doubt: Some Questions About the Assassination." *The New Republic* 149 (December 21, 1963): 14-20; 150 (January 11, 1964): 28-30.

Newcomb, Fred T., and Perry Adams. "Did Someone Alter the Medical Evidence?" *Skeptic* No. 9 (August 1975): 25-27.

Nichols, John. "Assassination of President Kennedy." *The Practioner* 211 (November 1973): 625- 33.

_____. "The Wounding of Governor Connally of Texas, November 22, 1963." *Maryland State Medical Journal* 26 (October 1977): 58-77.

Olson, Don, and Ralph F. Turner. "Photographic Evidence and the Assassination of President John F. Kennedy" *Journal of Forensic Sciences* 16 (October 1971): 399-419.

Petty, Charles. "JFK-An Allonge." *Journal of the American Medical Association* 269 (March 24/31 1993): 1552-53.

Posner, Michael. "Another Strand In An Unending Mystery." *Maclean's* 93 (December 15, 1980): 34-35.

Ragan, Charles A. "Editorial: On the Assassination and Autopsy of John F. Kennedy." *Resident and Staff Physician* (May 1972): 11-12.

_____. "A New Report on the Assassination of John F. Kennedy." *Medical Times* 102 (November 1974): 2.

Randall, Teri. "Clinicians' Forensic Interpretations of Fatal Gunshot Wounds Often Miss the Mark." *Journal of the American Medical Association* 269 (April 28, 1993): 2058, 2061.

Salandria, Vincent J. "A Philadelphia Lawyer Analyzes the Shots, Trajectories, and Wounds." *Liberation* 9 (January 1965): 13-18.

_____. "The Warren Report?: A Philadelphia Lawyer Analyzes the President's Back and Neck Wounds." *Liberation* 10 (March 1965): 14-32.

_____. "*Life* Magazine and the Warren Commission." *Liberation* 11 (October 1966): 44.

Schonfeld, Maurice W. "The Shadow of a Gunman: An Account of a Twelve-Year Investigation of a Kennedy Assassination Film." *Columbia Journalism Review* 14 (July/August 1975): 46-50.

Schroeder, Randall L. "Social Sciences: *High Treason 2: The Great Cover-Up*." *Library Journal* 117 (May 15, 1992): 104.

Schwartz, Benjamin L. "Another View [A Challenge to Richard E. Sprague]." *Computers and Automation* 20 (March 1971): 35-39.

Schweisheimer, W. "Die Wirbelsaulen-Erkrankung Prasident Kennedys [President Kennedy's Ailing Spinal Injury]." *Medizinische Klinik. Wochenschrift fur Klinik und Praxis* (Berlin) 59 (1964): 1927.

Seelye, John. "Mute Witness." *The New Republic* 172 (June 14, 1975): 22-24.

Silver, Isidore. "The Contemporary Scene: *The Assassination Tapes*." *Library Journal* 100 (April 15, 1975): 744.

Smith, Jack A. "New Break on Oswald's Gun." *National Guardian* 16 (February 27, 1964): 1, 8-9.

Smith, Wayne S. "The Injuries to JFK." *Journal of the American Medical Association* 268 (October 7, 1992), 1683-84.

_____. "Opinion: *JAMA* Knows Best." *Columbia Journalism Review* 32 (September/October 1993): 49-50.

Snider, Arthur J. "The Assassination: A New Medical Opinion." *Science Digest* 61 (February 1967): 35-36.

Sprague, Richard E. "The Assassination of President John F. Kennedy: The Application of Computers to the Photographic Evidence." *Computers and Automation* 19 (May 1970): 29-60; 19 (June 1970): 7; 19 (July 1970): 36; 20 (March 1971): 44; 20 (May 1971): 27-29.

_____. "Computer-Assisted Analysis of Evidence Regarding the Assassination of President John F. Kennedy: Progress Report." *Computers and Automation* 19 (September 1970): 48.

Steck, Henry. "Social Science: Law & Criminology: *Best Evidence.*" *Library Journal* 106 (April 1, 1981): 808-09.

Stolley, Richard B. "The Zapruder Film: Shots Seen Round the World." *Entertainment Weekly* 101 (January 17, 1992): 22-23, 25.

Telford, V. Q. "The Injuries to JFK." *Journal of the American Medical Association* 268 (October 7, 1992): 1682.

Thomas, Evan. "National Affairs: Who Shot JFK?" *Newsweek* 122 (September 6, 1993): 14-17.

Thompson, Josiah. "The Crossfire That Killed President Kennedy." *The Saturday Evening Post* 240 (December 2, 1967): 27-31, 46, 50-55.

Tooley, Jo Ann. "Enterprise: Jack Ruby's Gun." *U.S. News and World Report* 111 (December 30, 1991/January 6, 1992): 24.

Warner, Ken. "Big Bargins in Rifles." *Mechanix Illustrated* 60 (October 1964): 89-91, 152-53.

Wecht, Cyril H. "A Critique of the Medical Aspects of the Investigation into the Assassination of President Kennedy." *Journal of Forensic Sciences* 2 (1966): 300-17.

_____. "Pathologist's View of JFK Autopsy: An Unsolved Case." *Modern Medicine* 40 (November 27, 1972): 28-32; Reprinted in *Medical Trial Technique Quarterly* 20 (Summer, 1973): 42-52.

_____. "Analysis of the Autopsy on President John F. Kennedy, and the Impossibility of the Warren Commission's Lone Assassin Conclusion." *Computers and Automation* 22 (February 1973): 26-28.

_____. "New Evidence Rekindles Old Doubts: JFK Assassination: 'A Prolonged and Willful Cover-Up'." *Modern Medicine* 42 (October 28, 1974): 40X-40FF.

_____. "A Civilian M. D. In On The Kennedy Autopsy Says More Than One Gun Killed JFK." *Physician's Management* 15 (October 1975): 14-23; 15 (November 1975): 37-40, 43-44.

_____. "JFK Revisited." *Journal of the American Medical Association* 269 (March 24/31 1993): 1507.

Wecht, Cyril H., and Robert P. Smith. "The Medical Evidence in the Assassination of President John F. Kennedy." *Forensic Science* 3 (April 1974): 105-28.

Wheeler, Keith. " 'Cursed Gun'---The Track of C2766." *Life* 59 (August 27, 1965): 62-65.

White, Anthony. "The Injuries to JFK." *Journal of the American Medical Association* 268 (October 7, 1992): 1683.

Wilber, Charles G. "Book Reviews: *Best Evidence*." *America* 144 (March 21, 1981): 235.

_____. "The Assassination of the Late President John F. Kennedy: An Academician's Thoughts." *The American Journal of Forensic Medicine and Pathology* 7 (March 1986): 52-58.

Wilson, Arthur J. "Letters: The Injuries to JFK." *Journal of the American Medical Association* 268 (October 7, 1992): 1681.

Wrone, David R. "Book Reviews: *Kennedy and Lincoln.*" *Civil War History* 31 (March 1985): 80- 81.

Unsigned Articles:

"Assassination Gives Impetus to Dodd's Gun Bill." *Advertising Age* 34 (December 2, 1963): 1-2.

"Inside the Archives." *American History Illustrated* 23 (January 1989): 18-19.

"The Sixth Floor." *American History Illustrated* 23 (February 1989): 42-43.

"A Physicist Examines the Kennedy Assassination Film." *American Journal of Physics* 44 (1976): 813-27.

"Classified Books: Social Sciences: *Six Seconds in Dallas.*" *Booklist* 64 (May 15, 1968): 1075.

"Nonfiction: History: *The Assassination Tapes.*" *Booklist* 72 (September 1, 1975): 16.

"Upfront: Advance Reviews: Adult Nonfiction: *Best Evidence.*" *Booklist* 77 (February 15, 1981): 776.

"This Week: *Six Seconds in Dallas.*" *The Christian Century* 85 (January 3, 1968): 52.

"The Warren Report: How to Murder the Medical Evidence." *Current Medicine for Attorneys* 12 (November 1965): 1-28.

"Books: The Historian As Criminologist: *Crime of the Century.*" *The Economist* 284 (July 31, 1982): 79.

"Give Me the Best You Can Buy . . . A Gift from Klein's." *Field & Stream* 68 (November 1963): 97.

"Washington News: Kennedy Shot Twice in the Back." *Journal of the American Medical Association* 187 (January 4, 1964): 15.

"Nonfiction: *Six Seconds in Dallas.*" *Kirkus Reviews* 35 (November 15, 1967): 1412.

"Nonfiction: *High Treason 2: The Great Cover-Up.*" *Kirkus Reviews* 60 (April 1, 1992): 446-47.

"A Matter of Reasonable Doubt [Zapruder Film]." *Life* 61 (November 25, 1966): 38-48A.

"Rebuttal by the Protagonist of the One Bullet Verdict." *Life* 61 (November 25, 1966): 48B, 53.

"Nov. 22, 1963, Dallas: Photos by Nine Bystanders." *Life* 63 (November 24, 1967): 87-97.

"New Clues in J. F. K. Assassination Photos: LRL Scientist's Persuasive Theory." *The Magnet: Lawrence Radiation Laboratory* 11 (July 1967): 1, 6-7.

"Reader Reaction to the Kennedy Autopsy Report." *Medical Times* 100 (December 1972): 28, 30, 32.

"Fresh Doubts on JFK Assassination." *Medical World News* 16 (June 2, 1975): 25-28.

"Editorials: Those Missing Exhibits." *The Nation* 203 (November 14, 1966): 500.

The Week: [Kennedys Restrict Access to Autopsy Materials]." *National Review* 18 (November 29, 1966): 1199.

"Where the Shots Came From." *The New Republic* 149 (December 28, 1963): 7.

"Kennedy Assassination." *The New Republic* 155 (November 12, 1966): 8-9.

"JFK Assassination." *The New Republic* 160 (February 1, 1969): 9-10.

"Kennedy Family Allowed to Control Autopsy Photos." *News Media and the Law* 20 (Winter 1996): 23.

"Medicine: How JFK Died." *Newsweek* 62 (December 30, 1963): 55.

"Press: A Big Sale." *Newsweek* 63 (March 2, 1964): 80.

"National Affairs: Assassination: The Missing Link." *Newsweek* 68 (November 14, 1966): 30-31.

"The Periscope: Inside Story: Solved--Mystery of the Missing Frames." *Newsweek* 69 (February 6, 1967): 17.

"Medicine: Post-Mortem on JFK." *Newsweek* 70 (July 24, 1967): 54.

"National Affairs: New Assassination Theory." *Newsweek* 70 (November 27, 1967): 29-30, 35.

"Notes and Comments [*Six Seconds in Dallas*]." *The New Yorker* 43 (December 9, 1967): 51

"PW Forecasts: Nonfiction: *Six Seconds in Dallas*." *Publishers Weekly* 192 (October 23, 1967): 51.

"PW Forecasts: Nonfiction: *The Assassination Tapes*." *Publishers Weekly* 207 (March 10, 1975): 50.

"PW Forecasts: Nonfiction: *Crime of the Century*." *Publishers Weekly* 221 (February 5, 1982): 378.

"PW Forecasts: Nonfiction: *High Treason 2: The Great Cover-Up*." *Publishers Weekly* 239 (April 13, 1992): 51.

"PW Forecasts: Nonfiction: *Killing Kennedy: And the Hoax of the Century*." *Publishers Weekly* 242 (September 11, 1995): 66.

"Reexamination of Accoustic Evidence in the Kennedy Assassination." *Science* 218 (October 8, 1982): 127-33.

"Addison's Disease: Pathologist Sleuth Reopens Kennedy Controversy." *Science News* 92 (July 22, 1967): 79-80.

"Warren Commission Report: Parafin Test Unreliable." *Science News Letter* 86 (October 10, 1964): 227.

"General Science: Model of Head Used in Assassination Study." *Science News Letter* 86 (October 10, 1964): 229.

"Medicine: Kennedy Alive in Hospital." *Science News Letter* 86 (October 10, 1964): 229.

"Killing Still Mystery: FBI Confused by Oswald's Loose Pistol Barrel." *Science News Letter* 86 (October 10, 1964): 230.

"Kein Meister traf den Kopf der Puppe. Die Schiessversuche mit Oswalds Mannlicher-Carcano Gewehr [Not Even a Master-Rifleman Hit the Puppy's Head. Trial Shots with Oswald's Gun]." *Der Spiegel* (Hamburg) 21 (1967): 104.

"Observations: The Assassination." *The Texas Observer* 60 (January 12, 1968): 15.

"Three Patients at Parkland." *Texas State Journal of Medicine* 60 (1964): 61-74.

"Medical History: Gunshot Wounds of Four Presidents." *Texas State Journal of Medicine* 60 (1964): 74-77.

"The Autopsy." *Time* 82 (December 27, 1963): 18.

"Historical Notes: Braced for Death?" *Time* 86 (October 8, 1965): 33.

"Assassinations: The Guns of Dallas." *Time* 87 (March 4, 1966): 28.

"Historical Notes: Into the Archives." *Time* 88 (November 11, 1966): 33.

"The Assassination: Shadow on a Grassy Knoll." *Time* 89 (May 26, 1967): 21.

"Nation: The FBI Story on J. F. K.'s Death." *Time* 90 (December 19, 1977): 18, 23.

"See Oswald's Lair-for $4." *Time* 133 (February 27, 1989): 25.

"The Gun That Jack Shot." *Time* 133 (May 29, 1989): 35.

"American Notes: Firearms: Have Gun Will Travel." *Time* 139 (April 13, 1992): 31.

"Not The Grassy Knoll?" *Time* 139 (June 1, 1992): 21.

"In the Works: Tighter Laws on Gun Sales." *U. S. News and World Report* 55 (December 9, 1963): 4.

"As the Assassination Inquiry Goes On . . . ." *U. S. News and World Report* 55 (December 23, 1963): 10.

"Problem: What to Do With Rifle That Killed JFK." *U. S. News and World Report* 58 (April 19, 1965): 8.

"To Be Disclosed Soon: More on JFK's Killing." *U. S. News and World Report* 58 (May 17, 1965): 22.

"Now U.S. Gets JFK Autopsy Photos." *U. S. News and World Report* 61 (November 14, 1966): 81.

"The JFK Killing . . . New Findings." *U. S. News and World Report* 66 (January 27, 1969): 4.

"JFK Killing: FBI Files Raise Questions, Give No Answers." *U. S. News and World Report* 83 (December 19, 1977): 15.

"The Cross fire Over Jack Ruby's Gun." *U. S. News and World Report* 107 (December 25, 1989): 10.

CONSPIRACY THEORIES

Books:

Anson, Robert Sam. *" 'They've Killed the President!' ": The Search for the Murderers of John F. Kennedy.* New York: Bantam, 1975.

Ashman, Charles. *The CIA-Mafia Link.* New York: Manor Books, 1975.

Blakey, G. Robert, and Richard N. Billings. *The Plot to Kill the President.* New York: Times Books, 1981. Re-titled *Fatal Hour: The Assassination of President Kennedy by Organized Crime.* Berkley Books, 1992.

Blumenthal, Sid, and Harvey Yazijian, eds. *Government by Gunplay: Assassination Conspiracy Theories from Dallas To Today.* New York: Signet, 1976.

Bringuier, Carlos. *Red Friday: Nov. 22nd 1963.* Chicago, Illinois: Charles Hallberg & Co., 1969.

Brown, Ray, and Don Lasseter. *Broken Silence: The Truth About Lee Harvey Oswald, LBJ and the Assassination of JFK.* New York: Pinnacle Books, 1996.

Brown, Walt. *Treachery In Dallas.* New York: Carroll & Graf Publishers Inc., 1995.

Buchanan, Thomas G. *Who Killed Kennedy?* New York: Putnam, 1964; London: Secker & Warburg, 1964; New York: MacFadden, 1965.

Calder, Michael. *JFK vs. CIA: Central Intelligence Agency's Assassination of the President.* Los Angeles, California: West LA Publishers, 1998.

Callahan, Bob. *Who Shot JFK? A Guide To The Major Conspiracy Theories.* New York: Simon & Schuster, 1993.

Camper, Frank. *The MK/Ultra Secret: An Account of CIA Deception.* Savannah, Georgia: Christopher Scott Publishing, 1996.

Canfield, Michael, and Alan J. Weberman. *Coup d' Etat in America: The CIA and the Assassination of John F. Kennedy.* New York: The Third Press, 1975, 1992; San Francisco, Quick American Archives, 1992.

Craig, John R., and Philip A. Rogers. *The Man on the Grassy Knoll.* New York: Avon Books, 1992.

Davies, Col. *Named! The Master Spy and Hitmen Who Shot JFK.* Melbourne, Australia: Bookman Press, 1993.

Davis, John H. *The Kennedy Contract: The Mafia Plot To Assassinate The President.* New York: Harper, 1993.

_____. *Mafia Kingfish: Carlos Marcello and the Assassination of John F. Kennedy.* New York: McGraw-Hill, 1988; Signet, 1989.

Downey, Durbin H. *After The Fact: The Piano Man's Story.* Princeton, Illinois: 4-D Publishing Co., 1998.

Eddowes, Michael. *Khrushchev Killed Kennedy.* Published by Author, 1975.

_____. *November 22: How They Killed Kennedy.* London: Neville Spearman Ltd., 1976.

_____. *The Oswald File.* New York: Clarkson N. Potter, 1977; Ace, 1978.

Evica, George M. *And We Are All Mortal: New Evidence and Analysis in the John F. Kennedy Assassination.* West Hartford, Connecticut: University of Hartford, 1978.

Furiati, Claudia. *ZR Rifle: The Plot to Kill Kennedy and Castro.* Melbourne, Australia: Ocean Press, 1994.

Goodman, Bob. *Triangle of Fire.* San Jose, California: Laquerian Publishing Co., 1993.

Gordon, Bruce. *One and One Make Two Sometimes: The Kennedy Assassination.* Fullerton, California, 1968.

Gun, Nerin E. *Red Roses from Texas.* London: F. Muller, 1964.

Hemenway, Phillip. *Riding The Tiger's Back.* Chico, California: Heidelberg Graphics, 1992.

Hepburn, James. *Farewell America.* Vaduz, Liechtenstein: Frontiers, 1968.

Hinckle, Warren, and William W. Turner. *The Fish Is Red: The Story of the Secret War Against Castro.* New York: Harper & Row, 1981. Re-titled *Deadly Secrets: The CIA-Mafia War Against Castro and the Assassination of JFK.* New York: Thunder's Mouth Press, 1992.

Hurt, Henry. *Reasonable Doubt: An Investigation into the Assassination of John F. Kennedy.* New York: Holt, Rinehart & Winston, 1986.

Keith, Jim, ed. *The Gemstone File.* Avondale Estates, Georgia: Illumi Press, 1992.

Lane, Mark. *Plausible Denial: Was the CIA Involved in the Assassination of JFK?* New York: Thunder's Mouth Press, 1991.

Lawrence, Lincoln. *Were We Controlled?* New Hyde Park, New York: University Books, 1967.

MacFarlane, Ian Colin A. *The Assassination of John F. Kennedy: A New Review.* Melbourne, Australia, 1974.

_____. *Proof of Conspiracy in the Assassination of President Kennedy.* Melbourne, Australia: Book Distributors, 1975.

Marks, Stanley. *Coup d' Etat!: November 22, 1963.* Los Angeles, California: Bureau of International Affairs, 1970.

_____. *Yes, Americans, A Conspiracy Murdered JFK!* Los Angeles, California: Bureau of International Affairs, 1992.

Marrs, Jim. *Crossfire: The Plot That Killed Kennedy.* New York: Carroll & Graf Publishers, Inc., 1989, 1990.

McDonald, Hugh C. *Appointment in Dallas: The Final Solution to the Assassination of JFK.* New York: H. McDonald Publishing Corp., and Zebra, 1975.

_____. *LBJ and the JFK Assassination Conspiracy.* New York: Condor Publishing, 1978.

Meek, Jeff. *A Chronology of the Circumstances Surrounding A Possible Organized Crime Conspiracy To Assassinate President John F. Kennedy.* Published by Author, 1994.

Morrow, Robert D. *Betrayal.* Chicago, Illinois: Regnery, 1976; New York Warner Books, 1976.

_____. *First Hand Knowledge: How I Participated In The CIA-Mafia Murder of President Kennedy.* New York: S. P. I. Books, 1992.

Moscovit, Andrei. *Did Castro Kill Kennedy?* Miami, Florida: Cuban American National Foundation, 1998.

Newcomb, Fred, and Perry Adams. *Murder From Within.* Santa Barbara, California: Probe, 1974.

North, Mark. *Act of Treason.* New York: Carroll & Graf Publishers, Inc., 1991.

Noyes, Peter. *Legacy of Doubt.* New York: Pinnacle Books, 1973.

Oglesby, Carl. *The JFK Assassination: The Facts and the Theories.* New York: Signet, 1992.

_____. *Who Killed JFK?* Berkeley, California: Odonian Press, 1992.

_____. *The Yankee and Cowboy War: Conspiracies from Dallas To Watergate.* Kansas City, Missouri: Sheed Andrews and McMeel, 1976; New York: Berkeley Publishing Corp., 1977.

Piper, Michael Collins. *Default Judgement: Questions, Answers and Reflections on the Crime of the Century: The Assassination of John F. Kennedy.* Washington, D. C.: Published by Author, 1997.

_____. *Final Judgement: The Missing Link in the JFK Assassination Conspiracy.*Washington, D. C.: The Wolfe Press, 1993, 1994.

Prouty, L. Fletcher. *JFK: The CIA, Vietnam, and the Plot to Assassinate John F. Kennedy.* New York: Birch Lane Press, 1992; Citadel Press, 1996.

Roberts, Craig. *Kill Zone.* Tulsa, Oklahoma: CPI, 1994.

Russell, Dick. *The Man Who Knew Too Much.* New York: Carroll & Graf Publishers Inc., 1992.

Sample, Glen, and Mark Collom. *The Men on the Sixth Floor.* Garden Grove, California: Sample Graphics, 1995.

Scheim, David E. *Contract on America: The Mafia Murders of John and Robert Kennedy.* New York: Shapolsky Publishers, 1988; Zebra Books, 1991.

Scott, Peter Dale. *Crime and Cover-Up: The CIA, the Mafia, and the Dallas-Watergate Connection.* Berkeley, California: Westworks, 1977.

_____. *Deep Politics and the Death of JFK.* Berkeley, California: University of California Press, 1993.

Smith, Matthew. *JFK: The Second Plot.* Edinburgh: Mainstream Publishing, 1992.

Summers, Anthony. *Conspiracy.* New York: McGraw-Hill, 1980, 1981; Paragon House, 1989. Re- titled *Not In Your Lifetime.* Marlowe & Company, 1998.

Truels, William P. *Breach of Faith: A Study of the Assassination of President John Fitzgerald Kennedy.* Oklahoma City, Oklahoma: Circulation Limited, 1996.

Waggoner, Jeffrey. *The Assassination of President Kennedy: Opposing Viewpoints.* San Diego, California: Greenhaven Press, Inc., 1989.

Weisberg, Harold. *Oswald in New Orleans: A Case for Conspiracy With the CIA.* New York: Canyon Books, 1967.

Yefimov, Igor. *Kennedy, Oswald, Castro, Khruschev.* Tenafly, New Jersey: Hermitage, 1987.

Zirbel, Craig I. *The Texas Connection: The Assassination of John F. Kennedy.* Scottsdale, Arizona: Wright & Company Publishers, 1991; New York: Warner Books, 1992.

Signed Articles:

Andronov, Iona. "On the Trail of a President's Killers." *New Times* (Moscow) (January 1977): No. 1, 27-30; No. 2, 26-30; No. 3, 27-30.

Barber, Gary D. "Social Science: Law & Criminology: *Mafia Kingfish.*" *Library Journal* 113 (December 1988): 127.

_____. "Social Sciences: Law & Crime: *Plausible Denial.*" *Library Journal* 116 (November 1, 1991): 118.

Belfrage, Cedric. "Four Assassinations: One Pattern." *The Minority of One* 6 (October 1964): 18-19.

Belin, David W. "*'They've Killed the President!'*: The Book You Shouldn't Read." *National Review* 28 (February 6, 1976): 81-85, 88-90.

Berkeley, Edmund C. "Confirmation of FBI Knowledge 12 Days Before Dallas of a Plot To Kill President Kennedy." *Computers and Automation* 19 (July 1970): 32-34.

_____. "The Assassination of President Kennedy: The Pattern of Coup d' Etat and Public Deception." *Computers and Automation* 20 (November 1971): 24-26, 29-30, 48.

Bernabei, Richard. "The New Books: The Kennedy Assassination: *'They've Killed the President!'.*" *Queen's Quarterly* 83 (Summer 1976): 510-11.

Bernt, H. H. "New Books Appraised: Reference: *Who Killed Kennedy?*" *Library Journal* 90 (January 1, 1965): 102-03.

Cartwright, Gary. "I Was Mandarin: Did Dallas Policeman Roscoe White Pull the Trigger on President Kennedy, or Is He Pulling Our Leg?" *Texas Monthly* 18 (December 1990): 129-30, 133, 160, 162, 164, 166-68, 170, 172, 174.

Catchpole, Terry. "Conspiracies: Out, Damned Plot." *Entertainment Weekly* 101 (January 17, 1992): 18-21.

Cohen, Jeff, and Donald Freed. "CIA Pins JFK Murder on Castro." [*National*] *Guardian* 29 (December 22, 1976): 7.

Crawford, Allan. "Leftists Stoking Fires of 'Conspiracy' Theory in JFK Death." *Human Events* 35 (January 4, 1975): 14.

Dirix, Bob. "Why Was JFK Shot?" *Atlas* 13 (May 1967): 10-13.

Evans, M. Stanton. "The Right Books: *'They've Killed the President!'*." *National Review* 28 (July 23, 1976), 796.

_____. "Dark Horses: *The Oswald File*." *National Review* 30 (April 14, 1978): 483.

Feldman, Harold. "The Johnson Murder Charge." *The Minority of One* 8 (December 1966): 21-22.

Fensterwald, Bernard, Jr. "The Case of Secret Service Agent Abraham W. Bolden-Who Wanted To Tell the Warren Commission About a Chicago Plot to Kill President Kennedy." *Computers and Automation* 20 (June 1971): 41-43.

Fraker, Susan. "National Affairs: Hints of the Mob." *Newsweek* 92 (October 9, 1978): 44, 47.

Gates, David. "The Kennedy Conundrum." *Newsweek* 112 (November 28, 1988): 46.

Gates, David, with Howard Manly. "The Arts: Movies: Bottom Line: How Crazy Is It?" *Newsweek* 118 (December 23, 1991): 52-54.

Hacker, Andrew. "The Case That Will Not Rest." *The New York Review of Books* 28 (July 17, 1980): 12.

Helicher, Karl. "Social Sciences: *JFK: The CIA, Vietnam, and the Plot to Assassinate John F. Kennedy.*" *Library Journal* 117 (August 1992): 128.

Jones, Kirby. "Unlikely Assassin." *The New Republic* 175 (July 3, 1976): 5-6.

Karel, Thomas A. "Social Sciences: Law & Crime: *Act of Treason.*" *Library Journal* 116 (November 1, 1991): 118.

Keisling, Phil. "Political Booknotes: *Contract on America.*" *The Washington Monthly* 15 (April 1983): 59.

Kister, Kenneth F. "Social Science: Law & Criminology: *'They've Killed the President!'.*" *Library Journal* 101 (February 15, 1976): 629.

Lynd, Staughton. "Is the Oswald Inquiry America's Dreyfus Case?" *National Guardian* 16 (February 27, 1964): 5.

Magnuson, Ed. "Did the Mob Kill J. F. K.?" *Time* 132 (November 28, 1988): 42-44.

Marquand, David. "Oswald Inc.?" *New Statesman* (London) 67 (May 8, 1964): 727, 730.

McKinven, Mary Jane. "Original Nonfiction Paperbacks: *'They've Killed the President!'.*" *Booklist* 72 (February 1, 1976): 752.

Murray, Hugh. "Book Review: *Mafia Kingfish.*" *Louisiana History* 31 (Spring 1990): 211-13.

Possony, Stefan T. "Clearing the Air." *National Review* 17 (February 9, 1965): 113-14, 116.

Preston, Gregor A. "History: *The Oswald File.*" *Library Journal* 102 (November 15, 1977): 2342-43.

Relation, A. Joseph. "Book Note: *The Plot To Kill The President.*" *Notre Dame Lawyer* 57 (1982): 620.

Rosenbaum, Ron. "History: Taking a Darker View." *Time* 139 (January 13, 1992): 54-56.

Russell, Dick. "From Dallas to Eternity." *Boston* 11 (November 1993): 62-65, 82, 85-88.

Salandria, Vincent J. "The Assassination of President John F. Kennedy: A Model for Explanation." *Computers and Automation* 20 (December 1971): 32-40.

Salholz, Eloise. "National Affairs: Did The Mob Kill JFK?" *Newsweek* 119 (January 27, 1992): 26- 27.

Sauvage, Leo. "Thomas Buchanan: Detective." *The New Leader* 47 (September 28, 1964): 10-15.

Schulz, Donald E. "Kennedy and the Cuban Connection." *Newsweek* 88 (September 6, 1976): 9.

Scott, Peter Dale. "From Dallas to Watergate: The Longest Cover-Up." *Ramparts* 12 (November 1973): 12-17, 20, 53-54.

Smith, Jack A. "Nagging Doubts on the 'Crime of the Century': Two Major Books on the Kennedy Assassination." *National Guardian* 16 (August 22, 1964): 5.

Sprague, Richard E. "More About Jim Hicks." *Computers and Automation* 19 (July 1970): 32.

Steck, Henry. "Political Science & International Affairs: *Conspiracy.*" *Library Journal* 105 (June 15, 1980): 1394.

_____. "Political Science & International Affairs: *The Plot to Kill the President.*" *Library Journal* 106 (February 15, 1981): 456.

_____. "Political Science: *Contract on America.*" *Library Journal* 109 (January 1984): 97-98.

_____. "Social Science: Law & Criminology: *Reasonable Doubt.*" *Library Journal* 3 (March 1, 1986): 104.

Thomas, Evan. "Bobby Kennedy's War on Castro." *The Washington Monthly* 27 (December 1995): 24-30.

Viorst, Milton. "The Mafia, the CIA, and the Kennedy Assassination." *Washingtonian* 11 (November 1975): 113-18.

Wecht, Cyril. "Book Reviews: *Reasonable Doubt.*" *The Journal of American History* 73 (September 1986): 437-38.

Welsh, David, and David Lifton. "The Case for Three Assassins." *Ramparts* 5 (January 1967): 77- 100.

Worsnop, Richard L. "JFK Assassination and the Mafia: Is There a Link?" *The CQ Researcher* 2 (March 27, 1992): 280.

Unsigned Articles:

"Nonfiction: Social Sciences: *The Oswald File.*" *Booklist* 74 (November 15, 1977): 510.

"Upfront: Advance Reviews: Adult Nonfiction: *Mafia Kingfish.*" *Booklist* 85 (September 15, 1988): 99-100.

"History, Geography, and Travel: North America: *The Plot to Kill the President.*" *Choice* 18 (July/August 1981): 1600.

"Political Science: *Contract on America.*" *Choice* 21 (April 1984): 1200.

"CIA: Who Killed Kennedy?" *The Economist* (London) 255 (May 3, 1975): 80.

"Books: A Second Murderer?" *The Economist* (London) 275 (May 24, 1980): 117-18.

"Were Kennedy, King Conspiracy Victims?" *Gallup Opinion Index* No. 139 (February 1977): 1-4.

"Nonfiction: *Mafia Kingfish*." *Kirkus Reviews* 56 (October 1, 1988): 1445.

"Nonfiction: *Crossfire*." *Kirkus Reviews* 57 (October 1, 1989): 1453.

"Nonfiction: *JFK: The CIA, Vietnam, and the Plot to Assassinate John F. Kennedy*." *Kirkus Reviews* 60 (July 15, 1992): 904.

"Nonfiction: *Deep Politics and the Death of JFK*." *Kirkus Reviews* 61 (August 15, 1993): 1059-60.

"A Theory on Kennedy Killing: Writer Postulates a Conspiracy Involving 7 Persons." *National Guardian* 16 (March 28, 1964): 1, 10.

"The Conspiracy Theories." *Newsweek* 122 (November 22, 1993): 98-99.

"Briefly Noted: *The Oswald File*." *The New Yorker* 53 (September 19, 1977): 142.

"PW Forecasts: Nonfiction: *The Oswald File*." *Publishers Weekly* 212 (August 1, 1977): 108.

"PW Forecasts: Nonfiction: *Conspiracy*." *Publishers Weekly* 217 (May 9, 1980): 45.

"PW Forecasts: Nonfiction: *The Plot to Kill the President*." *Publishers Weekly* 219 (January 16, 1981): 68.

"PW Forecasts: Nonfiction: *Reasonable Doubt*." *Publishers Weekly* 228 (November 22, 1985): 45.

"PW Forecasts: Nonfiction: *Mafia Kingfish*." *Publishers Weekly* 234 (October 7, 1988): 99.

"PW Forecasts: Nonfiction: *Crossfire*." *Publishers Weekly* 236 (October 20, 1989): 46.

"PW Forecasts: Nonfiction: *Plausible Denial*." *Publishers Weekly* 238 (September 6, 1991): 92.

"PW Forecasts: Nonfiction: *Act of Treason.*" *Publishers Weekly* 238 (September 20, 1991): 119.

"PW Forecasts: Nonfiction: *JFK: The CIA, Vietnam, and the Plot to Assassinate John F. Kennedy.*" *Publishers Weekly* 239 (July 13, 1992): 42.

"PW Forecasts: Nonfiction: *Deep Politics and the Death of JFK.*" *Publishers Weekly* 240 (September 20, 1993): 57.

"The Assassination and the Cover-Up: What Really Happened?" *Tikkun* 7 (March/April 1992): 40- 48.

"Historical Notes: The Mythmakers." *Time* 88 (November 11, 1966): 33-34.

"The Kennedys: Another Death Plot?" *Time* 95 (April 20, 1970): 17-18.

"Why a Plot Was Feared When Kennedy Was Shot." *U. S. News and World Report* 56 (January 6, 1964): 7.

"Charged: A Cover-Up In Kennedy Killing." *U. S. News and World Report* 81 (July 5, 1976): 21.

"John Kennedy's Death: The Debate Still Rages." *U. S. News and World Report* 95 (November 21, 1983): 49-50.

"Conspiracy News." *WIN* 10 (February 7, 1974): 19.

JIM GARRISON AND THE CLAY SHAW TRIAL

Books:

Associated Professional Services, ed. *Death of the President: The Warren Report on Trial in New Orleans!* Covina, California: Collectors Publications, 1967.

Brener, Milton E. *The Garrison Case: A Study in the Abuse of Power.* New York: Clarkson N. Potter, 1969.

Davis, William H. *Aiming for the Jugular in New Orleans.* Port Washington, New York: Ashley Books, 1976.

Davy, William. *Through The Looking Glass: The Mysterious World of Clay Shaw.* Published by Author, 1995.

DiEugenio, James. *Destiny Betrayed: JFK, Cuba, and the Garrison Case.* New York: Sheridan Square Press, 1992.

Epstein, Edward Jay. *Counterplot.* New York: Viking Press, 1969.

Flammonde, Paris. *The Kennedy Conspiracy: An Uncommissioned Report on the Jim Garrison Investigation.* New York: Meredith Press, 1969.

Garrison, Jim. *A Heritage of Stone.* New York: Putnam, 1970; Berkeley, 1972.

_____. *On The Trail of the Assassins.* New York: Sheridan Square Press, 1988; Warner Books, 1988, 1991.

James, Rosemary, and Jack Wardlaw. *Plot or Politics?: The Garrison Case and Its Cast.* New Orleans, Louisiana: Pelican Publishing House, 1967.

Joesten, Joachim. *The Garrison Enquiry: Truth & Consequences.* London: Dawnay, 1967.

Kirkwood, James. *American Grotesque: An Account of the Clay Shaw-Jim Garrison Affair in the City of New Orleans.* New York: Simon & Schuster, 1970; Harper, 1992.

Seigenthaler, John. *A Search for Justice.* Nashville, Tennessee: Aurora Publishers, 1970.

Sproesser, Louis. *The Garrison Investigation.* Connecticut: Published by Author, 1995.

Weisberg, Harold. *Oswald in New Orleans.* Foreward by Jim Garrison. New York: Canyon Books, 1967.

Signed Articles:

[Arnoni, M. S.]. "An Assassination's Retroactivity." *The Minority of One* 9 (April 1967): 9.

Arnoni, M. S. "Garrison and Warren: Anything in Common?" *The Minority of One* 9 (October 1967): 11-12.

[Arnoni, M. S.]. "Of Demonologists and Eunuchs." *The Minority of One* 10 (September 1968): 8-9.

Abrams, Garry. "Billion Buck Brawl: The Estate of Jim Garrison Is Locked In Legal Combat With Hollywood Studios In a Massive Profit-Participation Lawsuit." *The Los Angeles Daily Journal* (*California Law Business Supplement*) 109 (May 28, 1996): S16, 18-19.

Allen, Robert L. "New Questions Raised On JFK Killing: New Orleans D. A. Charges Conspiracy." *National Guardian* 19 (March 18, 1967): 1, 9.

Autry, James. "The Garrison Investigation: How and Why It Began." *New Orleans Magazine* 1 (April 1967): 8-9, 50-51.

Aynesworth, Hugh. "The JFK 'Conspiracy'." *Newsweek* 69 (May 15, 1967): 36-40.

Barber, Gary D. "Social Sciences: *Destiny Betrayed.*" *Library Journal* 117 (August 1992): 123-24.

Bennett, Liz. "Mrs. Garrison Talks About Home Life in the Midst of It All." *New Orleans Magazine* 1 (April 1967): 10-11, 48.

Bernt, H. H. "The Contemporary Scene: *The Kennedy Conspiracy.*" *Library Journal* 94 (January 1, 1969): 57.

_____. "Social Science: Law, Crime, & Criminal Procedure: *Counterplot.*" *Library Journal* 94 (March 1, 1969): 1012.

_____. "Social Science: Law, Crime, & Criminal Procedure: *The Garrison Case.*" *Library Journal* 94 (October 15, 1969): 3662.

_____. "Social Science: Law, Crime, & Criminal Procedure: *American Grotesque.*" *Library Journal* 95 (October 15, 1970): 3484.

_____. "Political Science & International Affairs: *A Heritage of Stone.*" *Library Journal* 95 (December 15, 1970): 4267.

Boothby, Paul. "Letters: Abuse of Powers." *The Nation* 208 (April 14, 1969): 450, 468.

Bowers, Faubion. "Books: The Garrison Saga." *The Village Voice* 16 (July 8, 1971): 23, 42.

Brady, Martin A. "Adult Nonfiction: History: *On The Trail of the Assassins.*" *Booklist* 85 (February 1, 1989): 909.

Chin, Sylvia Fung. "Federal Courts: Federal Common Law Created to Allow Survival of Section 1983 Action to Decedant's Executor [Shaw's]." *Fordham Law Review* 44 (December 1975): 666-74.

Cook, I. "Profile in Courage." *Amex-Canada* 2 (February 1971): 40.

Coyne, J. R. "Books in Brief: *A Heritage of Stone.*" *National Review* 23 (April 6, 1971): 382-83.

Cuff, Sergeant. "Criminal Record: Fact: *The Kennedy Conspiracy.*" *Saturday Review* 52 (March 29, 1969): 37.

_____. "Criminal Record: Fact: *Counterplot.*" *Saturday Review* 52 (April 26, 1969): 63.

Epstein, Edward Jay. "A Reporter at Large: Garrison." *The New Yorker* 44 (July 13, 1968): 35-40, 42, 44, 49-52, 54-56, 58-60, 62-76, 79-81.

_____. "Postscript: Shots in the Dark." *The New Yorker* 68 (November 30, 1992): 47-55, 57-58.

Feldman, Harold, Maggie Field, Sylvia Meagher, Penn Jones, Jr., and Leo Sauvage. "From Readers' Letters: 'Garrison and Warren: Anything in Common?'," *The Minority of One* 9 (December 1967): 29-30.

Fensterwald, Bernard, Jr.. "Jim Garrison, District Attorney, Orleans Parish vs The Federal Government." *Computers and Automation* 20 (August 1971): 37-42.

Fife, Darlene. "Mark Lane on Oswald." [*National*] *Guardian* 20 (April 6, 1968): 6.

_____. "Shaw Trial Opens." [*National*] *Guardian* 21 (February 15, 1969): 6.

Frankel, Haskel. "Criminal Record: Fact: *American Grotesque.*" *Saturday Review* 53 (December 26, 1970): 27.

Frewin, Anthony. "Late Breaking News on Clay Shaw's United Kingdom Contacts." Published by Author, 1994.

Gershman, Bennett L. "Will The Real Jim Garrison Please Stand Up?" *New York Law Journal* 207 (January 27, 1992): 2.

Giquel, Bernard. "Bientot Toutes les Preuves [Soon All of the Evidence]." *Paris Match* 935 (March 11, 1967): 44-47.

_____. "Le Mystere Kennedy--Le Procureur Garrison: 'J'irai Jusgu' au Bout' [The Kennedy Mystery: Attorney Garrison: 'I will go to the bitter end']." *Paris Match* 934 (March 4, 1967): 52-54.

Gun, Nerin E. "Le Mystere Kennedy--La Veille de sa Mort Ferrie m' a dit 'Oswald? Connais pas!' [The Kennedy Mystery: On the Eve of His Death, Ferrie Said to Me: 'Oswald? I Don't Know Him!']" *Paris Match* 934 (March 4, 1967): 67-68.

Hager, Steven. "Heritage of Stone." *High Times* (September 1991): 32-35, 50-54.

Jackson, Donald. "Book Review: A Heritage of Smoke." *Life* 69 (December 4, 1970): 16.

Jackson, John J. "State-Federal Relations: Enjoinment of State Criminal Prosecutions." *Loyola Law Review* 18 (1972): 207-16.

Joesten, Joachim. "Jim Garrison klagt an. Sieben Jahre nach dem Mord an Prasident Kennedy [Jim Garrison's Litigation Seven Years After Kennedy's Murder]." *Stimme der Gemeinde zum kirchlichen Leben, zur Politik, Wirtschaft und Kultur* (Frankfurt/Main) 23 (1971): 10-12.

Kerby, Phil. "Please Mail Your Check Promptly to the Conspiracy of Your Choice." *Frontier* 18 (February 1967): 12-13.

Kirkwood, James. "Surviving: So Here You Are, Clay Shaw . . . ." *Esquire* 70 (December 1968): 218-21, 254-61.

Knabb, Wayne M. "Shaw's Trial Covered by Reporters in Teams." *Editor & Publisher* 102 (February 15, 1969): 12.

Lane, Mark. "J'espere que Garrison est Fort/ses Ennemis sont sans Pitie" [I Hope That Garrison Is Strong: His Enemies Are Merciless]." *Paris Match* 934 (March 4, 1967): 69.

Lemann, Nicholas. "The Case Against Jim Garrison." *GQ* 62 (January 1992): 68-75.

Lowney, Douglas. "Another JFK Conspiracy." *California Lawyer* 16 (February 1996): 19.

Macdonald, Neil. "District Attorney Jim Garrison on the Assassination of President Kennedy: A Review of *Heritage of Stone*." *Computers and Automation* 20 (March 1971): 45-46.

Maddox, Henry. "The Plot According to Garrison." *New Orleans Magazine* 1 (July 1967): 18-19, 52-53.

Meagher, Sylvia. "Books: *The Kennedy Conspiracy.*" *Commonweal* 89 (March 7, 1969): 712-14.

Olds, Greg. "In My Opinion: Assassination." *The Texas Observer* 60 (July 26, 1968): 15.

Phelan, James. "A Plot To Kill Kennedy? Rush To Judgement in New Orleans." *The Saturday Evening Post*, 204 (May 6, 1967): 21-25.

Popkin, Richard H. "Garrison's Case." *New York Review of Books* 9 (September 14, 1967): 19-29.

Powledge, Fred. "Is Garrison Faking?: The D. A., the CIA, and the Assassination." *The New Republic* 156 (June 17, 1967): 13-18.

Rogers, Warren. "The Persecution of Clay Shaw." *Look* 33 (August 26, 1969): 53-56, 58-60.

Rohe, Terry Flettrich. "Our Friend Was a Suspect." *New Orleans Magazine* 25 (June 1991): 56-57.

Ruge, Gerd. "Wie starb John F. Kennedy? Im Prozess von New Orleans geht es um Aufklarung, aber auch um handfeste Interessen [How did Kennedy Die? There Is Clarification from Proceedings in New Orleans-But Also a Sturdy Self-Interest]." *Die Zeit* (Hamburg) 24 (1969): 2.

Schwelien, Joachim. " 'Enthullungen' uber den Kennedy-Mord. Die Kampagne des Staatsanwaltes Garrison ['Disclosures' About Kennedy's Murder. District Attorney Garrison's Campaign]." *Die Zeit* (Hamburg) 22 (1967): 6.

Scott, Liz. "Past Tense: Jim Garrison and the Kennedy Question." *New Orleans Magazine* 25 (November 1990): 78-81.

Sprague, Richard E. "Walter Sheridan--Democrats' Investigator? or Republicans' Countermeasure?" *Computers and Automation* 21 (November 1972): 29-31.

Taylor, Gilbert. "Adult Books: Nonfiction: Social Sciences: *Destiny Betrayed.*" *Booklist* 88 (July 1992): 1902.

Theis, William H. "Shaw v. Garrison: Some Observations on 42 U. S. C. 1988 and Federal Common Law." *Louisiana Law Review* 36 (Winter 1976): 681-91.

Turner, William W. "The Plot Thickens." *Ramparts* 5 (April 1967): 8-9.

_____. "The Inquest." *Ramparts* 5 (June 1967): 17-29.

_____. "The Press Versus Garrison." *Ramparts* 6 (September 1967): 8-12.

_____. "The Garrison Commission on the Assassination of President Kennedy." *Ramparts* 6 (January 1968): 2, 43-68.

_____. "Shaw Verdict: Garrison Out, Investigation On." [*National*] *Guardian* 21 (March 22, 1969): 15.

Ward, Nathan. "The Time Machine: 1967: Twenty-Five Years Ago: Rush To Judgement." *American Heritage* 43 (May/June 1992): 45-46.

Young, Roger. "The Investigation: Where It Stands Today." *New Orleans Magazine* 1 (July 1967): 16-17, 54-59.

Unsigned Articles:

"Classified Books: Social Sciences: *A Heritage of Stone*." *Booklist* 67 (April 1, 1971): 633.

"Classified Books: Social Sciences: *A Search For Justice*." *Booklist* 68 (November 15, 1971): 260.

"Garrison to Seek Equal Time." *Broadcasting* 72 (June 26, 1967): 72-73.

"Will Garrison Take Half of Equal Time?" *Broadcasting* 73 (July 10, 1967): 71.

"Sheridan to Answer Garrison in New Orleans." *Broadcasting* 73 (July 17, 1967): 48.

"Political Science: *American Grotesque.*" *Choice* 8 (October 1971): 1088.

"The New Orleans Portion of the Conspiracy to Assassinate President John F. Kennedy." *Computers and Automation* 22 (April 1973): 34-39; 22 (May 1973): 30-32.

"Garrison Under Fire." *The Economist* (London) 222 (February 25, 1967): 730.

"Tales of Garrison." *The Economist* (London) 222 (March 25, 1967): 1145.

"Plot Thickening?" *The Economist* (London) 223 (April 29, 1967): 468.

"Garrison's Way Out?" *The Economist* (London) 228 (July 20, 1968): 40.

"Who's on Trial?" *The Economist* (London) 230 (January 25, 1969): 21-22.

"Endless Trials." *The Economist* (London) 230 (March 8, 1969): 40-43.

"District Attorney Miffed by Scoop on JFK Probe." *Editor & Publisher* 100 (February 25, 1967): 10.

"Nonfiction: *The Kennedy Conspiracy.*" *Kirkus Reviews* 36 (September 15, 1968): 1084.

"Nonfiction: *American Grotesque.*" *Kirkus Reviews* 38 (September 1, 1970): 1009.

"Social Science: Law, Crime, & Criminal Procedure: *A Search for Justice.*" *Library Journal* 96 (March 15, 1971): 974.

"The Theory of an Oswald Conspiracy." *Life* 62 (March 3, 1967): 33.

"Lenta Disparitie din Scena a lui Jim Garrison [Slow Disappearance from the Scene by Jim Garrison]." *Lumea* (Bucharest) 5 (June 22, 1967): 97-100.

"Editorials: Verdict in New Orleans." *The Nation* 208 (March 17, 1969): 324-25.

"Report to Readers: Death and Intrigue in New Orleans." *National Guardian* 19 (March 4, 1967): 1- 2.

"Shaw Faces Trial in Kennedy Killing: Action by Judge Panel at New Orleans." *National Guardian* 19 (April 1, 1967): 3.

"Shaw Trial Will Open." [*National*] *Guardian* 21 (December 21, 1968): 9.

"New JFK Evidence Unearthed." [*National*] *Guardian* 28 (November 26, 1975): 7.

"JFK Prober Jailed for Releasing Tape." *The National Law Journal* 18 (February 26, 1996): A8.

"This Week: In a Blaze of Publicity . . . ." *National Review* 19 (March 7, 1967): 229.

"What Garrison Proved." *The New Republic* 160 (March 15, 1969): 9.

"Reporter Fined for Story About '69 Kennedy Assassination Investigation." *News Media and the Law* 20 (Spring 1996): 22-23.

"National Affairs: Assassination: Carnival in New Orleans." *Newsweek* 69 (March 6, 1967): 32-34.

"National Affairs: Assassination: History or Headlines?" *Newsweek* 69 (March 13, 1967): 44, 47.

"Press: A Taste for Conspiracy." *Newsweek* 69 (March 20, 1967): 76.

"National Affairs: The Assassination: Thickening the Plot." *Newsweek* 69 (March 27, 1967): 37-38.

"National Affairs: The Assassination: A Charge of Conspiracy." *Newsweek* 69 (April 3, 1967): 36-37.

"National Affairs: New Orleans: Sleight of Hand." *Newsweek* 69 (May 22, 1967): 40, 42.

"TV-Radio: Two for the Seesaw." *Newsweek* 70 (July 3, 1967): 82.

"National Affairs: The Assassination: Law Unto Himself." *Newsweek* 71 (January 8, 1968): 25-26.

"National Affairs: Investigations: Back in Business." *Newsweek* 72 (August 5, 1968): 26.

"National Affairs: Trials: Curtains for the D. A." *Newsweek* 73 (January 27, 1969): 27.

"National Affairs: Trials: Mardi Gras Season." *Newsweek* 73 (February 17, 1969): 34.

"National Affairs: Trials: What Conspiracy?" *Newsweek* 73 (February 24, 1969): 33.

"National Affairs: Trials: Fact and Opinion." *Newsweek* 73 (March 10, 1969): 36.

"Press: Covering Big Jim." *Newsweek* 73 (March 17, 1969): 105.

"The Periscope: D. A. Garrison's Re-Election Fight." *Newsweek* 74 (August 18, 1969): 14.

"Newsmakers: U.S. Justice Dept. Arrests Jim Garrison on Bribery Charges." *Newsweek* 78 (July 12, 1971): 52.

"Newsmakers: Federal Government Prosecution of Jim Garrison Continues." *Newsweek* 78 (December 13, 1971): 61.

"Newsmakers: Acquittal of Jim Garrison on Federal Charges of Bribery." *Newsweek* 82 (October 8, 1973): 64-65.

"The Periscope: Dallas Revisited?" *Newsweek* 82 (October 22, 1973): 23.

"Transition: Died: Clay L. Shaw, 60." *Newsweek* 84 (August 26, 1974): 43.

"PW Forecasts: Nonfiction: *The Kennedy Conspiracy.*" *Publishers Weekly* 194 (September 23, 1968): 94.

"PW Forecasts: Nonfiction: *The Garrison Case.*" *Publishers Weekly* 196 (August 18, 1969): 69.

"PW Forecasts: Nonfiction: *A Heritage of Stone.*" *Publishers Weekly* 198 (September 14, 1970): 64.

"PW Forecasts: Nonfiction: *American Grotesque.*" *Publishers Weekly* 198 (October 5, 1970): 60.

"PW Forecasts: Nonfiction: *A Search For Justice.*" *Publishers Weekly* 199 (April 26, 1971): 59.

"Kennedy Assassination: New Orleans Plot?" *Senior Scholastic* 90 (April 14, 1967): 18-19.

"JFK Assassination Plot?: Jury Clears Shaw." *Senior Scholastic* 94 (March 21, 1969): 16.

" 'Kennedy starb im Kreuzfeuer'. Spiegel-Gesprach mit dem Oberstaatsanwalt von New Orleans Jim Garrison {'Kennedy Died in a Crossfire'. Interview with D. A. Jim Garrison]." *Der Spiegel* (Hamburg) 21 (1967): 108-20.

"Political Intelligence: New Orleans." *The Texas Observer* 58 (March 3, 1967): 10.

"The Assassination: Bourbon Street Rococo." *Time* 89 (March 3, 1967): 26.

"Louisiana: Odd Company." *Time* 89 (March 10, 1967): 24-25.

"Investigations: The D. A. Wins a Round." *Time* 89 (March 24, 1967): 17-18.

"Medicine: Drugs: Sifting Fact from Fantasy." *Time* 89 (March 31, 1967): 41.

"The Assassination: Closing In." *Time* 90 (July 7, 1967): 17.

"The Law: Trials: Shutting Up Big-Mouth." *Time* 90 (August 25, 1967): 48-51.

"The Law: District Attorneys: Jolly Green Giant in Wonderland." *Time* 92 (August 2, 1968): 56-57.

"Trials: More Than a Man in the Dock." *Time* 93 (February 14, 1969): 26-29.

"Trials: Dallas Revisited." *Time* 93 (February 21, 1969): 18-19.

"Trials: Garrison's Last Gasp." *Time* 93 (March 7, 1969): 23.

"Trials: Garrison v. Everybody." *Time* 102 (October 8, 1973): 36.

"JFK Death: A New Investigation, But---." *U. S. News and World Report* 62 (March 13, 1967): 16.

"Order for a Trial in Assassination 'Plot'." *U. S. News and World Report* 62 (March 27, 1967): 10.

"More on the Kennedy Assassination Charges." *U. S. News and World Report* 62 (June 12, 1967): 55-56.

HOUSE SELECT COMMITTEE ON ASSASSINATIONS: 1976-1979

Official Printings:

U. S. House of Representatives. *Select Committee on Assassinations. Investigation of the Assassination of President John F. Kennedy: Appendix to Hearings Before the Select Committee on Assassinations of the U. S. House of Representatives.* 7 vols., 95th Cong., 2nd Session. Washington, D. C.: Government Printing Office, 1979.

_____. *Investigation of the Assassination of President John F. Kennedy: Hearings Before the Select Committee on Assassinations of¹ the U. S. House of Representatives.* 5 vols., 95th Cong., 2nd Session. Washington, D. C.: Government Printing Office, 1978-79.

_____. *Report of the Select Committee on Assassinations. 94th Cong., 2nd Session.* Washington, D. C.: Government Printing Office, 1979.

Other Printing:

U. S. House of Representatives. *The Final Assassinations Report: Report of the Select Committee on Assassinations.* Foreword by Tom Wicker, Introduction by G. Robert Blakey. New York: Bantam Books, 1979.

Books:

Cornwell, Gary. *Real Answers.* Spicewood, Texas: Paleface Press, 1998.

Fonzi, Gaeton. *The Last Investigation.* New York: Thunder's Mouth Press, 1993, 1994.

Gandolfo, Ted. *The House Committee on Assassinations Cover-Up.* Published by Author, 1987.

Scally, Christopher. *So Near...And Yet So Far: The House Select Committee on Assassinations' Investigation into the Murder of President John F. Kennedy.* New York: Aries, 1980.

Signed Articles:

Alpern, David M. "National Affairs: Self-Inflicted Wounds." *Newsweek* 89 (February 21, 1977): 18, 21.

_____. "National Affairs: Are There New Leads?" *Newsweek* 89 (April 11, 1977): 32, 37.

_____. "JFK: A Telltale Tape?" *Newsweek* 92 (January 1, 1979): 21.

Baker, John F. "New JFK Book Continues PGW's Sales Thrust [Fonzi's *The Last Investigation*]." *Publishers Weekly* 240 (July 26, 1993): 29-30.

Belin, David W. "The Kennedy Assassination: The Second-Gunman Syndrome." *National Review* 31 (April 27, 1979): 534-36, 553-55.

Berlow, Alan. "Law Enforcement/Judiciary: No 'Smoking Gun': House Rebuffs Effort to Cut Assassinations Panel Funding Until It Documents Progress." *Congressional Quarterly Weekly Report* 36 (March 18, 1978): 698.

Fonzi, Gaeton. "Who Killed Kennedy?" *Washingtonian* 16 (November 1980): 157-86, 190-92, 194- 97, 200-15, 218-37.

_____. "David Atlee Phillips and the Conspiracy to Assassinate President Kennedy." *The Pennsylvania Gazette* 92 (November 1993): 20-21.

Fraker, Susan, and Stephan Lesher. "Investigations: Back to Square One." *Newsweek* 88 (December 6, 1976): 32-35.

Gelman, David, and Elaine Shannon. "JFK: Settling Some Doubts." *Newsweek* 92 (September 18, 1978): 29-30.

_____. " 'A Tremendous Insanity'." *Newsweek* 92 (October 2, 1978): 62.

Goldman, Peter. "Rush To Judgement." *Newsweek* 93 (January 15, 1979): 26-27.

Hager, Barry. "Law Enforcement/Judiciary: House Move Reflects Questions on Cost of Assassination Probe." *Congressional Quarterly Weekly Report* 35 (January 8, 1977): 46-48.

_____. "Law Enforcement/Judiciary: House Revives Assassinations Panel." *Congressional Quarterly Weekly Report* 35 (February 5, 1977): 201-02.

_____. "Law Enforcement/Judiciary: Gonzalez Fires Sprague But Remains on Job." *Congressional Quarterly Weekly Report* 35 (February 12, 1977): 292.

_____. "Law Enforcement/Judiciary: Gonzalez Quits as Committee Chairman." *Congressional Quarterly Weekly Report* 35 (March 5, 1977): 410-11.

_____. "Law Enforcement/Judiciary: Bickering Ends: Stokes Named to Head Assassinations Committee." *Congressional Quarterly Weekly Report* 35 (March 12, 1977): 447, 449.

_____. "Law Enforcement/Judiciary: Sprague Quits: House Extends Life of Assassination Panel." *Congressional Quarterly Weekly Report* 35 (April 2, 1977): 618.

Kidder, Tracy. "Washington: The Assassination Tangle." *The Atlantic Monthly* 243 (March 1979): 4, 6-8, 10, 13-16, 24, 26, 28.

Lardner, George, Jr. "Congress and the Assassinations." *Saturday Review* 4 (February 19, 1977): 14- 17.

Livernash, Bob. "Kennedy Hearings Continue: House Votes Extra Funds For Assassination Unit." *Congressional Quarterly Weekly Report* 36 (September 16, 1978): 2497-98.

_____. "Hearings to End: Assassinations Unit to Probe Ruby's Links to Organized Crime; Hears Ford on FBI." *Congressional Quarterly Weekly Report* 36 (September 23, 1978): 2581.

_____. 'Hearings End: Assassination Panel Probes Ruby Ties to Crime Figures." *Congressional Quarterly Weekly Report* 36 (September 30, 1978): 2627.

_____. "Law Enforcement/Judiciary: House Panel Concludes Conspiracies Probably Part of Kennedy, King Deaths." *Congressional Quarterly Weekly Report* 37 (January 6, 1979): 19-20.

Morganthau, Tom. "National Affairs: Tales Of Conspiracy." *Newsweek* 94 (July 30, 1979): 37-38.

Segal, Jeff. "Assassination Probe: Counsel Named." *[National] Guardian* 29 (October 27, 1976): 11.

_____. "New Leads in Kennedy, King Probe?: Investigators Angle for Big Budget." *[National] Guardian* 29 (January 12, 1977): 6.

_____. "JFK, King Probe Falters in Congress." *[National] Guardian* 29 (March 20, 1977): 5.

_____. "New Light Shed on J. F. K. Murder." *[National] Guardian* 29 (April 13, 1977): 3.

Ungar, Sanford J. "A New Man on Two Old Cases." *The Atlantic Monthly* 239 (February 1977): 8, 12, 14.

Whitaker, Charles. "Ebony Interview with Rep. Louis Stokes: Chairman, Select Committee on Assassinations." *Ebony* 47 (April 1992): 24-26, 28.

Unsigned Articles:

"Assassination Committee: Controversy Continues." *Congressional Quarterly Weekly Report* 35 (January 15, 1977): 94.

"Assassination Committee Still Without a Budget." *Congressional Quarterly Weekly Report* 35 (January 29, 1977): 169-70.

"Law Enforcement/Judiciary: Gonzalez vs. Sprague: Assassinations Committee's Future Remains in Doubt." *Congressional Quarterly Weekly Report* 35 (February 19, 1977): 335-36.

"Henry Gonzalez: Standing Alone." *Congressional Quarterly Weekly Report* 35 (February 19, 1977): 336.

"Assassinations: Committee Seeks Support For Kennedy-King Probes." *Congressional Quarterly Weekly Report* 35 (March 19, 1977): 514.

"Inside Congress: Dealing with the Press." *Congressional Quarterly Weekly Report* 35 (April 2, 1977): 592.

"Law Enforcement/Judiciary: Assassinations Panel Funded." *Congressional Quarterly Weekly Report* 35 (April 30, 1977): 834.

"Law Enforcement/Judiciary: Committee History." *Congressional Quarterly Weekly Report* 36 (August 19, 1978): 235.

"Law Enforcement/Judiciary: Assassination Hearings." *Congressional Quarterly Weekly Report* 36 (September 9, 1978): 2420.

"The Sprague Circus." *The Economist* (London) 262 (February 26, 1977): 49.

"Assassinations: To Be Continued." *The Economist* (London) 263 (April 9, 1977): 31.

"The World: American Survey: The Ghost That Cannot Be Laid." *The Economist* (London) 268 (September 16, 1978): 41-42.

"National Report: Rep. Stokes Raps FBI on Kennedy Murder Plot." *Jet* 59 (December 25, 1980): 6.

"Umbrella Cover-Up." *The New Republic* 179 (October 7, 1978): 7-8.

"Periscope: Pruning the Probers." *Newsweek* 89 (January 31, 1977): 13.

"National Affairs: Congress: Death Trip." *Newsweek* 89 (February 14, 1977): 29.

"PW Forecasts: Nonfiction: *The Last Investigation*." *Publishers Weekly* 240 (September 20, 1993): 52.

"Investigations: Sprague's Sprawl." *Time* 109 (January 10, 1977): 17.

"Investigations: Shrinking Sprague." *Time* 109 (February 14, 1977): 24.

"Congress: Assassination: Now a Suicide Talks." *Time* 109 (April 11, 1977): 20.

"Nation: Lone Assassins: Decisions on the Deaths of Kennedy and King." *Time* 112 (September 18, 1978): 23-24.

"Nation: Dousing a Popular Theory." *Time* 112 (October 2, 1978): 22.

"Nation: The President and the Capo." *Time* 112 (October 9, 1978): 31-32.

"Nation: A Fourth Shot?: New Mystery in the JFK Case." *Time* 113 (January 1, 1979): 61-62.

"Why the JFK Case is Coming Back to Life." *U. S. News and World Report* 82 (January 17, 1977): 28-30.

"One More Theory On Kennedy Murder." *U. S. News and World Report* 87 (July 30, 1979): 6.

HOLLYWOOD AND THE JFK ASSASSINATION

Books:

Simon, Art. *Dangerous Knowledge: The JFK Assassination in Art and Film*. Philadelphia, Pennsylvania: Temple University Press, 1996.

Stone, Oliver, and Zachary Sklar. *JFK: The Book of The Film*. New York: Applause Books, 1992.

Signed Articles:

Ansen, David. "A Troublemaker For Our Times." *Newsweek* 118 (December 23, 1991): 50.

_____. "The Arts: Movies: What Does Oliver Stone Owe History?" *Newsweek* 118 (December 23, 1991): 49.

Anson, Robert Sam. "The Shooting of JFK." *Esquire* 116 (November 1991): 93-98, 100, 102, 174- 76.

Auchincloss, Kenneth, with Ginny Carroll. "The Arts: Movies: Twisted History." *Newsweek* 118 (December 23, 1991): 46-49.

Bancroft, Bill. "Outlook: Dateline: Past-Tense Production." *U. S. News and World Report* 110 (May 27, 1991): 19.

Barra, Allen, and Ty Burr. "*JFK.*" *Entertainment Weekly* 101 (January 17, 1992): 12-16.

Bart, Peter. "Film: Oliver's Twist." *Variety* (Weekly) 346 (January 20, 1992): 7, 159.

Belin, David W. "Which Work Is The Fiction?" *The National Law Journal* 14 (February 3, 1992): 17-19.

_____. "The Big 'Lies' of *JFK*." *New York* 25 (February 17, 1992): 44-47.

Bethell, Tom. "Books, Arts & Manners: Conspiracy to End Conspiracies." *National Review* 43 (December 16, 1991): 48-50.

Billson, Anne. "Film: Shots in the Dark." *New Statesman* (London) 5 (January 24, 1992): 35.

Bodovitz, Sandra. "*JFK* Required Complex Contracts, Clearances." *The Los Angeles Daily Journal* (*California Law Business Supplement*) 105 (January 13, 1992): S5.

Breo, Dennis L. "Sequel: Examining *JFK*." *People Weekly* 37 (June 8, 1992): 49-50.

Bruning, Fred. "An American View: A Ticking Bomb at the Movies." *Maclean's* 105 (January 13, 1992): 11.

Cockburn, Alexander. "Beat the Devil." *The Nation* 254 (January 6/13, 1992): 6-7.

_____. "American Diary: The Kooks Have It." *New Statesman* (London) 5 (January 17, 1992): 14.

_____. "Exchange: Cockburn Replies." *The Nation* 254 (May 18, 1992): 678-80.

Cohen, Jacob. "Yes, Oswald Alone Killed Kennedy." *Commentary* 93 (June 1992): 32-40.

Collier, Peter. "Ollie uber Alles." *The American Spectator* 25 (April 1992): 28-31.

Conant, Jennet. "The Man Who Shot *JFK*." *GQ* 62 (January 1992): 61-67, 137-39.

Corliss, Richard. "Cinema: Who Killed JFK?" *Time* 138 (December 23, 1991): 66-70.

Corn, David. "Beltway Bandits." *The Nation* 154 (January 27, 1992): 80.

Crist, Judith. "This Week's Movies: *The Trial of Lee Harvey Oswald*." *TV Guide* 25 (September 24, 1977): A-9.

Crowdus, Gary. "Clarifying the Conspiracy: An Interview With Oliver Stone." *Cineaste* 19 (1992): 25-27.

_____. "Getting the Facts Straight: An Interview With Zachary Sklar." *Cineaste* 19 (1992): 28- 32.

_____. "Striving for Authenticity: An Interview With Jane Rusconi." *Cineaste* 19 (1992): 33-34.

Cummins, Ken. "Capital Comment: For Specter, The Single Bullet Strikes Again." *Washingtonian* 27 (February 1992): 10.

Daly, Steve. "Camera Obscura." *Entertainment Weekly* 101 (January 17, 1992): 16-17.

Denby, David. "Movies: Thrill of Fear." *New York* 25 (January 6, 1992): 50-51.

Denton, Tommy. "Hopefully, Movie Will Force Debate Over Official Secrecy." *The Los Angeles Daily Journal* 105 (January 3, 1992): 6.

Dowell, Pat. "Last Year at Nuremberg: The Cinematic Strategies of *JFK*." *Cineaste* 19 (1992): 8-11.

Ephron, Nora. "Books & The Arts: The Tie That Binds." *The Nation* 154 (April 6, 1992): 453-55.

Epstein, Edward Jay. "The Second Coming of Jim Garrison." *The Atlantic Monthly* 271 (March 1993): 89-92, 94.

Evica, George M.. "Deconstructing the DA: The Garrison Image in *JFK*." *Cineaste* 19 (1992): 17-19.

Felberbaum, A. "Letter/*Executive Action*." *Cineaste* 6 (Fall 1974): 42.

Fisher, Bob. "The Whys and Hows of *JFK*." *American Cinematographer* 73 (February 1992): 42- 46, 48, 50, 52.

Fleming, Charles, "Film: Conspiracy Over *JFK* Buttons?" *Variety* (Weekly) 346 (January 27, 1992): 10.

_____, and David Kissinger. "Film: WB: Pub Hubbub OK for *JFK.*" *Variety* (Weekly) 345 (November 11, 1991): 6, 76.

Frook, John Evan. "Film: MPAA's Valenti Lets Rip on *JFK.*" *Variety* (Weekly) 346 (April 6, 1992): 5, 14.

Gardels, Nathan, and Leila Conners. "Splinters To The Brain [Interview with Oliver Stone]." *New Perspectives Quarterly* 9 (Spring 1992): 51-53.

Georgakas, Dan. "The 'Threat' to the New Frontier: The Kennedy Image in *JFK.*" *Cineaste* 19 (1992): 19-20.

Gerard, Jeremy. "Film: Stone Holds Own in Gotham *JFK* Debate." *Variety* (Weekly) 346 (March 9, 1992): 5, 23.

Giglio, James N. "Oliver Stone's *JFK* in Historical Perspective." *Perspectives* 30 (April 1992): 18- 19.

Gitlin, Todd. "The Stoning of Oliver and the Fascination of *JFK.*" *Tikkun* 7 (March/April 1992): 52- 55.

Green, Philip. "Exchange: Hunkered In The Bunker." *The Nation* 254 (May 18, 1992): 676-80.

Green, Stephen. "Oliver Stone's Lies in *JFK* May Smoke Out Documents That People Have a Right To See." *The Los Angeles Daily Journal* 105 (February 24, 1992): 6.

Grenier, Richard. "On the Trail of America's Paranoid Class: Oliver Stone's JFK." *National Interest* No. 27 (Spring 1992): 76-84.

Griffin, Sean. "Shooting Down the Lone-Director Theory." *The Los Angeles Daily Journal* 105 (January 15, 1992): 6.

Gross, Ken. "Up Front: Dallas Revisited." *People Weekly* 35 (May 13, 1991): 50-52.

Grundmann, Roy, and Cynthia Lucia. "Gays, Women, and Abstinent Hero: The Sexual Politics of *JFK.*" *Cineaste* 19 (1992): 20-22.

Grunwald, Lisa. "Why We Still Care: Oliver Stone's Latest Film, *JFK*, Revives An American Obsession." *Life* 14 (December 1991): 34-36, 38, 40-44, 46.

Jarvis, Jeff. "This Week: Hits & Misses: Fatal Deception." *TV Guide* 41 (November 13, 1993): 49.

Johnson, Brian D. "Films: Who Killed JFK?" *Maclean's* 104 (December 30, 1991): 25.

Kauffman, Stanley. "Books & The Arts: Yes, *JFK* Again." *The New Republic* 206 (April 6, 1992): 26-27.

Keller, James R. "Oliver Stone's *JFK* and the 'Circulation of Social Energy' and the 'Textuality of History'." *Journal of Popular Film and Television* 21 (Summer 1993): 72-78.

Kellogg, Mary Alice. "*The Marina Oswald Story*." *TV Guide* 41 (November 13, 1993): 26-28.

Klawans, Stuart. "Films: JFK." *The Nation* 254 (January 20, 1992): 62-63.

Kopkind, Andrew. "Editorials: *JFK*: The Myth." *The Nation* 254 (January 20, 1992): 40-41.

_____. "Vogue Arts: Movies: Thirty Years Later, Hollywood Is Unleashing Five New Films That Deal With The Kennedy Assassination." *Vogue* 182 (January 1992): 64-67.

Leo, John. "On Society: Oliver Stone's Paranoid Propaganda." *U. S. News and World Report* 112 (January 13, 1992): 18.

Liebeler, Wesley J. "Exchange: Liebeler Replies." *The Nation* 254 (May 18, 1992): 678.

Loebs, Bruce. "Mass Media: Kennedy, Vietnam, and Oliver Stone's Big Lie." *USA Today* (Periodical) 121 (May 1993): 88-91.

Luckinbill, Lawrence. "Letter: Say No to *JFK*." *Variety* (Weekly) 346 (March 16, 1992): 82.

MacKenzie, John P. "Oliver Stone Makes a Hero of a Malicious Prosecutor." *The Los Angeles Daily Journal* 105 (January 3, 1992): 6.

Mailer, Norman. "Footfalls In The Crypt." *Vanity Fair* 55 (February 1992): 124-29, 171.

Marshall, Alex. "Dead Again and Again." *Movieline* 3 (January /February 1992): 38-42.

Mellen, Joan. " *Executive Action*: The Politics of Distortion." *Cineaste* 6 (1974): 8-12.

Morrow, Lance. "Essay: When Artists Distort History." *Time* 138 (December 23, 1991): 84.

Morrow, Lance, and Martha Smilgis. "Cinema: Plunging into the Labyrinth." *Time* 138 (December 23, 1991), 74-76.

Newman, John. "Exchange: Loose Bazooka." *The Nation* 254 (May 18, 1992): 650, 676.

Novak, Ralph. "Picks & Pans: Screen: *Ruby*." *People Weekly* 37 (April 6, 1992): 16, 21, 22.

Oglesby, Carl. "Who Killed JFK? The Media Whitewash." *Lies of Our Times* 2 (September 1991): 3-6.

O'Sullivan, John. "From the Editor: *JFK*." *National Review* 44 (July 6, 1992): 6.

Petras, James. "The Discrediting of the Fifth Estate: The Press Attacks on *JFK*." *Cineaste* 19 (1992): 15-17.

Pickard, Roy. "Does This Movie Expose the Real Truth Behind the Kennedy Killing?" *Photoplay* (March 1974): 26-28.

Pilger, John. "Death in Dallas: Rightwingers Plotted to Kill JFK, A New Film Says." *New Statesman* (London) 120 (October 4, 1991): 10.

_____. "Shaming the System: Why the Critics Don't Like *JFK*." *New Statesman* (London) 5 (February 7, 1992): 10-11.

Pond, Steve. "Double Impact [*JFK's* Beata Pozinak and Gary Oldman]." *Harper's Bazaar* No. 3360 (December 1991): 137, 158.

Raskin, Marcus. "*JFK* and the Culture of Violence." *The American Historical Review* 97 (April 1992): 487-99.

Rieland, Randy, ed. "Capital Comment: The JFK Story Continues But Now It's Ruby's Turn." *Washingtonian* 27 (February 1992): 11.

Robach, M. " *Executive Action*: Hollywood Rediscovers Politics." *Ramparts* 12 (December 1973): 48-50.

Rogin, Michael. " *JFK*: The Movie." *The American Historical Review* 97 (April 1992): 500-05.

Romanowski, William D. "Oliver Stone's *JFK*: Commercial Filmmaking, Cultural History, and Conflict." *Journal of Popular Film and Television* 21 (Summer 1993): 63-71.

Rosenbaum, Ron. "History: Taking a Darker View." *Time* 139 (January 13, 1992): 54-56.

Rosenstone, Robert A. "*JFK*: Historical Fact/Historical Film." *The American Historical Review* 97 (April 1992): 506-11.

Schiller, Herbert. "JFK: The Movie." *Lies of Our Times* 2 (September 1991): 6-7.

Schorr, Daniel. "Washington Notebook: An Open Letter To Oliver Stone." *The New Leader* 75 (January 13-27, 1992): 5.

Seal, Mark. "Can Hollywood Solve JFK's Murder?" *Texas Monthly* 19 (December 1991): 128-33, 158, 160, 162, 164, 166, 168.

Sharrett, Christopher. "The Reel World: Media vs. Oliver Stone." *USA Today* (Periodical) 120 (May 1992): 37.

_____. "Debunking the Official History: The Conspiracy Theory in *JFK*." *Cineaste* 19 (1992): 11-14.

_____. "The Reel World: Revisionism, History, and Hollywood." *USA Today* (Periodical) 123 (July 1994): 83.

Simon, Art. "The Making of Alert Viewers: The Mixing of Fact and Fiction in *JFK*." *Cineaste* 19 (1992): 14-15.

Sklar, Zachary. *"Time* Magazine's Continuing Cover-Up." *Lies of Our Times* 2 (September 1991): 7- 8.

Sloan, Jane E. "[Book Review]: *The JFK Assassination in Art and Film.*" *Library Journal* 121 (February 1, 1996): 77, 80.

Smolla, Rodney A. "Harlots Ghost and *JFK*: A Fictional Conversation With Norman Mailer, Oliver Stone, Earl Warren, and Hugo Black." *Suffolk University Law Review* 26 (Fall 1992): 587-618.

Steel, Ronald. "Mr. Smith Goes to the Twilight Zone." *The New Republic* 206 (February 3, 1992): 30-32.

Stone, Oliver. "Letters: Oliver Stone's *JFK*." *Time* 37 (July 1, 1991): 4.

_____. "The Sound and the Fury: Stone Shoots Back." *Esquire* 116 (December 1991): 42.

_____. "Oliver Stone Talks Back." *Premier* 5 (January 1992): 66-70, 72.

_____. "Exchange: A Stone's Throw." *The Nation* 254 (May 18, 1992): 650.

_____. "Who Defines History?" *Cineaste* 19 (1992): 23-24.

Toplin, Robert Brent, ed. "Forum: Oliver Stone's *JFK*." *Journal of American History* 79 (December 1992): 1262-68.

Tyrrell, R. Emmett. "Stone Dead." *The American Spectator* 25 (February 1992): 11-12.

Wall, James M. "Editorials: *JFK*: A Series of Evocative Possibilities." *The Christian Century* 109 (January 22, 1992): 59-60.

Waters, Harry F. "Television: Recipe for Paranoia." *Newsweek* 90 (October 3, 1977): 64-65.

Wells, Jeffrey. "Fights: Riling Stone." *Entertainment Weekly* 104 (February 7, 1992): 12.

Wharton, Dennis. "Film: Stone on Capital Hill." *Variety* (Weekly) 346 (March 9, 1992): 23.

Zaller, Robert. "Shilling for the Warren Report." *Seven Arts* 2 (January 1994): 25-26, 28.

Zimmerman, Paul D. "Movies: The Killing of JFK." *Newsweek* 82 (November 26, 1973): 104.

Zoglin, Richard. "Cinema: More Shots in Dealey Plaza." *Time* 137 (June 10, 1991): 64, 66.

Unsigned Articles:

"Action Replay [*JFK*]." *The Economist* (London) 318 (March 30, 1991): 25.

"American Survey: Lexington: Oliver Stone and The Appetite For Conspiracies." *The Economist* (London) 321 (December 21, 1991): 32.

"Reviews: *Executive Action.*" *Films and Filming* 20 (February 1974): 37.

"Editorials: Stone's Opening" *The Nation* 254 (February 17, 1992): 184-85.

"Editorials: Recapturing the Past." *The Nation* 254 (March 23, 1992): 361.

"Movies: The Killing of JFK." *Newsweek* 82 (November 26, 1973): 104.

"Newsmakers: *The Trial of Lee Harvey Oswald.*" *Newsweek* 90 (July 11, 1977): 52; 90 (August 15, 1977): 7-9.

"Gaffe Squad: The Eyes Have It [*JFK*]." *Premier* 5 (June 1992): 16.

"Gaffe Squad: The Eyes Have It [*JFK*]." *Premier* 5 (October 1992): 23.

"Media News: *JFK: The Book of The Film*." *School Library Journal* 38 (September 1992): 129.

"Cinema: Tragedy Trivialized." *Time* 102 (December 24, 1973): 71, 73.

"People: That Haunting, Half-Familiar Figure With the Rifle Is Not Lee Harvey Oswald, But Actor John Pleshette . . . ." *Time* 110 (July 11, 1977): 45.

"Television: Garbling History: *The Trial of Lee Harvey Oswald*, ABC, Sept. 30 & Oct. 3." *Time* 110 (October 3, 1977): 91.

"Best of 1991 Cinema: *JFK*." *Time* 139 (January 6, 1992): 79.

"*JFK* Review Killed, So Critic Quits." *Variety* (Weekly) 346 (January 27, 1992): 16.

"With *JFK*, Stone Makes A Splash But Some Don't Buy Oliver's Story." *Washingtonian* 27 (January 1992): 7.

THE JFK ASSASSINATION RECORDS
COLLECTION ACT

Official Printings:

U. S. House of Representatives. *The Assassination Materials Disclosure Act.* Hearings Before the Subcommittee on Economic and Commercial Law of the Committee on the Judiciary on H. J. Res. 454. 102nd Cong., 2nd Sess., May 20, 1992. Washington, D. C.: Government Printing Office, 1992.

_____. *Assassination Materials Disclosure Act of 1992.* House Report 102-625, Part I & Part II, Report of the House Government Operations Committee to accompany House Joint Resolution 454, the Assassination Materials Disclosure Act of 1992. 102nd Cong., 2nd Sess. Washington, D. C.: Government Printing Office, 1992.

_____. *The Effectiveness of Public Law 102-526; The President John F. Kennedy Assassination Records Collection Act of 1992.* Hearings Before the Subcommittee on Legislation and National Security of the Committee on Government Operations. 103rd Cong., 1st Sess., November 17, 1993. Washington, D. C.: Government Printing Office, 1994.

U. S. Senate. *The Assassination Materials Disclosure Act of 1992.* Hearings Before the Committee on Governmental Affairs. 102nd Cong., 2nd Sess., May 12, 1992. S. Hearing 102-721. Washington, D. C.: Government Printing Office, 1992.

_____. *Assassination Materials Disclosure Act of 1992.* Senate Report 102-328. Report of the Senate Governmental Affairs Committee to Accompany, S. 3006. 102nd Cong., 2nd Sess. Washington, D. C.: Government Printing Office, 1992.

Signed Articles:

Cope, Virginia. "JFK Assassination: Justice's Opposition May Slow Release of Long-Secret Files." *Congressional Quarterly Weekly Report* 50 (May 2, 1992): 1138.

_____. "JFK Assassination: FBI, CIA Keep Key To Unlock Files." *Congressional Quarterly Weekly Report* 50 (May 16, 1992): 1324.

_____. "Investigations: Panel Tries To End JFK Files Impasse." *Congressional Quarterly Weekly Report* 50 (July 25, 1992): 2152.

_____. "Investigations: Senate Votes for Release of Secret JFK Files." *Congressional Quarterly Weekly Report* 50 (August 1, 1992): 2250.

_____. "Investigations: House Finally Passes JFK Bill, But Obstacles Remain." *Congressional Quarterly Weekly Report* 50 (August 15, 1992): 2434.

Corn, David. "The J. F. K. Files-II: Secrets From the CIA Archives." *The Nation* 257 (November 29, 1993): 656-60.

Hall, Kermit L. "The Virulence of The National Appetite For Bogus Revelation." *Maryland Law Review* 56 (1993): 1-56.

Hernandez, Debra Gersh. "Opening The Kennedy Assassination Files." *Editor & Publisher* 126 (December 18, 1993): 17, 47.

Kuntz, Phil. "Investigations: Congress Moving To Open Files On Kennedy Assassination." *Congressional Quarterly Weekly Report* 50 (January 25, 1992): 155.

Peterson, Roger S. "Declassified [Documents Released by Assassination Records Review Board]." *American History* 31 (July/August 1996): 22-26, 54-57.

Sanders, Charles J., and Mark S. Zaid. "Declassification of Dealey Plaza: After Thirty Years, A New Disclosure Law At Last May Help to Clarify the Facts of the Kennedy Assassination." *South Texas Law Review* 34 (October 1993): 407-41.

Thomas, Evan. "Who Shot JFK?" *Newsweek* 122 (September 6, 1993): 14-17.

Webster, Vanessa L. "Truth, Justice and the American Way--Revelation Comes Due For J. F. K.: The John F. Kennedy Assassination Records Collection Act of 1992." *Seton Hall Legislative Journal* 17 (January 1993): 261-302.

Unsigned Articles:

"JFK Assassination: Measure May Free Information." *Congressional Quarterly Weekly Report* 50 (March 28, 1992): 788.

"Section Notes: Release of JFK Files Progresses in House." *Congressional Quarterly Weekly Report* 50 (May 30, 1992): 1519.

"Section Notes: Compromise Bill Approved on Release of JFK Files." *Congressional Quarterly Weekly Report* 50 (June 6, 1992): 1587.

"Section Notes: Senate Panel Approves Bill To Release JFK Files." *Congressional Quarterly Weekly Report* 50 (June 27, 1992): 1858.

"Issue: JFK Assassination Documents." *Congressional Quarterly Weekly Report* 50 (September 5, 1992): 2603-04.

"Investigations: JFK Disclosures Cleared by Hill." *Congressional Quarterly Weekly Report* 50 (October 3, 1992): 3018.

"Issue: JFK Assassination Documents." *Congressional Quarterly Weekly Report* 50 (October 31, 1992): 3456.

"World Notes: Clearing the Air." *Maclean's* 105 (February 10, 1992): 21.

"World Notes: Opening the Files." *Maclean's* 105 (May 25, 1992): 21.

"World Notes: The JFK Papers." *Maclean's* 106 (September 6, 1993): 19.

EYEWITNESS ACCOUNTS:
NOVEMBER 22-24, 1963

Books:

Brennan, Howard, with Edward J. Cherryholmes. *Eyewitness to History.* Waco, Texas: Texian Press, 1987.

Connally, John. *In History's Shadow.* New York: Hyerion, 1993.

Crenshaw, Charles A., with Jens Hansen, and J. Gary Shaw. *JFK Conspiracy of Silence.* New York: Signet, 1992.

Curry, Jesse. *JFK Assassination File.* Dallas, Texas: American Poster and Printing Company, 1969.

Feldman, Harold. *Fifty-One Witnesses: The Grassy Knoll.* San Francisco, California: Idlewild Publishers, 1965.

Hampton, Wilborn. *Kennedy Assassinated!: The World Mourns: A Reporter's Story.* Cambridge, Massachusetts: Candlewick Press, 1997.

Hlavach, Laura, and Darwin Payne, eds. *Reporting the Kennedy Assassination: Journalists Who Were There Recall Their Experiences.* Dallas, Texas: Three Forks Press, 1996.

Hoffman, Ed, and Ron Friedrich. *Eyewitness.* Grand Prairie, Texas: JFK Lancer Productions and Publications, 1995, 1996, 1997.

Johnson, Lyndon B. *The Vantage Point: Perspectives on the Presidency 1963-1969.* New York: Holt, Rinehart & Winston, 1971.

Lincoln, Evelyn. *My Twelve Years with John F. Kennedy.* New York: David McKay, 1965; Bantam, 1966.

MacNeil, Robert. *The Right Place at the Wrong Time.* Boston, Massachusetts: Little, Brown & Company, 1982.

Oliver, Beverly, with Coke Buchanan. *Nightmare In Dallas.* Lancaster, Pennsylvania: Starburst Publishers, 1994.

Palmara, Vincent M. *The Third Alternative: Survivor's Guilt: The Secret Service and the JFK Murder.* Published by Author, 1993; Grand Prairie, Texas: JFK Lancer Productions and Publications, 1997.

Rather, Dan, with Mickey Herskowitz. *The Camera Never Blinks: Adventures of a TV Journalist.* New York: William Morrow and Company, Inc., 1977.

Sloan, Bill. *JFK: Breaking the Silence.* Dallas, Texas: Taylor Publishing, 1993.

_____, with Jean Hill. *JFK: The Last Dissenting Witness.* Gretna, Louisiana: Pelican Publishing, 1992.

Smith, Merriman. *The Murder of the Young President.* New York: United Press International, 1963.

Sneed, Larry. *No More Silence: An Oral History of the Assassination of President Kennedy.* Dallas, Texas: Three Forks Press, 1998.

Wicker, Tom. *On Press.* New York: Viking Press, 1978.

Wise, Dan, and Marietta Maxfield. *The Day Kennedy Died.* San Antonio, Texas: Naylor, 1964.

Youngblood, Rufus W. *20 Years in the Secret Service.* New York: Simon & Schuster, 1973.

Signed Articles:

Connally, John. "Why Kennedy Went to Texas." *Life* 63 (November 24, 1967): 86A-86B, 100A- 100B, 103-04.

_____. " 'I Knew I Had Been Hit'." *Texas Monthly* 21 (October 1993): 122-23, 185-86, 188, 202-203.

Connally, Mrs. John. "Since That Day In Dallas." *McCall's* 91 (August 1964): 78-79, 141-42.

Dudman, Richard. "Commentary of An Eyewitness." *The New Republic* 149 (December 21, 1963): 18.

Feldman, Harold. "Fifty-One Witnesses: The Grassy Knoll." *The Minority of One* 7 (March 1965): 16-25.

Hughes, Sarah T. "The President Is Sworn In." *The Texas Observer* 55 (November 29, 1963): 7.

Jones, Wyman. "On the Grindstone: November in Dallas." *Library Journal* 89 (January 1, 1964): 72.

Roberts, Charles. "National Affairs: Eyewitness in Dallas." *Newsweek* 68 (December 5, 1966): 26- 29.

Sidey, Hugh. "The Assassination: A Shattering Afternoon in Dallas." *Time* 132 (November 28, 1988): 45.

Smith, A. Merriman. "U. P. I. Reporter [Eyewitness Account]." *Editor & Publisher* 96 (November 30, 1963): 8-10.

Towner, Tina. "View From the Corner." *Teen* 12 (June 1968): 46-49, 90.

Unsigned Articles:

"The Reporters' Story." *Columbia Journalism Review* 24 (Winter 1964): 6-17.

"National Affairs: Ex-Presidents: LBJ on the Assassination." *Newsweek* 75 (May 11, 1970): 41.

"In The Kennedy Car." *U. S. News and World Report* 55 (December 9, 1963): 12.

REMEMBERING JFK

Books:

Ballot, Paul. *Memorial to Greatness.* Island Park, New York: Aspen Corp., 1964.

Bergquist, Laura, and Stanley Tretick. *A Very Special President.* New York: McGraw-Hill, 1965.

Berry, Wendell, and Ben Shahn. *November Twenty Six, Nineteen Hundred Sixty Three.* New York: George Braziller, 1964.

Bradlee, Benjamin. *That Special Grace.* Philadelphia: Lippincott, 1964.

Cournos, John. *The Lost Leader.* New York: Twayne, 1964.

Duheme, Jacqueline. *John F. Kennedy: A Book of Paintings.* New York: Atheneum, 1967.

Fine, William M., ed. *That Day With God.* Foreword by Richard Cardinal Cushing. New York: McGraw-Hill, 1963.

Gardner, Francis V. *Rest Assured, John Kennedy.* McLean, Virginia: Published by Author, 1973.

Gardune, Joseph A. *Museum for a President.* New York: Carleton, 1966.

Glikes, Edwin A., ed., with Paul Schwaber. *Of Poetry and Power: Poems Occasioned by the Presidency and by the Death of John F. Kennedy.* New York: Basic Books, 1964.

Goldman, Alex J. *John Fitzgerald Kennedy: The World Remembers.* New York: Fleet, 1968.

Gronouski, John S. *Address by John A. Gronouski, Postmaster General, at the Dedication of the John Fitzgerald Kennedy Memorial Stamp, Boston, Mass., May 29, 1964.* Washington, D. C.: U. S. Post Office Department, 1964.

Hunt, Conover. *JFK: For A New Generation.* Dallas: Southern Methodist University Press, 1996.

John Fitzgerald Kennedy: The Last Full Measure. Washington, D. C.: National Geographic, 1964.

John Fitzgerald Kennedy: A Tribute . . . From the Youth of the United States for the Youth of the World. Philadelphia: U. S. National Student Association, 1964.

A John F. Kennedy Memorial. New York: MacFadden-Bartell, 1964.

John F. Kennedy Memorial Edition: Life. Chicago: Time, Inc., 1963.

Kazan, Molly. *Kennedy.* New York: Stein and Day, 1963.

Kellner, Abraham, ed. *Sunset at Mid-day: A Tribute to the Late John Fitzgerald Kennedy.* New York: K' Das Publishing Co., 1964.

Klein, Harry T., ed. *President Kennedy Commemorative Anthology.* Los Angeles: Swordsman Press, n. d.

Levy, Clifford V. *Twenty-Four Personal Eulogies on the Late President John F. Kennedy 1917- 1963.* San Francisco, 1963.

Lowe, Jacques. *JFK Remembered.* New York: Random House, 1993.

Lowe, Jacques, and Wilfrid Sheed. *The Kennedy Legacy: A Generation Later.* New York: Viking Studio Books, 1988.

Lowe, Jacques. *The Kennedy Years.* New York: Viking Press, 1964.

MacNeil, Robert. *The Way We Were: 1963, The Year Kennedy Was Shot.* New York: Carroll & Graf Publishers, Inc., 1988.

Manchester, William. *One Brief Shining Moment: Remembering Kennedy.* Boston: Little, Brown, 1983.

Mansfield, Michael J. *John Fitzgerald Kennedy: Eulogies to the Late President Delivered in the Rotunda of the United States Capitol, November 24, 1963, by Mike Mansfield, Earl Warren, and John W. McCormack.* Washington, D. C.: U. S. Government Printing Office, 1963.

Marten, Paul. *Kennedy Requiem.* Toronto: Weller, 1963.

Matthews, James P., ed. *In Memoriam.* Los Angeles: *Matador Magazine*, 1964.

Mayhew, Aubrey. *The World's Tribute to John F. Kennedy in Medallic Art.* New York: Morrow, 1966.

Murray, Norbert. *Legacy of an Assassination.* New York: Pro-People Press, 1964.

Salinger, Pierre, and Sander Vanocur, eds. *A Tribute to John F. Kennedy.* Foreword by Theodore C. Sorenson; Dedication by Lyndon B. Johnson. Chicago: Encyclopedia Britannica, 1964; New York: Dell, 1965.

Schmidt, (Sister Mary) Bernadette, ed. *The Trumpet Summons Us--- John F. Kennedy.* New York: Vantage Press, 1964.

Stewart, Charles J., and Bruce Kendall, eds. *A Man Named John F. Kennedy: Sermons on His Assassination.* Glen Rock, New Jersey: Paulist Press, 1964.

Strior, Murray. *The Historic Significance of the Assassination of President John F. Kennedy.* Flushing, New York: Spinoza Institute of America, 1963.

United Nations. *Homage to a Friend: A Memorial Tribute by the United Nations for President John F. Kennedy.* New York: The U. S. Commission, with the United Nations Office of Public Information, 1964.

United States Congress. *Memorial Addresses in the Congress of the United States and Tributes in Eulogy of John Fitzgerald Kennedy Late President of the United States.* Washington, D. C.: U. S. Government Printing Office, 1964.

Vilnis, Aija. *The Bearer of the Star Spangled Banner: In Memory of President John Fitzgerald Kennedy.* Translated by Lilija Pavars. New York: Speller, 1964.

Walsh, William G., ed. *Children Write About John F. Kennedy.* Brownsville, Texas: Springman- King, 1964.

Signed Articles:

Allis, Sam. "Nation: Of Myth and Memory: Dreaming of 1960 in the New World." *Time* 132 (October 24, 1988): 21-24, 27.

Alsop, Joseph. "The Legacy of John F. Kennedy: Memories of an Uncommon Man." *The Saturday Evening Post* 237 (November 21, 1964): 15-19.

Alter, Jonathan. "Between The Lines: Less Profile, More Courage." *Newsweek* 122 (November 1, 1993): 33.

d' Apollonia, L. "Reflexions sur une Tragedie [Reflections on a Tragedy]." *Relations* (Montreal) 24 (January 1964): 27.

Ascoli, Max. "Editorial: The 22nd of November." *The Reporter* 29 (December 5, 1963): 19.

Attwood, William. "In Memory of John F. Kennedy." *Look* 27 (December 31, 1963): 11-13.

Augstein, Rudolf. "Der Prasident der Starke und des Friedens [The President of the Strong and Peaceful]." *Der Spiegel* (Hamburg) 48 (1963): 22-23.

Barone, Michael, and Katia Hetter. "The Lost World of John Kennedy." *U. S. News and World Report* 115 (November 15, 1993): 38-40, 42-44.

Berendt, John. "A Look at the Record: What the School Books Are Teaching Our Kids About J. F. K." *Esquire* 80 (November 1973): 140, 263-65.

Berger, Kurt Martin. "Das Ende einer 'Fuhrungsmacht' [The End of a 'Unique Leadership']." *Zeitschrift fur Geopolitik* (Heidelberg) 34 Hefte 11-12 (1963): 339-42.

Bergquist, Laura. "John Fitzgerald Kennedy . . . 1917-1963." *Look* 28 (November 17, 1964): 33-35.

Bettiza, Enzo. "The Kennedy Myth [From *L' Espresso,* Rome]." *Atlas* 7 (January 1964): 9.

Booker, Simeon. "How JFK Surpassed Abraham Lincoln." *Ebony* 19 (February 1964): 25-34.

Boorstin, Daniel J. "JFK: His Vision: Then and Now." *U. S. News and World Report* 105 (October 24, 1988): 30-31.

Borch, Herbert von. "Wird Kennedys Erbe uberleben? [Will the Kennedy Heritage Survive?]." *Aussenpolitik Zeitschrift fur internationale Fragen* (Stuttgart) 15 (1964): 1-4.

Bosworth, Patricia. "The Arts: Film/Books/Dance: John F. Kennedy Remembered." *Working Woman* 8 (November 1983): 234, 236.

Bruning, Fred. "An American View: The Grief Has Still Not Gone Away." *Maclean's* 101 (November 28, 1988): 13.

Carleton, William G. "Kennedy in History: An Early Appraisal." *The Antioch Review* 24 (Fall 1964): 277-99.

Carter, Manfred A. "November 22, 1963: [Four Poems]." *The Christian Century* 80 (December 11, 1963): 1540.

Chamberlin, Anne. "The Legacy of John F. Kennedy: The Commercialization of J. F. K." *The Saturday Evening Post* 237 (November 21, 1964): 20-21.

Clarke, Gerald. "JFK--Bitter Memories of a Cold Day: Camelot in Retrospect." *The New Republic* 164 (January 16, 1971): 13-15.

Clifford, G. "Warren Report: A New Boost for the Kennedy Memorabilia Industry." *Maclean's* (Toronto) 77 (November 2, 1964): 3.

Cousins, Norman. "The Legacy of John F. Kennedy." *Saturday Review* 46 (December 7, 1963): 21- 17.

_____. "Can Civilization Be Assassinated?" *Saturday Review* 46 (December 21, 1963): 14, 32.

Donhoff, Marion (Grafin). "Was wird bleiben? John F. Kennedys Politik fur die Welt von morgen [What Will Remain? John F. Kennedy's Politics for the World of Tomorrow]." *Die Zeit* (Hamburg) 18 (1963): 1.

Elfin, Mel. "Beyond the Generations." *U. S. News and World Report* 105 (October 24, 1988): 32-33.

Endt, Frisco. "Washington 25 November 1963." *Revu* [Netherlands] 10 (March 11, 1967): 18-20.

Ferguson, Andrew. "Burning the Flame for JFK." *The American Spectator* 21 (December 1988): 56.

Ferlinghetti, Lawrence. "Assassination Raga." *Ramparts* 7 (August 24, 1968): 38-39.

Forbes, Malcolm S. "Fact and Comment: Can You Believe That 20 Years Have Passed." *Forbes* 132 (December 5, 1983): 26.

Freund, Hugo. "Zum Tode John F. Kennedys [On the Death of John F. Kennedy]." *Stadtehygiene* 15 (1964): 1.

Gappert, Gary. "Correspondence: [Tribute from Students in Tanganyika]." *Atlas* 7 (January 1964): 64.

Givens, Ron. "Update: JFK: A Flood of Memories." *Newsweek* 112 (December 5, 1988): 8.

Gold, Victor. "Looking Back: Summer of '63." *Washingtonian* 28 (May 1993): 27, 29-32, 35.

Goldman, Peter. "Kennedy Remembered: After 20 Years, A Man Lost In His Legend." *Newsweek* 102 (November 28, 1983) 60-64.

Gotte, Fritz. "Nach John F. Kennedys Tod [After John F. Kennedy's Death]." *Die Drei. Monatsschrift fur Anthroposophie, Dreigliederung und Goetheanismus* (Stuttgart) 34 (1964): 143-45.

Greenfield, Meg. "The Way Things Really Were." *Newsweek* 112 (November 28, 1988): 98.

Halberstam, David. "When the Best and the Brightest Were Young." *Newsweek* 121 (January 11, 1993): 36-37.

Hamill, Pete. "JFK: The Real Thing." *New York* 21 (November 28, 1988): 44-51.

Harrison, Barbara Grizzuti. "The Private Eye: Was JFK As Wonderful As We Remember?" *Mademoiselle* 89 (November 1983): 102.

Hart, L. "A Year of Progress With a Sorrowful Close." *Columbia* 44 (January 1964): 16.

Hessel, Dieter. "To Heal the Wounds." *The Christian Century* 81 (January 1, 1964): 15-16.

Howard, Jane. "The Day That Changed Our World." *Ladies' Home Journal* 100 (November 1983): 114, 170, 172.

Joesten, Joachim. "Der Kennedy-Merd als 'politische Walrheit' [Kennedy's Murder as 'Political Truth']." *Frankfurter Hefte. Zeitschrift fur Kul tur und Politik* (Frankfurt/Main) 21 (August 1966): 534-40.

Kaiser, David E. "The Politician." *The New Republic* 189 (November 21, 1983): 15, 18-19.

Kempton, Murray. "Looking Back on the Anniversary." *The Spectator* (London) No. 7119 (December 4, 1964): 778-79.

King, Peter. "Point After: The Blackest Sunday." *Sports Illustrated* 79 (November 22, 1993): 76.

Koch, Thilo. "Der Tod des Prasidenten [The Death of the President]." *Die Zeit* (Hamburg) 18 (1963): 2.

Kopkind, Andrew. "J. F. K.'s Legacy." *The Nation* 247 (December 5, 1988): 589.

Krippendorff, Ekkehart. "John F. Kennedy--Ruckblick nach einem Jahr {Retrospect on a Year]." *Zeitschrift fur Politik* (Berlin) 11 (1964): 309-22.

Kurnoth, Rudolf. "Gedanken um den Tod John F. Kennedys [Thoughts on the Death of John F. Kennedy]." *Frankenstein Munsterberger Heimatblatt* (Lengerich) 10 (1963): 2.

Levin, Bernard. "The Bell Tolls in Dallas: From BBC-TV 'That Was the Week That Was'." *The Listener* (London) 70 (December 5, 1963): 914.

Logan, Andy. "JFK: The Stained Glass Image." *American Heritage* 18 (August 1967): 4-7, 75-78.

Lohmar, Ulrich. "Kennedys Vermachtnis [Kennedy's Legacy]." *Kirche und Mann. Monatszeitung fur Mannerarbeit der Evangelische Kirche in Deutschland* (Gutersloh) 16 (1963): 2.

Lowe, Jacques, and Wilfrid Sheed. "The Kennedy Legacy." *Ladies' Home Journal* 105 (August 1988): 35-38.

Manchester, William. "One Brief Shining Moment: Remembering Kennedy." *McCall's* 111 (November 1983): 102-05, 177-84, 187-88, 190.

Mayer, Milton. "November 22, 1963." *The Progressive Magazine* 28 (December 1964): 21-25.

McLaughlin, M. "Paris, November 22nd, 1963." *Immaculate Heart Crusader* 28 (November 1964): 8-9.

McNaspy, C. J. "Apres la Mort de Kennedy: l'Amerique Devant Elle-Meme [After Kennedy's Death: America Facing Herself]." *Etudes: Revue Catholique d' interet general* 320 (1964): 27-37.

Medved, Michael, and David Wallechinsky. "November 22, 1963 . . . as Remembered by the Class of '65." *Senior Scholastic* 109 (November 18, 1976): 15, 30.

Moore, Thomas, and Marianna I. Knight. "Idealism's Rebirth." *U. S. News and World Report* 105 (October 24, 1988): 37-38, 40.

Morrow, Lance. "J. F. K.: After 20 Years, The Question: How Good a President?" *Time* 122 (November 14, 1983): 58-60, 63-67.

Moynihan, Daniel Patrick. "The Democrats, Kennedy, and the Murder of Dr. King." *Commentary* 14 (1968): 15-29.

Muggeridge, Malcolm. "The Apotheosis of John F. Kennedy." *The New York Review of Books* 3 (January 28, 1965): 1, 3-4; 4 (March 11, 1965): 28.

O'Brien, Conor Cruise. "The Life and Death of Kennedy." *New Statesman* (London) No. 1818 (January 14, 1966): 50-51.

Osbaine, Cecil. "Five Years Later: Kennedy--The Making of a Myth." *National Review* 20 (November 5, 1968): 1113-14.

Peyer, Tom, and Hart Seely. "Shouts and Murmurs: The Day The Stars Cried." *The New Yorker* 69 (November 22, 1993): 128.

Plummer, William, and David Grogan. "November 22, 1963." *People Weekly* 30 (November 28, 1988): 54-64, 69-70.

Pouillon, Jean. "De l'assassinat a l'enterrement [From the Assassination to the Burial]." *Temps moderness* (Paris) No. 218 (1964): 184-92.

Reeves, Richard. "History: They Just Don't Get Him." *Time* 142 (November 22, 1993): 62-63.

_____. "Why Camelot and Kennedy Endure on TV." *TV Guide* 41 (November 20-26, 1993): 22- 25.

Remus, Bernhard. "Erinnerung an John F. Kennedy [Memories of John F. Kennedy]." *Weltwoche* (Zurich) 31 (1963): 1, 3.

Rendulic, Lothar. "Das Erbe nach Kennedy und die Krise des Westens [The Kennedy Heritage and the Western World's Crisis]." *Berichte und Informationen des Osterreichischen Forschungsinstitutes fur Wirtschaft und Politik* (Salzburg) 19 (1964): 1-3.

Roddy, Joseph. "Ireland: They Cried the Rain Down That Night." *Look* 28 (November 17, 1964): 75-76, 79.

Salinger, Pierre. "John Kennedy Then and Now." *Maclean's* 96 (November 28, 1983): 2, 18-30.

_____. "Kennedy Remembered." *McCall's* 115 (June 1988): 36-40.

Schlesinger, Arthur M., Jr. "A Eulogy: John Fitzgerald Kennedy." *The Saturday Evening Post* 236 (December 14, 1963): 32-32a; 248 (July/August 1976): 74.

_____. "J. F. K.: What He Was Really Like." *Ladies' Home Journal* 100 (November 1983): 115, 168, 170.

_____. "What The Thousand Days Wrought." *The New Republic* 189 (November 21, 1983): 20- 22, 25, 28, 30.

Sidey, Hugh. "The Presidency: He Asked Me to Listen to the Debate." *Time* 122 (November 14, 1983): 69.

_____. "The Assassination: A Shattering Afternoon in Dallas." *Time* 132 (November 28, 1988): 45.

_____. "The Presidency: A Sly and Wry Humor." *Time* 142 (November 22, 1993): 63.

Stahl, Walter. "Correspondence: A German Writes About Kennedy." *Atlas* 7 (February 1964): 127.

Stanglin, Douglas. "A Time For Self-Interest." *U. S. News and World Report* 105 (October 24, 1988): 35-36.

Strout, Richard L. "J. F. K. Remembered." *Esquire* 189 (November 21, 1983): 24.

Styron, William. "The Short, Classy Voyage of JFK." *Esquire* 100 (December 1983): 124-26, 129- 30.

Thomas, J. "Le 'monde libre' et le crime de Dallas [The 'Free World' and the Dallas Crime]." *La nouvelle revue internationale* (Paris) 7 (February 1964): 83-88.

Tschappat, R. "Das geistige Erbe Kennedys [Kennedy's Spiritual Heritage]." *Schweizerisches kaufmannisches Zentralblatt* (Zurich) 67 (1963): 1.

Ulam, Adam B. "Lost Frontier." *The New Republic* 189 (November 21, 1983): 10, 12, 14.

Weisman, John. "An Oral History: Remembering JFK . . . Our First TV President." *TV Guide* 36 (November 19-25, 1988): 2-4, 6-8.

Whitmore, Reed. "Books and the Arts: Poetry of the Assassination." *The New Republic* 151 (November 21, 1964): 17-19.

Unsigned Articles:

"Memorial Outdoor Boards Are Posted." *Advertising Age* 34 (December 2, 1963): 112.

"May He Rest In Peace." *America* 109 (December 7, 1963): 728-29.

"Zum Tode von Prasident John F. Kennedy [On the Death of President John F. Kennedy]." *Blatter fur deutsche und internationale Politik* (Cologne) 8 (1963): 904-05.

"Kennedys Vermachtnis [The Kennedy Legacy]." *Bulletin des Presse- und Informationsamtes der Bundesregierung* (Bonn) No. 208 (1963): 1843.

"Editorial: In 1963, We Survived." *The Christian Century* 80 (December 25, 1963): 1599-01.

"The Kennedy Legacy: The People's Task." *Commonweal* 79 (December 13, 1963): 335-36.

"Backstage: [Editorial Tribute to JFK]." *Ebony* 19 (January 1964): 19.

"*Ebony* Photo-Editorial: A Tribute to John F. Kennedy." *Ebony* 19 (January 1964): 90-1.

"Letters to the Editor: Kennedy and Lincoln." *Ebony* 19 (April 1964): 10-16.

"Anniversary Fever." *The Economist* (London) 221 (November 26, 1966): 914.

"Ten Years Later: Where Were You? Nobody Forgets." *Esquire* 80 (November 1973): 136-37.

"Ten Years Later: Who Was He?: Not Everybody Remembers." *Esquire* 80 (November 1973): 138- 39.

"Dossier: John Fitzgerald Kennedy." *Esquire* 100 (December 1983): 131.

"In Memoriam Kennedy." *Forum. Osterreichische Monatsblatter fur Kulturelle Freiheit* (Vienna) 11 (1964): 230.

"John F. Kennedy zum Gedachtnis [Memories of John F. Kennedy]." *Katholischer Digest. Internationale* katholische Monatsrundschan (Aschaffenburg) 18 (1964): 10-12.

"John F. Kennedy: In Memoriam." *The Nation* 197 (December 14, 1963): 404-05.

"Camelot Revisited." *The Nation* 237 (November 19, 1983): 483-84.

"BB Overseas Mourn JFK." *National Jewish Monthly* 78 (January 1964): 24-26.

"The Week: Dallas, November 22, 1963." *National Review* 40 (December 9, 1988): 13.

"The Day Kennedy Died." *Newsweek* 62 (December 2, 1963): 20-26.

"An End and a Beginning." *Newsweek* 62 (December 9, 1963): 19-20.

"Business and Finance: Enterprise: Memorial Boom." *Newsweek* 62 (December 30, 1963): 49-50.

"Music: The Prodigal Returns [Leonard Bernstein's *Kaddish*, for JFK." *Newsweek* 63 (February 10, 1964): 77.

"The Assassination: Birch View of JFK." *Newsweek* 63 (February 24, 1964): 29-30; (March 30, 1964): 73.

"Music: When a Just Man Dies." *Newsweek* 63 (April 20, 1964): 75.

"National Affairs: And Then It Was November 22 Again." *Newsweek* 64 (November 30, 1964): 25- 28.

"Music: Orchestra of Record [Roy Harris's Epilogue for JFK]." *Newsweek* 67 (March 21, 1966): 102- 05.

"Where Are They Now?: Black Friday--Five Years Later." *Newsweek* 72 (November 25, 1968): 22- 23.

"National Affairs: The Kennedy Years: What Endures?" *Newsweek* 77 (February 1, 1971): 20-22.

"Ideas: JFK: Visions and Revisions." *Newsweek* 82 (November 19, 1973): 76-92.

"Newsmakers: [Annual Memorial Ceremonies at Site of JFK Assassination." *Newsweek* 88 (November 29, 1976): 52.

"What JFK Meant to Us: Thirty Americans Reflect on the Kennedy Legacy." *Newsweek* 102 (November 28, 1983): 65-66, 71-72, 75-76, 78-80, 83-84, 86, 91.

"Kennedys Tod bringt die Welt zur Besinnung [Kennedy's Death Brings the World to Recollection]." *Paulinus. Trierer Bistumblatt* (Trier) 89 (1963): 6.

"Tribute: Nov. 22, 1963: A Day Beyond Forgetting." *People Weekly* 20 (November 28, 1983): 12, 22, 26, 30-31, 33-34, 40, 44-45.

"L' occidente e la morte di Kennedy [The Western World and Kennedy's Death]." *Rivista di studi politici internazionali* (Florence) 30 (1963): 323-26.

"Letters to the Editor: With Editorial Comment." *Senior Scholastic* 83 (January 10, 1964): 18.

"This Week in History: Tragic Day in Texas." *Senior Scholastic* 89 (November 18, 1966): 7.

"Historical Notes: 'Land of Kennedy'." *Time* 82 (December 13, 1963): 27.

"Music: Composers: To J. F. K." *Time* 86 (August 6, 1965): 69.

"Art: Murals: Assassination in Boston." *Time* 88 (August 26, 1966): 60.

"Visitors to the Kennedy Grave--An Endless Line." *U. S. News and World Report* 56 (May 25, 1964): 79-81.

"For John F. Kennedy: Birthday Tributes." *U. S. News and World Report* 56 (June 8, 1964): 10-11.

"1963-1973: 10 Years That Shook the World [Triggered by JFK Murder]." *U. S. News and World Report* 75 (November 26, 1973): 38-53.

"A Great President?: Experts Size Up JFK." *U. S. News and World Report* 95 (November 21, 1983): 51-52, 54.

"Nur tausend Tage. Ein Jahr nach der Ermordung John F. Kennedys [Only a Thousand Days. One Year After John F. Kennedy's Murder]." *Weltwoche* (Zurich) 32 (1964): 1.

FICTION ASSOCIATED WITH THE JFK ASSASSINATION

Books:

Andrews, David. *The Magic Bullet.* Baltimore, Maryland: Planetary Press, 1980.

Aubrey, Edmund. *Sherlock Holmes in Dallas.* New York: Dodd, Mead and Company, 1980. Retitled *The Case of the Murdered President.* New York: Congdon & Weed, Inc., 1980.

Balling, L. Christian. *The Fourth Shot.* Boston, Massachusetts: Atlantic, 1982.

Barkus, G. Z. A. *Incident at Credibility Gap and the Innocent Child.* Greenwich, Connecticut: Paper Bag Books, 1967.

Bealle, Morris A. *Guns of the Regressive Right, or How to Kill a President.* Washington, D. C.: Columbia Publishing Co., 1964.

Bernau, George. *Promises To Keep.* New York: Warner Books, 1988.

Bourjaily, Vance. *The Man Who Knew Kennedy.* New York: Dial Press, 1967.

Brown, Walt. *The People v. Lee Harvey Oswald.* New York: Carroll & Graf Publishers, Inc., 1992.

Buckley, William F., Jr. *Mongoose R. I. P.* New York: Random House, 1987.

Collins, Max Allan. *In The Line of Fire.* New York: Jove Books, 1993.

Condon, Richard A. *The Manchurian Candidate.* New York: McGraw-Hill, 1959.

_____. *Winter Kills.* New York: Dial Press, 1974; Dell, 1974, 1984.

Delillo, Dan. *Libra.* New York: Viking, 1988; Penguin Books, 1989.

Dimona, Joseph. *Last Man at Arlington*. New York: Arthur Fields Books, Inc., 1973; Dell, 1975; London: Futura Publications, Ltd., 1974.

Fox, Victor. *The White House Case: A Sequel to the Pentagon Case*. Pleasantville, New York: Fargo Press, 1968.

Fraley, Oscar. *The Director*. New York: Award Books, 1976.

Freed, Donald, and Mark Lane. *Executive Action: Assassination of a Head of State*. New York: Dell, 1973; London: Charisma Books, 1973.

Freedman, Nancy. *Joshua Son of None*. New York: Delacorte Press, 1973; Dell, 1978.

Frewin, Anthony. *Sixty-Three Closure*. United Kingdom: No Exit Press, 1998.

Garrison, Jim. *The Star Spangled Contract*. New York: McGraw-Hill, 1976; Warner Books, 1977, 1992.

Gerson, Jack. *The Back of the Tiger*. Beaufort, South Carolina: Beaufort Books, 1984.

Harrington, William. *Columbo: The Grassy Knoll*. New York: Forge, 1993.

Harris, Ruth. *Modern Women*. New York: St. Martin's Press, 1989.

Heath, Peter. *Assassins From Tomorrow*. New York: Lancer Books, 1967.

Kritzberg, Constance, and Larry Hancock. *November Patriots*. Colorado Springs, Colorado: Undercover Press, 1998.

La Fountaine, George. *Flashpoint*. New York: Coward, McCann & Geoghegan Inc., 1976.

Malzberg, Barry N. *The Destruction of the Temple*. New York: Pocket Books, 1974.

_____. *Scop*. New York: Pyramid, 1976.

McCarry, Charles. *The Tears of Autumn.* New York: Dutton & Co., 1975; Saturday Review Press, 1975; Signet Books, 1984.

Morris, Wright. *One Day: This Being the Day in November the Word From Dallas Was Heard in Escondido.* New York: Atheneum, 1965.

Names, Larry D. *Twice Dead.* New York: Leisure Books, 1978.

O'Donnell, M. K. *You Can Hear the Echo.* New York: Simon & Schuster, 1965.

Shapiro, Stanley. *A Time To Remember.* New York: Random House, 1986; Signet, 1988.

Shrear, Arnold. *Chase to Dallas.* New York: Vantage Press, 1990.

Singer, Loren. *The Parallax View.* Garden City, New York: Doubleday, 1970.

Sloan, Bill. *The Other Assassin.* New York: S. P. I. Books, 1992.

Stevens, James, and David Bishop. *Doctor Who: Who Killed Kennedy.* London: Virgin Publishing, 1996.

Tannenbaum, Robert K. *Corruption of Blood.* New York: Signet, 1996.

Thomas, D. M. *Flying Into Love.* New York: Scribners, 1992.

Thompson, Robert E. *The Trial of Lee Harvey Oswald.* New York: Ace Books, 1977.

Thornley, Kerry W. *The Idle Warriors.* Lilburn, Georgia: Illuminet Press, 1991.

Thurston, Wesley S. *The Trumpets of November.* New York: Bernard Geis Associates, 1966.

Warren, David M. *The Plot to Kill J. F. K.* Chicago, Illinois: Novel Books, 1965.

Webb, Lucas. *The Attempted Assassination of John F. Kennedy: A Political Fantasy.* San Bernardino, California: Borgo Press, 1976. Retitled *If J.F.K. Had Lived: A Political Scenario.* San Bernardino, California: Borgo Press, 1982.

Woolley, Bryan. *November 22.* New York: Seaview Books, 1981.

Signed Articles:

Ackroyd, Peter. "Fiction: Old Lines: *Winter Kills.*" *The Spectator* (London) 233 (September 21, 1974): 372-73.

Aldridge, John W. "The Kennedy Drama: Matrix Novelists [*The Man Who Knew Kennedy*]." *Life* 62 (February 3, 1967): 8.

Andrews, Charles R. "Fiction: *Winter Kills.*" *Library Journal* 99 (April 15, 1974): 1148.

Aroeste, Jean. "Fiction: *Joshua Son of None.*" *Library Journal* 98 (August 1973): 2332.

Bergonzi, Bernard. "New Novels: *One Day.*" *The New York Review of Books* 4 (March 11, 1965): 19-20.

Berolzheimer, Hobart F. "Fiction: *One Day.*" *Library Journal* 90 (April 15, 1965): 1933-34.

Booth, Wayne C. "Reviews: *One Day.*" *The Kenyon Review* 27 (Summer 1965): 569-70.

Carroll, Mary. "Fiction: Mystery: *Corruption of Blood.*" *Booklist* 92 (November 1, 1995): 458.

Clemons, Walter. "Appointment in Dallas: JFK's Murder As Fiction [*Libra*]." *Newsweek* 112 (August 15, 1988): 59-60.

Crinklaw, Don. "Books: *The Man Who Knew Kennedy.*" *Commonweal* 86 (June 16, 1967): 373-74.

Cunningham, Valentine. "Books & Arts: Mercenaries: *Winter Kills.*" *New Statesman* (London) 88 (September 20, 1974): 389.

Donadio, Stephen. "Books: The Day That Was: *One Day*." *Partisan Review* 32 (Summer 1965): 466-68.

Donahugh, Robert H. "Fiction: *The Man Who Knew Kennedy*." *Library Journal* 91 (December 15, 1966): 6108.

_____. "Fiction: *The Fourth Shot*." *Library Journal* 108 (January 15, 1983): 144.

Dunn, Robert. "Books In Brief: Oswald As Anti-Hero: *Libra*." *Mother Jones* 13 (September 1988): 50.

Glynn, Lenny. "Books: The Mind of An Assassin [*Libra*]." *Maclean's* 101 (August 29, 1988): 50-51.

Grandmaison, Ann M. "Fiction: *Sherlock Holmes in Dallas*." *Library Journal* 105 (October 1, 1980): 2103.

Gray, Paul. "Books: Reimagining Death in Dallas [*Libra*]." *Time* 132 (August 1, 1988): 65.

Gray, Simon. "Fiction: Myth and Magic: *The Man Who Knew Kennedy*." *New Statesman* (London) 71 (June 16, 1967): 840.

Hayward, E. B. "Fiction: *The Trumpets of November*." *Library Journal* 92 (June 15, 1967): 2435.

Hicks, Granville. "Literary Horizons: Time Stops and the World Goes On [*One Day*]." *Saturday Review* 48 (February 20, 1965): 23-24.

_____. "Literary Horizons: The Generation of the Assassination [*The Man Who Knew Kennedy*]." *Saturday Review* 50 (February 4, 1967): 35-36.

Hill, William. "Fiction: *One Day*." *America* 112 (May 8, 1965): 677-78.

_____. "Fiction: *The Man Who Knew Kennedy*." *America* 116 (May 6, 1967): 700.

Jackson, Katherine Gauss. "Books In Brief: Fiction: *One Day.*" *Harper's Magazine* 230 (May 1965): 145-46.

_____. "Books In Brief: Fiction: *The Man Who Knew Kennedy.*" *Harper's Magazine* 234 (February 1967), 114.

Kister, Kenneth F. "Fiction: *The Star Spangled Contract.*" *Library Journal* 101 (May 15, 1976): 1224.

LaSalle, Peter. "A November Day In Dallas [*Libra*]." *Commonweal* 115 (November 4, 1988): 598- 99.

Leonard, John. "Books & The Arts: Scripts, Plots and Codes: *Libra.*" *The Nation* 247 (September 19, 1988): 205-08.

Linklater, Andro. "Books: Borrow A Drama and Add Sex: *Flying Into Love.*" *The Spectator* (London) 268 (February 8, 1992): 28.

Miller, Warren. "Books: *One Day.*" *Commonweal* 81 (March 12, 1965): 769-70.

Orr, Leonard. "VLS: *Winter Kills.*" *The Village Voice* 19 (June 27, 1974): 29.

Radin, Victoria. "Jack Junk: *Flying Into Love.*" *New Statesman* 5 (February 14, 1992): 39.

Rafferty, Terrence. "Books: *Libra.*" *The New Yorker* 64 (September 26, 1988): 108-10.

Richler, Mordecai. "Books & Things: Spooks, Mobsters, Lee Harvey Oswald and His Mother [*Libra*]." *GQ* 58 (August 1988): 111, 114-15.

Saylor, V. Louise. "Fiction: *Promises To Keep.*" *Library Journal* 113 (October 15, 1988): 100.

Skow, John. "Books: Obscurity Now: *Winter Kills.*" *Time* 103 (June 24, 1974): 91-92.

Unsigned Articles:

"The Atlantic Bookshelf: *One Day.*" *The Atlantic Monthly* 215 (April 1965): 154-56.

"Fiction: *Joshua Son of None.*" *Booklist* 70 (November 15, 1973): 320.

"Adult Fiction: *The Fourth Shot.*" *Booklist* 79 (September 15, 1982): 90.

"Adult Fiction: *A Time To Remember.*" *Booklist* 82 (August 1986): 1663.

"Upfront: Advance Reviews: *Promises To Keep.*" *Booklist* 84 (August 1988): 1865.

"Upfront: Advance Reviews: *Flying Into Love.*" *Booklist* 89 (September 1, 1992): 5.

"Language and Literature: English and American: *One Day.*" *Choice* 2 (July/August 1965): 299.

"Fiction: *You Can Hear the Echo.*" *Kirkus Reviews* 33 (December 1, 1965): 1205-06.

"Fiction: *The Man Who Knew Kennedy.*" *Kirkus Reviews.* 34 (November 15, 1966): 1191.

"Fiction: *The Trumpets of November.*" *Kirkus Reviews* 35 (January 15, 1967): 82.

"Fiction: *Joshua Son of None.*" *Kirkus Reviews* 41 (July 1, 1973): 703.

"Fiction: *Last Man at Arlington.*" *Kirkus Reviews* 41 (September 15, 1973): 1052.

"Fiction: *Winter Kills.*" *Kirkus Reviews* 42 (March 15, 1974): 320.

"Fiction: *The Star Spangled Contract.*" *Kirkus Reviews* 44 (March 15, 1976): 342.

"Fiction: *Flashpoint*." *Kirkus Reviews* 44 (May 15, 1976): 609.

"Fiction: *Sherlock Holmes in Dallas*." *Kirkus Reviews* 48 (July 15, 1980): 942.

"Fiction: *The Fourth Shot*." *Kirkus Reviews* 50 (November 1, 1982): 1199-1200.

"Fiction: *A Time To Remember*." *Kirkus Reviews* 54 (July 15, 1986): 1061.

"Fiction: *Libra*." *Kirkus Reviews* 56 (June 15, 1988): 843-44.

"Fiction: *Promises To Keep*." *Kirkus Reviews* 56 (August 15, 1988): 1170-71.

"Fiction: *Flying Into Love*." *Kirkus Reviews* 60 (August 1, 1992): 946.

"Fiction: *Corruption of Blood*." *Kirkus Reviews* 63 (September 1, 1995): 1217.

"Mystery, Detective, & Suspense: *The Parallax View*." *Library Journal* 95 (August 1970): 2725.

"Mystery, Detective, & Suspense: *Last Man at Arlington*." *Library Journal* 98 (December 1, 1973): 3581.

"Mystery, Detective, & Suspense: *Flashpoint*." *Library Journal* 101 (July 1976): 1560.

"Books: Escondido, Nov. 22, 1963 [*One Day*]." *Newsweek* 65 (February 22, 1965): 97-98.

"Books: Melted Snow [*The Man Who Knew Kennedy*]." *Newsweek* 69 (January 30, 1967): 94.

"Books: *Flying Into Love*." *New York* 25 (September 14, 1992): 110.

"Books: Briefly Noted: Fiction: *The Man Who Knew Kennedy*." *The New Yorker* 43 (May 27, 1967): 149-50.

"PW Forecasts: Fiction: *The Trumpets of November.*" *Publishers Weekly* 191 (January 16, 1967): 75.

"PW Forecasts: Fiction: *The Man Who Knew Kennedy.*" *Publishers Weekly* 192 (November 27, 1967): 44.

"PW Forecasts: Fiction: *The Parallax View.*" *Publishers Weekly* 197 (April 20, 1970): 56.

"PW Forecasts: Fiction: *Last Man at Arlington.*" *Publishers Weekly* 204 (September 10, 1973): 42.

"PW Forecasts: Science Fiction: *The Destruction of the Temple.*" *Publishers Weekly* 205 (January 7, 1974): 56.

"PW Forecasts: Paperbacks: *Joshua Son of None.*" *Publishers Weekly* 205 (June 24, 1974): 61.

"PW Forecasts: Fiction: *Winter Kills.*" *Publishers Weekly* 206 (July 15, 1974): 1227-28.

"PW Forecasts: Fiction: *Flashpoint.*" *Publishers Weekly* 209 (May 17, 1976): 46.

"PW Forecasts: Espionage and Intrigue: *The Star Spangled Contract.*" *Publishers Weekly* 209 (June 1, 1976): 1391.

"PW Forecasts: Fiction: *Sherlock Holmes in Dallas.*" *Publishers Weekly* 217 (June 27, 1980): 83-84.

"PW Forecasts: Fiction: *The Fourth Shot.*" *Publishers Weekly* 222 (November 5, 1982): 58.

"PW Forecasts: Fiction: *The Back of the Tiger.*" *Publishers Weekly* 227 (May 3, 1985): 64.

"PW Forecasts: Fiction: *Promises To Keep.*" *Publishers Weekly* 234 (August 26, 1988): 76.

"PW Forecasts: Fiction: *Flying Into Love.*" *Publishers Weekly* 239 (August 3, 1992): 61.

"PW Forecasts: Fiction: *Corruption of Blood.*" *Publishers Weekly* 242 (September 25, 1995): 42.

"Books: Also Current: *One Day.*" *Time* 85 (March 26, 1965): 103-04.

"Books: Intimations of Mortality: *The Man Who Knew Kennedy.*" *Time* 89 (February 10, 1967): 100.

"Notes on Current Books: Fiction: *One Day.*" *The Virginia Quarterly Review* 41 (Summer 1965): R81.

REFERENCE BOOKS

Books:

Adamson, Bruce Campbell. *The JFK Assassination Timeline Chart.* Published by Author, 1995.

Benson, Michael. *Who's Who in the JFK Assassination: An A-to-Z Encyclopedia.* New York: Citadel Press, 1993.

Brazil, Martin. *J. F. K. Quick Reference Guide.* Hurst, Texas: Published by Author, 1990.

Brown, Walt. *Referenced Index Guide To The Warren Commission.* Wilmington, Delaware: Delmax, 1995.

Ciccone, Craig. *Schematic of Dealey Plaza.* Michigan: Published by Author, 1992.

_____. *Schematic of Oak Cliff, Texas.* Michigan: Published by Author, 1992.

Committee to Investigate Assassinations. *American Political Assassinations: A Bibliography of Works Published 1963-1970.* Washington, D. C., 1973.

_____. *Coincidence or Conspiracy?* New York: Zebra Books, 1977.

_____. *Selective Bibliography on Assassinations.* Washington, D. C., 1969.

Crown, James Tracy. *The Kennedy Literature: A Bibliographical Essay on John F. Kennedy.* New York: New York University Press, 1968.

Duffy, James P., and Vincent L. Ricci. *The Assassination of John F. Kennedy: A Complete Book of Facts.* New York: Thunder's Mouth Press, 1992.

Frewin, Anthony. *The Assassination of John F. Kennedy: An Annotated Film, TV, and Videography, 1963-1992.* Westport, Connecticut: Greenwood Press, 1993.

Giglio, James N. *John F. Kennedy: A Bibliography.* Westport, Connecticut: Greenwood Press, 1995.

Guiochet, Joel Charles. *A General Index of Persons, Places, and Facts.* Paris: J.C. Guiochet, 1984.

Guth, Delloyd J., and David R. Wrone. *The Assassination of John F. Kennedy: A Comprehensive Historical and Legal Bibliography, 1963-1979.* Westport, Connecticut: Greenwood Press, 1980.

Holz, Denice, ed. *Conspiracy in Dallas!* Shreveport, Louisiana: Fairchild Publishing, 1981.

Irwin, T. H., and Hazel Hale. *A Bibliography of Books, Newspaper, and Magazine Articles, Published in English Outside the United States of America, Related to the Assassination of John F. Kennedy.* Belfast: Published by Author, 1975; Supplementary ed., 1978, 1980.

Joesten, Joachim. *Why, When and How I Wrote Eight Printed Books and Three Mimeographed Reports About the Assassination of President Kennedy: A Biographical Bibliography.* Munich, Germany: Published by Author, 1968.

Johnson, Marion M. *Inventory of the Records of the President's Commission on the Assassination of President Kennedy.* Washington, D. C.: National Archives, 1973.

Meagher, Sylvia. *Master Index to the JFK Assassination Investigation: The Reports and Supporting Volumes of the House Select Committee on Assassinations and the Warren Commission.* Metuchen, New Jersey: Scarecrow Press, 1980.

_____. *Subject Index to the Warren Report and Hearings and Exhibits.* Metuchen, New Jersey: Scarecrow Press, 1966; Ann Arbor, Michigan: University Microfilms, 1971.

Miller, Tom. *The Assassination Please Almanac*. Chicago, Illinois: H. Regnery Co., 1977.

Newcomb, Joan I. *John F. Kennedy: An Annotated Bibliography*. Metuchen, New Jersey: Scarecrow Press, 1977

Phillips, Robert A. *Assassination Bibliography: November 22, 1963-November 22, 1982*. Clayton, California: Published by Author, 1982.

Rice, William R. *John & Robert Kennedy: Assassination Bibliography*. Orangevale, California: Published by Author, 1975; rev. ed., 1976.

Ritchie, Raymond E. *A Comprehensive Listing Of JFK Documents In The House Select Committee On Assassinations Volumes*. Randolph, Maine: Spindrift Publications, 1988.

Roberts, Craig, and John Armstrong. *JFK: The Dead Witnesses*. Tulsa, Oklahoma: Consolidated Press International, 1995.

Sable, Martin H. *A Bio-Bibliography of the Kennedy Family*. Metuchen, New Jersey: The Scarecrow Press, Inc., 1969.

Sawa, James P., and Glenn A. Vasbinder. *A Compilation of the Books Relating to the Life and Assassination of President John F. Kennedy.* Published by Author, 1998.

Shearer, Russ. *JFK Index*. Published by Author, 1995.

Thompson, William Clifton. *A Bibliography of Literature Relating to the Assassination of President John F. Kennedy*. San Antonio, Texas: Published by Author, 1968; rev. ed., 1971.

U. S. Library of Congress. *The Kennedy Assassination and the Warren Report: Selected References*. Washington, D. C.: U. S. Government Printing Office, 1966.

Who Killed Kennedy? Bibliography of Assassination Literature. Beaconsfield, Quebec, Canada: Collector's Archives, 1976.

Wrone, David R.   *The Assassination of John Fitzgerald Kennedy: An
Annotated Bibliography.* Madison, Wisconsin: Historical Society of
Wisconsin, 1972.

DISSERTATIONS AND THESES

Bradley, Richard M. "From Kennedy to Nixon: American Political Mythology." Ph.D. diss., University of Illinois, Urbana-Champaign, 1997.

Brossmann, Brent Gene. "Rhetorical Hermeneutics and Oliver Stone's *JFK*: A Method and An Application." Ph.D. diss., University of Kansas, 1995.

Brown, Robert S. "Football as a Rhetorical Site of National Reassurance: Managing the Crisis of the Kennedy Assassination." Ph.D. diss., Indiana University, 1996.

Love, Ruth L. "Television and the Death of a President: Network Decisions in Covering Collective Events." Ph.D. diss., Columbia University, 1969.

McCaffrey, Raymond Aloysius. "Assassination of American Presidents: An Analysis of the Literature." Ph.D. diss., Fordham University, 1982.

McKinney, Bruce C. "Decision-Making in the President's Commission on the Assassination of President Kennedy: A Descriptive Analysis Employing Irving Janis' Groupthink Hypothesis." Ph.D. diss., Penn State University, 1985.

Schubert, Gregory Kent. "A Compilation and Evaluation of Selected Positive and Negative Reactions to the Three and One-Half Day Television News Coverage Which Followed the Assassination of President John F. Kennedy." Master's thesis, Miami University, 1964.

Selesnick, Herbert Lawrence. "The Diffusion of Crisis Information: A Computer Simulation of Soviet Mass Media Exposure During the Cuban Missile Crisis and the Aftermath of President Kennedy's Assassination." Ph.D. diss., Massachusetts Institute of Technology, 1970.

Simon, Arthur. "The Site of Crisis: Representation and the Assassination of JFK." Ph.D. diss., New York University, 1993.

Stone, Nancy. "A Conflict of Interest: The Warren Commission, the FBI, and the CIA." Ph.D. diss., Boston College, 1987.

Tagg, Carl Francis. "Fidel Castro and the Kennedy Assassination." Master's thesis, Florida Atlantic University, 1982.

Van Der Karr, Richard. "Crisis in Dallas: An Historical Study of the Activities of Dallas Television Broadcasters During the Period of President Kennedy's Assassination." Master's thesis, Indiana University, 1965.

Zelizer, Barbie. "Covering the Body: The Kennedy Assassination and the Establishment of Journalistic Authority." Ph.D. diss., University of Pennsylvania, 1990.

AUDIOVISUALS

Audiocassettes:

Air Force One: November 22, 1963. [Radio conversations between Air Force One, Andrews Air Force Base, and the White House], 120 minutes, n. d.

Candlelight Vigil, Dallas. (November 20, 1993), 60 minutes. Distributed by Citizens for Truth About the Kennedy Assassination, 1995.

Case Closed: Lee Harvey Oswald and the Assassination of JFK. 180 minutes. Read by Gerald Posner, Produced by Jessica Kaye. The Publishing Mills, Inc., 1993.

The Grassy Knoll Witnesses: Who Shot JFK? 60 minutes. Compiled by Henry Yardum, n. d.

JFK Assassination Fascination. 180 minutes. Read by Dan Sarver. History Mystery Productions, 1994.

JFK Assassination: The Gangster Nature of the State. 54 minutes. Distributed by People's Video, n. d.

JFK: Conspiracy. 120 minutes. Narrated by Edwin Newman, Produced by Public Interest Affiliates, Inc., Audio Renaissance Tapes, 1990.

Jim Garrison on the Tonight Show. (January 31, 1968), 45 minutes. Distributed by Citizens for Truth About the Kennedy Assassination, 1995.

John Newman: McNamara & Vietnam, Oswald and the CIA. (August 17, 1995), 30 minutes. Distributed by Citizens for Truth About the Kennedy Assassination, 1995.

John Newman on Oswald and the CIA. (June 25, 1995), 85 minutes. Distributed by Citizens for Truth About the Kennedy Assassination, 1995.

Mortal Error: The Shot That Killed Kennedy. 180 minutes. Read by John Hockenberry, Produced and Directed by Sandy Moore. Simon & Schuster Audioworks, 1992.

Murder Made to Order: A New Look at the Assassination of John F. Kennedy & Other Acts of Infamy. 90 minutes. Distributed by Texe Marrs.

November 22, 1963: The Fateful Hours. 47 minutes. Distributed by VIA-TEL, Inc., 1993.

On The Trail of The Assassins. 180 minutes. Read by Edward Asner, Produced by Bill Hartley. Audio Renaissance Tapes, 1991.

Oswald's Tale: An American Mystery. 360 minutes. Read by Norman Mailer and Norris Church Mailer, Produced by Robert Kessler. Random House AudioBooks, 1995.

Plausible Denial: Was the CIA Involved in the Assassination of JFK? 180 minutes. Read by Paul Soles, Produced by Robert Kessler. Bantam Audio Publishing, 1992.

The Probe Interview: Bob Tanenbaum. (May 27, 1996) 60 minutes. Distributed by Citizens for Truth About the Kennedy Assassination, 1996.

The Sixth Floor: John F. Kennedy and the Memory of a Nation. 35 minutes. Narrated by Pierce Allman, Produced by Antenna. Antenna & Dallas County Historical Foundation, 1989.

Who Shot 1st & Keystone Cops; Sound Bites From the Warren Commission Report. 60 minutes. Compiled by Walt Brown, Delmax Productions, 1995.

The Two Assassinations of John Kennedy. (May 31, 1995), 50 minutes. Distributed by Citizens for Truth About the Kennedy Assassination, 1995.

Voices: The JFK Assassination. 180 minutes. Pratt Productions, 1992.

Documentaries on Videocassette:

The Assassination Films. 60 minutes. Narrated by Robert J. Groden, Produced by Robert J. Groden. New Frontier Productions, 1995.

The Assassination of JFK. 78 minutes. Narrated by Warren Leming, Produced by Waleed B. Ali and Malik B. Ali. MPI Home Video, 1992.

Best Evidence: The Research Video. 35 minutes. Narrated by David S. Lifton, Produced by David S. Lifton. Rhino Home Video, 1990.

Beyond JFK: The Question of Conspiracy. 90 minutes. Narrated by Ike Pappas, Directed by Barbara Kopple and Danny Schechter. Warner Home Video, 1992.

CIA Killed Kennedy! 60 minutes Hosted by Mike Marino. Distributed by Paul Kangas, n. d.

Confession of An Assassin. 76 minutes. Produced by Bob Vernon. MPI Home Video, 1996.

The Dallas Police JFK Files. 9 minutes. Presented by Jim Marrs, Produced by Perry Tong and Jack White, Directed by Ron Youngblood. Third Coast Productions, 1992.

Declassified: The Plot To Kill President Kennedy. 58 minutes. Narrated by Larry McCann, Produced by John Sharnik. VidAmerica, Inc., 1988. Re-titled *The Plot To Kill JFK.* Sterling Entertainment Group, 1993.

Deep Politics in the United States. 55 minutes. Hosted by Jack Robinson, Produced and Directed by William P. Ashlin. Starlynx Productions, 1993.

Eyewitness Video Tape: Real JFK Facts (Part I). 122 minutes. Distributed by Mark A. Oakes, 1992.

Eyewitness Video Tape: Real JFK Facts (Part II). 121 minutes. Distributed by Mark A. Oakes, 1995.

Eyewitness Video Tape: Real JFK Facts (Part III). 117 minutes. Distributed by Mark A. Oakes, 1998.

Fake. 50 minutes. Hosted by Craig Mauer, Produced by Perry Tong, Directed by Jim Marrs. Third Coast Productions, 1990.

Films From The Sixth Floor: John F. Kennedy and the Memory of a Nation. 44 minutes. Narrated by Doc Morgan, Produced and Directed by Allen Mondell and Cynthia Salzman Mondell. Dallas County Historical Foundation, 1989.

Four Days In November. 123 minutes. Narrated by Richard Basehart, Produced and Directed by Mel Stuart. MGM/UA Home Video, 1988.

He Must Have Something: The Real Story of Jim Garrison's Investigation of the Assassination of JFK. 88 minutes. Narrated by Ron Small, Produced and Directed by Stephen Tyler. NOVAC, 1992.

Image Of An Assassination: A New Look At The Zapruder Film. 45 minutes. Narrated by Peter Dean, Produced by Malik B. Ali and Waleed B. Ali. MPI Home Video, 1998.

JFK: The Assassination, the Cover-Up, and Beyond. 265 minutes. Directed by James H. Fetzer. James H. Fetzer, 1994.

The JFK Assassination: The Jim Garrison Tapes. 90 minutes. Produced by Fred Weintraub, Directed by John Barbour. Vestron Video, 1992.

JFK: The Case For Conspiracy. 103 minutes. Narrated by Mark Crouch, Produced and Directed by Robert J. Groden. New Frontier Video, 1993, 1995.

JFK: The Day The Nation Cried. 52 minutes. Narrated by James Earl Jones, Produced and Directed by Bruce Halford. View Video, 1989.

JFK: The Investigations. 120 minutes. Hosted by David Starks, Produced by David Starks. Imagi- Vision, Inc., 1994.

Kennedy in Texas. 30 minutes. International Historic Films, 1984.

The Killing of President Kennedy. 80 minutes. Narrated by Bob Sherman, Produced by Anthony Summers. VidAmerica, Inc., 1978. Retitled *The J. F. K. Conspiracy*, MNTEX Entertainment, Inc., 1993.

Lee Harvey Oswald, JFK and Me: An Interview with Ron Lewis. 98 minutes. Hosted by Henry Kreuter, Produced by Martin Nelson and Henry Kreuter, 1995.

The Many Faces of Lee Harvey Oswald. 60 minutes. Narrated by Craig Mauer, Produced by Perry Tong, Directed by Jim Marrs. Third Coast Productions, 1991.

The Mind of L. Flethcher Prouty (Mr. X Identifies General Y). 60 minutes. Produced by Brian Guig. Distributed by Prevailing Winds Research, 1992.

The Mystery FBI Man. 30 minutes. Produced by Mark A. Oakes, 1993.

Oswald: Self-Portrait. 25 minutes. Narrated by John Wilson, Produced by Paul J. Yacich, Directed by Terry Gerstner. INAC, 1994.

The Plot To Kill JFK: Rush To Judgement. 98 minutes. Narrated by Mark Lane, Produced by Emile de Antonio and Mark Lane, Directed by Emile de Antonio. MPI Home Video, 1988.

Reasonable Doubt: The Single-Bullet Theory and the Assassination of John F. Kennedy. 60 minutes. Narrated by Mike Buchanan, Produced and Directed by Chip Selby. White Star, 1988.

The Scene of the Crime: The Dallas Police Recordings. 40 minutes. Distributed by Greg Jaynes, 1998.

The Search For The Truth. 50 minutes. Narrated by Kelly Burly, Produced and Directed by David Daugherty. Independent Video Services, 1992.

Two Men in Dallas. 48 minutes. Hosted by Mark Lane, Produced by Lincoln Carle and Mark Lane, Directed by Lincoln Carle. Tapeworm Distributors, 1987.

Who Didn't Kill JFK? 60 minutes. Narrated by Craig Mauer, Produced by Perry Tong, Directed by Jim Marrs. 3-G Productions, 1992.

ZR Rifle Cuban Documentary. 54 minutes. Produced by Tony Valdes and Directed by Reinaldo Taladrid. Cubanvision International, n. d.

Lectures on Videocassette:

Beyond Dallas: The Real Politics of the Kennedy Assassination. 123 minutes. With Ralph Schoenman, Distributed by Prevailing Winds Research, n. d.

Dallas To Oklahoma City: The Deep Politics (2-parts). 178 minutes. With Peter Dale Scott, John Newman, and Donald Freed (June 26, 1995). Distributed by Prevailing Winds Research.

The JFK Assassination. 360 minutes. With John Judge and Wendy Govier (August 10, 1991). Distributed by Prevailing Winds Research.

JFK Symposium. 31 minutes. Sudbury, Canada, (August 19-22, 1993).

National Archives: Hearings on the JFK Assassination. 223 minutes. With Peter Dale Scott, John Judge, and John Newman, Distributed by Prevailing Winds Research, n. d.

Who Killed Kennedy & Why? 113 minutes. Featuring Ralph Schoenman and John Judge (February 23, 1992). Distributed by Prevailing Winds Research.

Motion Pictures on Videocassette:

Blow Out. 107 minutes, 1981. Produced by George Litto, Directed and Written by Brian DePalma, Distributed by Good Times Home Video. The Players: John Travolta, Nancy Allen, John Lithgow, and Dennis Franz.

Executive Action. 91 minutes, 1973. Produced by Edward Lewis, Directed by David Miller, Screenplay by Dalton Trumbo, based upon the novel by Mark Lane and Donald Freed. Distributed by Warner Home Video. The Players: Burt Lancaster, Robert Ryan, Will Geer, Gilbert Green, and John Anderson.

Greetings. 90 minutes, 1968. Produced by Charles Hirsch, Directed by Brian DePalma, Screenplay by Charles Hirsch and Brian DePalma. Distributed by StarMaker. The Players: Robert DeNiro, Jonathan Warden, Gerrit Graham, and Megan McCormick.

In The Line of Fire. 127 minutes, 1993. Produced by Jeff Apple, Directed by Wolfgang Peterson, Written by Jeff Maguire. Distributed by Tristar Home Video. The Players: Clint Eastwood, John Malkovich, Rene Russo, Dylan McDermott, and John Mahoney.

JFK. 189 minutes (Special Edition: Director's Cut 206 minutes), 1991. Produced by A. Kitman Ho and Oliver Stone, Directed by Oliver Stone, Screenplay by Oliver Stone and Zachary Sklar. Distributed by Warner Home Video. The Players: Kevin Costner, Sissy Spacek, Gary Oldman, Jack Lemmon, Joe Pesci, Tommy Lee Jones, and Kevin Bacon.

Love Field. 104 minutes, 1992. Produced by Sarah Pillsbury and Midge Sanford, Directed by Jonathan Kaplan, Written by Don Roos. Distributed by Orion Home Video. The Players: Michelle Pfeiffer, Dennis Haysbert, Stephanie McFadden, Brian Kerwin, and Louise Latham.

The Manchurian Candidate. 126 minutes, 1962. Produced and Directed by John Frankenheimer and George Axlerod, Screenplay by George Axlerod, based upon the novel by Richard A. Condon. Distributed by MGM/UA Home Video. The Players: Frank Sinatra, Laurence Harvey, Janet Leigh, Angela Lansbury, Henry Silva, and James Gregory.

The Parallax View. 102 minutes, 1974. Produced and Directed by Alan J. Pakula, Screenplay by David Giler. Distributed by Paramount Home Video. The Players: Warren Beatty, Paula Prentiss, William Daniels, Walter McGinn, and Hume Cronyn.

Ruby. 111 minutes, 1992. Produced by Sigurjon Sighvatsson, Directed by John Mackenzie, Screenplay by Stephen Davis. Distributed by Columbia Tristar Home Video. The Players: Danny Aiello, Sherilynn Fenn, Arliss Howard, Tobin Bell, David Duchovny, and Willie Garson.

Winter Kills. 97 minutes, 1979. Produced by Leonard J. Goldberg and Robert Sterling, Directed by William Richert, Screenplay by William Richert. Distributed by Embassy Home Entertainment. The Players: Jeff Bridges, John Huston, Anthony Perkins, Sterling Hayden, and Eli Wallach.

Tele-Movies on Videocassette:

Flashpoint. 94 minutes, 1984. Produced by Skip Short, Directed by William Tannen, Screenplay by Dennis Shryack and Michael Butler, Edited by David Garfield. Distributed by Thorn-EMI Video. The Players: Kris Kristofferson, Treat Williams, Rip Torn, Tess Harper, and Kevin Conway.

Running Against Time. 120 minutes, 1990. Produced by David Roessell, Directed by Bruce Seth Greene, Screenplay by Robert Glass and Stanley Shapiro. Distributed by MCA Universal Home Video. The Players: Robert Hays, Catherine Hicks, Sam Wanamaker, James DeStefano, and Brian Smiar.

The Trial of Lee Harvey Oswald. 192 minutes, 1976. Produced by Richard Freed, Directed by David Greene, Written by Robert E. Thompson. Distributed by Worldvision Home Video Inc. The Players: Lorne Greene, Ben Gazzara, and John Pleshette.

Yuri Nosenko, KGB. 90 minutes, 1986. Produced by Graham Massey, Directed by Mick Jackson, Screenplay by Stephen Davis. Distributed by HBO-Cannon Video. The Players: Tommy Lee Jones, Oleg Rudnik, Josepf Sommer, Ed Lauter, Alexandra O'Karma, and Stephen D. Newman.

Television Programs on Videocassette:

Assassination & Aftermath: The Death of JFK and The Warren Report. 50 minutes, *20th Century With Mike Wallace.* Hosted by Mike Wallace, Produced by Sam Roberts. A&E Home Video, 1996.

Assignment Oswald. 34 minutes, *C-Span.* With James Hosty (March 26, 1996). Public Affairs Video Archives, Purdue University.

Booknotes: Oswald's Tale: An American Mystery. 58 minutes, *C-Span.* Hosted by Bryan Lamb, Produced by Sarah Trahern, Directed by Kevin King (May 2, 1995). Public Affairs Video Archives.

Coalition on Political Assassinations. 42 minutes, *C-Span.* With Daniel Alcorn, Philip Melanson, and Wayne Smith (June 13, 1997). Public Affairs Video Archives, Purdue University.

Equal Time: Gerald Posner. 30 minutes, *CNBC.* Hosted by Torie Clarke and Gloria Borger, Produced by Andy Friendly (October 3, 1994). CNBC Inc.

Jack Anderson: JFK, The Mob and Me. 50 minutes. Hosted by Bill Kurtis, Produced by Barbara Newman. A&E Home Video, 1994.

JFK Assassination Files. 34 minutes, *Nightline.* Hosted by Ted Koppel, Produced by Tom Bettag (January 22, 1992). MPI Home Video.

JFK Assassination Film Status. 141 minutes, *C-Span.* With Jeremy Gunn, James Lesar, and Josiah Thompson (April 2, 1997). Public Affairs Video Archives, Purdue University.

The JFK Conspiracy. 98 minutes. Hosted by James Earl Jones, Produced by George Paige, Directed by Bill Davis. BMG Video, 1992.

JFK: The End of Camelot. 90 minutes. Produced by George Carey, Directed by Steve Ruggi. Discovery Program Enterprises, 1993.

JFK, Hoffa and The Mob. 60 minutes, *Frontline.* Narrated by Mike McNally, Produced by Charles C. Stuart. PBS Home Video, 1993.

JFK and its Depiction of History. 118 minutes, *C-Span.* With Henry Gonzalez, Dan Moldea, and Col. Fletcher Prouty (January 22, 1992). Public Affairs Video Archives, Purdue University.

John F. Kennedy Assassination. 19 minutes, *C-Span.* With John Connally, Pierre Salinger, and Jack Valenti (November 22, 1993). Public Affairs Video Archives, Purdue University.

Journalists Remember JFK Assassination (6-parts). 338 minutes, *C-Span*. With Eddie Barker, Tom Dillard, and Darwin Payne (November 20, 1993). Public Affairs Video Archives, Purdue University.

The Kennedy Assassination: Coincidence or Conspiracy. 90 minutes. Hosted by Robert Conrad, Produced by George Paige, Directed by Phil Olsman. All-American Communications, 1992.

The Kennedy-Johnson Transition. 5 minutes, *C-Span*. (December 12, 1989). Public Affairs Video Archives, Purdue University.

The KGB Oswald Files. 39 minutes, *Nightline*. Hosted by Ted Koppel, Produced by Tom Bettag (November 22, 1991). MPI Home Video.

Making the Movie JFK. 60 minutes, *C-Span*. With Oliver Stone (January 15, 1992). Public Affairs Video Archives, Purdue University.

The Men Who Killed Kennedy (5-parts). 250 minutes. Narrated by Bill Kurtis, Produced and Directed by Nigel Turner. A&E Home Video, 1992.

The Men Who Killed Kennedy: The Truth Shall Make You Free . . . 50 minutes. Narrated by Hilary Minster, Produced and Directed by Nigel Turner. A&E Home Video, 1995.

Oliver Stone's JFK. 23 minutes, *Nightline*. Hosted by Forrest Sawyer, Produced by Tom Bettag (December 19, 1991). MPI Home Video.

President Kennedy Assassination Exhibit. 2 minutes, *C-Span*. With Bob Porter (January 14, 1994). Public Affairs Video Archives, Purdue University.

Who Killed JFK? Facts, Not Fiction. 70 minutes, *48 Hours*. Hosted by Dan Rather, Produced by Liza McGuirk, Directed by Eric Shapiro. CBS Video, 1992.

Who Shot President Kennedy? 60 Minutes, *NOVA*. Narrated by Walter Cronkite, Produced and Directed by Robert Richter. Films for the Humanities & Sciences Inc., 1992.

Who Was Lee Harvey Oswald? (3-parts). 175 minutes, *Frontline*. Narrated by Will Lyman, Produced and Directed by William Cran and Ben Loeterman. PBS Video, 1992.

Phonographic Recordings:

The Actual Voices and Events of Four Days That Shocked the World. New York: Colpix Records CP2500, 1963.

A Time to Keep: NBC Reporting by Robert MacNeil, Chet Huntley, and Tom Pettit. New York: RCA Victor LOC-1088, 1963.

The Assassination of A President: The Four Black Days: November 22-25, 1963. Beverly Hills, California: American Society of Recorded Drama, n. d.

Can't Keep From Crying: Topical Blues on the Death of President Kennedy. Testament Records, 1974.

The Controversy: The Death: The Warren Report. Los Angeles, California: Capitol Records, 1967.

A Documentary: John F. Kennedy: The Presidential Years. New York: 20th Century-Fox Records, n. d.

The Fateful Hours: Actual Unforgettable News Reports of Friday, November 22nd, 1963 by KLIF Dallas. Hollywood, California: Capitol Records RB-2278, n. d.

John F. Kennedy: Years of Lightning, Day of Drums. Capitol Records, n. d.

John Fitzgerald Kennedy: A Memorial Album. New York: Premier Album, Inc., n. d.

John Fitzgerald Kennedy . . . As We Remember Him. Columbia Records Legacy Collection L2L 1017, n. d.

November 22: Dialogue in Dallas: The Assassination of President Kennedy as Reported by Newsmen Malcolm Kilduff, J. F. Terhorst, Robert Donovan, and Sid Davis, With Jim Snyder as Moderator. WBC 2692-2693, 1964.

November 22nd 1963: An Historical Document in Sound. American Broadcasting News. n. d.

Oswald: Self Portrait in Red. Eyewitness Records EW 1001, 1967.

Rush To Judgement: The Living Testimony By the Actual Witnesses on the Original Soundtrack of the Emile de Antonio and Mark Lane Film. New York: Vanguard VRS 92-42, 1967.

That Was The Week That Was: The British Broadcasting Corporation's Tribute To John Fitzgerald Kennedy. n. d.

CD-ROMs:

The Clay Shaw Trial Court Transcripts. Dallas, Texas: L. M. P. Systems, 1996.

The Collected Works of Colonel L. Fletcher Prouty. Osanic, Canada, 1997.

Encyclopedia of the JFK Assassination. Dallas, Texas: Zane Publishing Inc., 1994, 1995.

Hearings Before the President's Commission on the Assassination of President Kennedy. Dallas, Texas: L. M. P. Systems, 1992-1994.

Hearings Before the Select Committee on Assassinations of the U.S. House of Representatives. Dallas, Texas: L. M. P. Systems, 1993.

J. F. K. Assassination: A Visual Investigation. Medio, 1993.

The JFK Assassination: The Dallas Papers. Addison, Texas: DFW Multimedia, 1995.

Mary Ferrell JFK Database. Grand Prairie, Texas: JFK Lancer Productions, 1998.

TV NEWS SEGMENTS: 1968-1997

ABC World News Tonight:

December 9, 1968: "JFK Assassination: Shaw-Garrison."

January 20, 1969: "Shaw Trial to Begin."

January 21, 1969: "Shaw Trial [Trial Begins in New Orleans]."

January 22, 1969: "Shaw Trial [Jury Selection]."

February 6, 1969: "Shaw Trial [Garrison Says Shaw Conspired to Kill Kennedy]."

_____: "Commentary: Shaw & Garrison."

February 7, 1969: "Shaw Trial [Vernon Bundy Testifies]."

February 10, 1969: "Shaw Trial [Perry Russo Testifies]."

February 11, 1969: "Shaw Trial [Russo Testimony]."

February 12, 1969: "Shaw Trial: Inaccurate Memo."

February 13, 1969: "Shaw Trial [Zapruder Film Shown]."

February 14, 1969: "Shaw Trial [Prosecution Pushes Conspiracy Theory]."

February 17, 1969: "Shaw Trial [William Newman Testifies]."

February 19, 1969: "Shaw Trial: John Connally."

February 21, 1969: "Shaw Trial: Defense Presents Case."

February 25, 1969: "Shaw Trial [Witness Claims He Lied to Warren Commission]."

February 27, 1969: "Shaw Trial [Shaw Testifies]."

_____: "Shaw Trial [Denial by Shaw]."

February 28, 1969: "Shaw Trial [Defense & Prosecution Plan Summaries]."

March 3, 1969: "Shaw Trial: Not Guilty."

June 30, 1971: "Garrison Arrested."

November 22, 1971: "[Kennedy Assassination: Eighth Anniversary]."

November 20, 1972: "The Shaw Case."

November 22, 1972: "Kennedy Memorial [Ninth Anniversary]."

November 23, 1972: "Commentary: JFK Assassination."

November 20, 1973: "Senator Mike Mansfield: Kennedy Remembrance."

November 21, 1973: "Rose Kennedy [10th Anniversary of JFK's Death]."

March 10, 1975: "Oswald [Discusses George O'Toole's *The Assassination Tapes*]."

October 21, 1975: "Kennedy Assassination: FBI."

November 14, 1975: "JFK Assassination: [12th Anniversary]."

November 27, 1975: "JFK Assassination [Ford Suggests Reopening Investigation]."

December 12, 1975: "FBI [The Oswald Letter]."

March 1, 1976: "Castro-Kennedys [Conspiracy Theory]."

March 20, 1976: "Warren Commission [CIA Memo]."

May 13, 1976: "Oversight Committee [JFK Assassination]."

May 14, 1976: "JFK Assassination [FBI & CIA]."

May 26, 1976: "Senate Report [Oswald's Motives]."

May 27, 1976: "Oversight Committee [JFK Assassination]."

June 23, 1976: "Senate Report [Critical of the Warren Report]."

June 24, 1976: "Commentary [Johnson Blames Castro For JFK's Death]."

September 17, 1976: "Kennedy-King Assassinations [New Investigations]."

November 15, 1976: "Kennedy-King Assassinations Probe."

November 16, 1976: "House Assassinations Committee; Missing Documents."

November 22, 1976: "JFK Assassination [13th Anniversary]."

_____: "Richard Sprague [Named House Assassinations Director]."

December 9, 1976: "Kennedy-King Assassinations: House Probe [Votes on Funding and Staff]."

December 31, 1976: "House Assassinations Committee [Conspiracy Theories]."

February 1, 1977: "House Assassinations Committee [Receives Extension]."

February 11, 1977: "Kennedy-King Assassinations Committee Dispute."

February 16, 1977: "House Assassinations Committee [Committee in Turmoil; Seeks Solutions]."

March 2, 1977: "House Assassinations Committee [Gonzalez Resigns]."

March 9, 1977: "House Assassinations Committee [Sprague Discusses New Evidence]."

March 16, 1977: "Assassinations Committee [Santos Trafficante Testifies]."

March 30, 1977: "Assassinations Committee [Sprague Resigns]."

March 31, 1977: "Assassinations Committee [Transcript Leaked]."

April 1, 1977: "Assassinations Committee [Dutch Journalist Testifies Regarding Plot]."

December 7, 1977: "Kennedy Assassination: FBI Files."

January 18, 1978: "Kennedy Assassination [FBI Releases More Files]."

July 25, 1978: "Kennedy Assassination [Cubans Allege CIA Involvement in JFK's Death]."

September 6, 1978: "House Assassinations Committee [John & Nellie Connally Testify]."

September 7, 1978: "House Assassinations Committee [Pathologists Support Single-Bullet Theory]."

September 8, 1978: "House Assassinations Committee [Ballistics Expert Supports Single-Bullet Theory]."

September 11, 1978: "House Assassinations Committee [Testimony Regarding Fourth Shot]."

September 12, 1978: "House Assassinations Committee [Testimony Supports Shots From Book Depository]."

September 13, 1978: "House Assassinations Committee [Marina Oswald Porter Testifies]."

September 14, 1978: "House Assassinations Committee [Oswald's Widow Says Husband Acted Alone]."

September 15, 1978: "House Assassinations Committee: [Backyard Photos of Oswald Discussed]."

September 19, 1978: "House Assassinations Committee [Panel Reviews Taped Interview With Castro]."

September 20, 1978: "House Assassinations Committee [FBI Inspector Testifies]."

September 21, 1978: "House Assassinations Committee [Former President Ford Testifies]."

September 22, 1978: "House Assassinations Committee [Former CIA Director Testifies]."

September 25, 1978: "House Assassinations Committee [Umbrella Man Testifies]."

September 26, 1978: "House Assassinations Committee [Jack Ruby's Brother Testifies]."

September 27, 1978: "House Assassinations Committee [Panel Examines Mob Link to Assassination]."

September 28, 1978: "House Assassinations Committee [Blakey Comments on Testimony of Trafficante]."

November 22, 1978: "House Assassinations Committee [Family Visits Grave on Anniversary]."

December 11, 1978: "House Assassinations Committee [FBI Director Testifies]."

December 20, 1978: "House Assassinations Committee [Scientific Report on Direction of Shots]."

December 21, 1978: "House Assassinations Committee [Panel Studies 4th-Shot Theory]."

December 22, 1978: "House Assassinations Committee [Panel Studies New Evidence]."

December 29, 1978: "House Assassinations Committee [Acoustics Expert Claims Fourth Shot]."

December 30, 1978: "House Assassinations Committee [Panel Concludes Kennedy-King Killings Were Probably the Result of a Conspiracy]."

January 1, 1979: "House Assassinations Committee [Panel Recommends Further Investigation of Cuban-Mob Figures]."

January 5, 1979: "House Assassinations Committee [Dallas Policeman Disputes Four-Shot Theory]."

March 25, 1979: "Kennedy Assassination [Oswald's Rifle Retested]."

July 17, 1979: "House Assassinations Committee [Panel Releases Final Report]."

October 19, 1979: "Oswald Controversy [British Author Claims Oswald Impersonator Killed JFK]."

August 14, 1980: "Oswald [Exhumation]."

September 19, 1980: "Oswald [Judge Blocks Exhumation of Oswald's Body]."

December 1, 1980: "JFK Assassination Probe [FBI Disputes House Committee's Findings]."

December 8, 1980: "Oswald [FBI Agent James Hosty]."

May 14, 1982: "Kennedy Assassination [Reexamination of House Committee's Second Gunman Theory]."

November 22, 1983: "Kennedy Assassination [20th Anniversary]."

November 22, 1984: "Kennedy Assassination [21st Anniversary]."

November 20, 1988: "Kennedy Assassination [Services Held on Eve of Anniversary]."

November 22, 1988: "Kennedy Assassination [25th Anniversary]."

February 20, 1989: "Dallas, Texas [Sixth Floor Museum Opens in the Texas School Book Depository]."

January 11, 1992: "JFK Assassination [Edward Kennedy Supports Release of JFK Files]."

May 19, 1992: "Kennedy Assassination: Doctor's Evidence."

October 21, 1992: "[Jim Garrison Dies]."

August 23, 1993: "Kennedy Assassination [Files Released by National Archives]."

November 21, 1993: "Kennedy Assassination [30th Anniversary]."

November 22, 1993: "Kennedy Assassination [Dealey Plaza Designated National Historical Landmark]."

December 1, 1993: "Kennedy Assassination: Johnson Audiotapes]."

April 1, 1994: "Kennedy Files."

April 15, 1994: "Kennedy Assassination Files: Johnson Tapes."

May 3, 1994: "Kennedy Assassination Files [Oswald]."

CBS Evening News:

November 22, 1968: "JFK Memorial."

December 11, 1968: "Shaw Trial [Supreme Court Rejects Efforts to Block Trial]."

January 20, 1969: "Shaw Trial to Begin."

January 21, 1969: "[Shaw Trial Starts Today]."

January 24, 1969: "Shaw Trial [Jury Selection]."

February 5, 1969: "Shaw Trial [Jury Chosen]."

February 6, 1969: "Shaw Trial: Garrison Charges Shaw With Conspiring to Kill JFK."

February 7, 1969: "Shaw Trial [Prosecution Witnesses Testify]."

February 10, 1969: "Shaw Trial [Perry Russo Testifies]."

February 11, 1969: "Shaw Trial: Russo Testimony."

February 12, 1969: "Shaw Trial: Sciambra Testimony."

February 13, 1969: "Shaw Trial: Zapruder Testimony."

February 14, 1969: "Shaw Trial [Garrison Tries to Prove Conspiracy]."

February 17, 1969: "Shaw Trial [Regis Kennedy Testifies]."

February 19, 1969: "Shaw Trial [Conflicting Testimony]."

February 20, 1969: "Shaw Trial: Prosecution Rests."

February 21, 1969: "Shaw Trial: Acquittal Denied."

February 24, 1969: "Shaw Trial: Kennedy Autopsy."

February 27, 1969: "Shaw Trial [Denial by Shaw]."

February 28, 1969: "Shaw Trial [Final Arguments]."

January 19, 1970: "Lee Harvey Oswald."

January 23, 1971: "Clay Shaw Acquitted on Perjury Charges."

June 30, 1971: "Garrison Indictment."

July 6, 1971: "[Distirct Attorney Jim Garrison: Countercharges]."

November 22, 1971: "[Kennedy Assassination: Eighth Anniversary]."

December 3, 1971: "Garrison [Indicted For Bribery]."

November 22, 1972: "Kennedy Memorial [Ninth Anniversary]."

November 22, 1973: "Kennedy Assassination: 10th Anniversary."

September 22, 1975: "[Senate Intelligence Committee Studying JFK Assassination]."

October 21, 1975: "Kennedy Assassination [The Oswald Letter]."

November 11, 1975: "Warren Commission [David Belin Talks to Congress About CIA Plots to Kill Castro]."

November 14, 1975: "Warren Commission Urged Secret Service to Rely on Local Law Enforcement After JFK Assassination."

November 25, 1975: "Only 15% Believe Warren Commission Report on JFK Assassination."

December 12, 1975: "[FBI Agent Told to Destroy Oswald's Letter]."

March 1, 1976: "Kennedy Assassinations: Castro."

May 10, 1976: "JFK Assassination: Castro."

May 13, 1976: "JFK Assassination: Senate Committee Proposes Reopening Investigation."

May 26, 1976: "Senate Report: JFK Assassination."

May 27, 1976: "Intelligence Committee [Reexamination of JFK Assassination Won't Come For Six Months]."

June 7, 1976: "Castro [Denies Involvement in JFK's Death]."

June 23, 1976: "JFK Assassination [Senate Report Says FBI & CIA Hampered Investigation]."

August 22, 1976: "Kennedy Assassination [Mob Lawyer Says Client's Death May Be Linked to JFK's Death]."

September 15, 1976: "Congressional Action Noted [Committee Votes on Reopening Kennedy-King Investigations]."

September 17, 1976: "Congressional Action Taken [House Votes to Reopen Kennedy-King Investigations]."

October 7, 1976: "Kennedy-King Assassinations [House Committee Begins Work Today]."

November 15, 1976: "House Committee on Kennedy-King Assassinations."

November 22, 1976: "Kennedy Memorial Service [13th Anniversary]."

_____: "Congressional Investigations: Kennedy-King."

December 9, 1976: "[House Assassinations Committee Requests Funding & Staff]."

December 10, 1976: "Analysis: House Assassinations Committee."

December 31, 1976: "[Select Committee Requests More Money For Kennedy-King Probes]."

January 27, 1977: "[Kennedy-King Probes Stalled]."

February 1, 1977: "House Assassinations Committee Receives Two-Month Extension."

February 10, 1977: "House Assassinations Committee [Gonzalez vs. Sprague]."

February 11, 1977: "Assassinations Committee [Gonzalez Tries to Fire Sprague]."

March 2, 1977: "House Assassinations Committee [Gonzalez Resigns]."

March 7, 1977: "[House Assassinations Committee Tries to Straighten Affairs]."

March 9, 1977: "[Sprague Claims Evidence of Conspiracy in Kennedy-King Murders]."

March 16, 1977: "[Santos Trafficante Testifies Before Assassinations Committee]."

March 28, 1977: "Assassinations Committee [Possible Connection Between Oswald and Anti-Cuban Forces]."

March 30, 1977: "Assassinations Committee: [Sprague Resigns]."

March 31, 1977: "Assassinations Committee: [Staffer Leaks Minutes of Secret Meeting]."

April 1, 1977: "Assassinations Committee: "[Dutch Journalist Testifies]."

_____: "Analysis: Assassination Conspiracies."

April 3, 1977: "Commentary: John F. Kennedy Murder."

April 11, 1977: "[Former Counsel Calls For Special Prosecutor in Kennedy-King Probes]."

June 20, 1977: "Assassinations Committee [Blakey Named Chief Counsel]."

October 12, 1977: "[Marina Oswald Porter Says Husband Killed JFK]."

November 2, 1977: "[House Assassinations Committee Probes Possibility That Frank Sturgis Was Second Gunman in Kennedy Killing]."

December 2, 1977: "Kennedy Assassination: FBI Files."

January 18, 1978: "[FBI Releases More JFK Assassination Files]."

February 15, 1978: "Assassinations Committee [Requests Funds]."

July 26, 1978: "Kennedy Assassination: Oswald Exhumation Request."

July 28, 1978: "[CIA Conspiracy to Blame Cuba For JFK's Death Alleged]."

August 3, 1978: "[Cubans Allege CIA Conspiracy to Frame Cuba For JFK's Assassination]."

August 10, 1978: "Kennedy & King Assassinations: Dallas Audiotape."

August 14, 1978: "House Assassinations Committee Hearings."

September 6, 1978: "[House Assassinations Committee Hears From Mr. & Mrs. John Connally]."

September 7, 1978: "House Assassinations Committee [Dr. Michael Baden Testifies]."

September 8, 1978: "House Assassinations Committee [Ballistics Expert Testifies]."

September 11, 1978: "House Assassinations Committee [Hears Testimony Regarding Fourth Shot]."

September 12, 1978: "House Assassinations Committee [Photoanalysis Supports Three Shots]."

September 13, 1978: "House Assassinations Committee [Oswald's Widow Testifies]."

September 14, 1978: "[Marina Oswald Porter Claims Husband Acted Alone]."

September 15, 1978: "House Assassinations Committee [CIA Official Questioned]."

September 21, 1978: "House Assassinations Committee [Former President Ford Testifies]."

September 22, 1978: "House Assassinations Committee [Former CIA Director Testifies]."

September 25, 1978: "[Assassinations Committee Hears Testimony Refuting Conspiracy Theories]."

September 27, 1978: "[House Assassinations Committee Explores Cuban-Mafia Links to Kennedy Assassination]."

September 28, 1978: "[Details Given About Mob Leader's Testimony Before House Assassinations Panel]."

November 22, 1978: "[Family Members Mark Anniversary at Gravesite]."

December 21, 1978: "House Assassinations Committee [Testimony Supporting Second Gun Theory]."

December 29, 1978: "House Assassinations Committee: 4th-Shot Theory."

January 4, 1979: "House Assassinations Committee [Dallas Police Officer Refutes Acoustical Evidence]."

March 16, 1979: "House Assassinations Committee: Hoffa."

July 17, 1979: "Assassinations Committee [Releases Findings]."

October 19, 1979: "[Dallas Medical Examiner Calls For Exhumation of Oswald's Body]."

August 14, 1980: "Oswald [Legal Wrangling Over Exhuming His Remains]."

September 19, 1980: "Oswald [Judge Denies Request to Exhume Oswald's Remains]."

December 1, 1980: "Kennedy Assassination Investigation [FBI Challenges House Committee's Findings]."

May 14, 1982: "Kennedy Assassination [Reexamining the Panel's Acoustical Study]."

November 7-9, 1983: "Kennedy: Myth & Reality."

November 20, 1983: "JFK Memorial [20th Anniversary]."

November 22, 1983: "Kennedy Assassination [20th Anniversary]."

November 14-23, 1988: "Assassination: Twenty-Five Years Later."

November 22, 1988: "Kennedy Assassination [25th Anniversary]."

August 6, 1990: "JFK Assassination Plot [Ricky White Links Father to Kennedy Killing]."

November 2, 1990: "Ruby Estate [Jules Mayer vs. Earl Ruby]."

November 22, 1991: "Kennedy Assassination [A Review on the 28th Anniversary]."

December 13, 1991: "Eye On America: The Movie *JFK*."

January 12, 1992: "Kennedy Assassination [Sealed Data]."

January 30, 1992: "Kennedy Assassination [Former Warren Commission Staffers Want JFK Files Opened]."

May 12, 1992: "Kennedy Assassination [CIA to Release Files on Lee Harvey Oswald]."

May 19, 1992: "Kennedy Assassination: *JAMA* Conclusion."

May 21, 1992: "Kennedy Assassination: AMA Conclusions."

August 23, 1993: "Kennedy Assassination [Files Released by National Archives]."

November 15, 1993: "Kennedy Assassination [Public Believes Oswald Did Not Act Alone]."

November 18, 1993: "Eye On America: Oswald."

November 22, 1993: "Kennedy Assassination [30th Anniversary]."

December 14, 1993: "FBI: Ruby Files."

April 15, 1994: "Kennedy Assassination Files: Johnson Audiotape."

April 3, 1995: "Fire Damage to the Texas Theater; Site of Lee Harvey Oswald's Arrest."

May 28, 1996: "JFK Assassination: Newly Discovered Film."

May 29, 1996: "Eye On America: Remembering JFK."

November 20, 1997: "Kennedy Assassination [34th Anniversary]."

NBC Nightly News:

December 9, 1968: "Shaw Trial [Shaw Charged With Conspiracy]."

December 11, 1968: "Shaw Trial."

January 20, 1969: "[Shaw Trial Set to Begin]."

January 21, 1969: "[Shaw Trial Starts Today]."

February 4, 1969: "Shaw Trial [Jury Selection]."

February 5, 1969: "Shaw Trial: Jury Selected."

February 6, 1969: "Shaw Trial [Garrison Says Shaw Conspired to Kill Kennedy]."

February 7, 1969: "Shaw Trial [Witnesses Say Shaw Knew Oswald]."

February 10, 1969: "Shaw Trial: Russo Testimony."

February 11, 1969: "Shaw Trial: Russo Testimony."

February 12, 1969: "Shaw Trial: Inaccurate Memo."

February 13, 1969: "Shaw Trial: Dallas Witnesses."

February 14, 1969: "Shaw Trial [FBI Photographic Expert Testifies]."

February 19, 1969: "Shaw Trial: Warren Commission Conflicts."

February 20, 1969: "Shaw Trial: Prosecution Rests."

February 21, 1969: "Shaw Trial: Acquittal Denied."

March 3, 1969: "Shaw Trial: Perjury Charges."

June 23, 1969: "JFK Assassination: Senate Report."

June 30, 1971: "Garrison Indictment."

November 22, 1971: "[Kennedy Assassination: Eighth Anniversary]."

June 6, 1972: "Kennedy Memorial."

November 22, 1972: "Kennedy Memorial [Relatives Visit Arlington Grave]"

November 22, 1973: "Kennedy Memorial [10th Anniversary]."

March 10, 1975: "Oswald: Not Kennedy's Assassin."

May 8, 1975: "Castro Claims Oswald Was Not a Pawn of Cuba."

June 10, 1975: "Rockefeller Commission: No Link Between CIA and JFK's Death."

October 21, 1975: "Kennedy Assassination: FBI."

May 13, 1976: "JFK Assassination: Intelligence Committee Wants Investigation of Oswald's Motives."

May 26, 1976: "[Senate Intelligence Committee: To Publish JFK Report]."

September 15, 1976: "House Rules Committee [Approves Establishment of Assassinations Committee]."

September 17, 1976: [House Votes to Set-Up Assassinations Committee]."

October 7, 1976: "[House Creates New Committee on Assassinations]."

November 15, 1976: "Kennedy-King Assassinations [First Meeting Held Today]."

November 18, 1976: "Kennedy Assassination Probe: Cuba."

November 19, 1976: "House Committee: Kennedy Assassination Investigation."

November 22, 1976: "Kennedy Assassination [13th Anniversary]."

November 26, 1976: "[Oswald Contacted Russian Embassy Eight Weeks Before Assassination]."

December 9, 1976: "Kennedy-King Assassination Probe."

January 11, 1977: "House Assassinations Committee [Future in Doubt]."

February 1, 1977: "House Assassinations Committee [Receives Two Month Extension]."

February 3, 1977: "House Assassinations Committee [Gonzalez Named Chairman]."

February 10, 1977: "[Conflict Between Gonzalez-Sprague]."

February 11, 1977: "Kennedy-King Assassinations Committee Dispute."

March 2, 1977: "House Assassinations Committee: Gonzalez Resigns."

March 3, 1977: "House Assassinations Committee [In Turmoil]."

March 9, 1977: "House Assassinations Committee [Comments by Richard Sprague]."

March 16, 1977: "Assassinations Committee: Trafficante."

March 23, 1977: "Assassinations Committee [Work Will Continue]."

March 30, 1977: "Assassinations Committee: Sprague Resigns."

March 31, 1977: "Assassinations Committee: Panel Releases Secret Material."

April 1, 1977: "Assassinations Committee [Dutch Journalist Testifies]."

April 11, 1977: "[Sprague Calls For Special Prosecutor to Investigate Kennedy-King Murders]."

December 7, 1977: "Kennedy Assassination: FBI Files."

January 18, 1978: "[FBI Releases Assassination Files]."

September 21, 1978: "House Assassinations Committee [Ford Testifies]."

September 22, 1978: "House Assassinations Committee [Former CIA Director Testifies]."

September 25, 1978: "House Assassinations Committee [Conspiracy Theories]."

September 28, 1978: "House Assassinations Committee [Trafficante Testifies]."

December 21, 1978: "House Assassinations Committee [4th-Shot Theory]."

December 29, 1978: "House Assassinations Committee: Acoustics Expert Testifies."

June 1, 1979: "Assassination Report."

June 17, 1979: "[Assassinations Committee Releases Final Report]."

October 19, 1979: "Oswald Controversy."

December 1, 1980: "JFK Assassination Investigation."

December 18, 1981: "John F. Kennedy Assassination: New Report."

November 21, 1983: "JFK Anniversary."

_____: "Kennedy Recalled."

November 22, 1983: "[Kennedy Assassination: 20th Anniversary]."

November 22, 1986: "[Kennedy Assassination: 23rd Anniversary]."

November 18, 1988: "Kennedy Mystique."

November 21, 1988: "Kennedy Assassination: 25 Years Later."

November 22, 1988: "Kennedy Assassination [25th Anniversary]."

August 25, 1988: "Kennedy-King Assassination: Justice Department Investigation."

February 20, 1989: "[JFK Museum Opens in Dallas]."

October 29, 1990: "[Court Battle Over Ruby's Gun]."

April 15, 1991: "[Kennedy Assassination: *JFK*]."

November 22, 1991: "Around The World: Kennedy Assassination."

January 30, 1992: "[Warren Commission Members Call For Release of JFK Documents]."

May 12, 1992: "Around The World: Oswald File Released."

May 18, 1992: "Kennedy Assassination: AMA Announcement."

May 19, 1992: "Kennedy Assassination: AMA Conclusion."

May 23, 1992: "Weekend Review: [Documents Released on JFK Assassination]."

October 21, 1992: "[Garrison Dies]."

June 17, 1993: "[Connally Dies]."

August 23, 1993: "Kennedy Assassination: CIA Files."

October 13, 1993: "[Dealey Plaza Designated National Landmark]."

November 20, 1993: "Kennedy Assassination Anniversary: Memories."

November 22-26, 1993: "Kennedy Assassination Anniversary."

November 30, 1993: "Kennedy Assassination Audiotapes."

April 15, 1994: "Kennedy Assassination Files: Johnson Tapes."

May 28, 1996: "JFK Assassination: Newly Discovered Film."

JOURNALS, NEWSLETTERS, AND QUARTERLIES

AARC Quarterly: Published by Jim Lesar, Assassination Archives and Research Center, 918 F Street, N. W., Washington, D. C. 20004, Tel: 202.393.1917 (No longer published).

Ahimsa News: Edited and Published by Tommy H. Bowden, 701 Commerce Street, Dallas, TX 75202, Tel: 214.741.3040.

Cover-Ups: Created by Larry Dunkel (aka Gary Mack) (No longer published).

The Continuing Inquiry: Journal of Assassination Research: Created by Penn Jones, Midlothian, TX 76065 (No longer published).

Dallas '63 Journal: Edited by Chris Mills, 76 Main Street, Nottingham, NG14 5EH, UK, Tel: 01159 314018.

Dateline Dallas: Published by the JFK Resource Group, 332 N. E. 5th Street, Grand Prairie, TX 75050 (No longer published).

Deep Politics Quarterly: Journal of JFK Assassination & Related Events: Published by Jan Stevens and Walt Brown, P. O. Box 174, Hillsdale, NJ 07642.

Echoes of Conspiracy: Published by Paul Hoch, 1525 Acton Street, Berkeley, CA 94702, Tel: 510.525.1980. (No longer published; back issues available).

The Fourth Decade: A Journal of Research on the John F. Kennedy Assassination: Edited and Published by Professor Jerry D. Rose, SUNY, Fredonia, NY 14063, Tel: 716.673.3205.

The Investigator: Edited and Published by Gary Rowell, 1501 Park Avenue, Bay City, MI 48708.

Kennedy Assassination Chronicles: JFK Lancer Productions, Grand Prairie, TX 75050, Tel: 888.259.6317, www.jfklancer.com.

Lobster: Edited and Published by Robin Ramsay, 214 West-bourne Avenue, Hull, HU5 3JB, UK, Tel: 01482 447558, http://www.knowledge.co.uk/xxx/lobster/.

Prevailing Winds: Prevailing Winds Research, P. O. Box 23511, Santa Barbara, CA 93121, Tel: 805.566.8016.

For hard-to-find titles, the following dealers are recommended:

All That Video
1551 Valley Forge Road
Lansdale, PA 19446
Tel: 215.368.8997

Almark and Co. Booksellers
P.O. Box 7
Thornhill, Ontario L3T 3N1
Tel: 905.764.2665

Cloak and Dagger Books
9 Eastman Avenue
Bedford, NH 03110
Tel: 603.668.1629
Fax: 603.626.0626
Email: cloakandspies@juno.com

JFK Lancer Productions & Publications
332 N. E. 5th Street
Grand Prairie, TX 75050
Tel: 888.259.6317
www.jfklancer.com

The Last Hurrah Bookshop
849 W. Third Street #1
Williamsport, PA 17701
Tel: 570.321.1150

The President's Box Bookshop
P.O. Box 1255
Washington, DC 20013
Tel: 703.998.7390

INDEX

A

Abrahamsen, David, 79
Abrams, Garry, 166
Abrams, Gus, 3
Abt, John J., 3
Ackroyd, Peter, 216
Acrobat, 3
Adamcik, John, 3
Adams, Francis W. H., 3
Adams, Perry, 144, 156
Adams, Victoria, 3
Adamson, Bruce Campbell, 223
Adelson, Alan, 99
Aguilar, Gary, 3, 139
Air Force One, 3
Akin, Gene C., 3
Alcock, James, 4
Alcorn, David S., 4
Aldridge, John W., 79, 216
Aleman, Jose, 4
Alexander, John, 139
Alexander, William F., 4
Allen, Robert L., 166
Allen, William, 4
Allis, Sam, 202
Alpern, David M., 178
Alsop, Joseph, 202
Alter, Jonathan, 202
Altgens, James, 4
Anderson, A. J., 79
Anderson, Alice, 99
Anderson, Jack, 4
Andrews Air Force Base, 4
Andrews, Charles R., 216
Andrews, David, 213
Andrews, Dean, 4
Andrews, Joseph L., 100
Andronov, Iona, 158
Angel, 4
Annin, Peter, 139
Ansbacher, Heinz, 79

Ansbacher, Rowena R., 79
Ansen, David, 183
Anson, Robert Sam, 4, 153, 183
Arce, Danny, 5
Armstrong, John, 225
Arnoni, M. S., 100, 114–15, 166
Aroeste, Jean, 216
Artwohl, Robert R., 139
Asbell, Bernard, 79
Aschkenasy, Ernest, 5
Ascoli, Max, 202
Ashman, Charles, 153
Assassination Archives And Research
    Center, 5
Assassination Information Bureau,
    5
Assassination Records Review
    Board, 5
Atkins, Thomas, 5
Attwood, William, 202
Aubrey, Edmund, 213
Auchincloss, Kenneth, 80, 183
Augstein, Rudolf, 202
Autry, James, 166
Aynesworth, Hugh, 80, 115, 166

B

Babushka Lady, 6
Bachmann, Ida, 80
Baden, Michael M., 6
Badgeman, 6
Bagdikian, Ben H., 80
Baker, John F., 140, 178
Baker, Marrion L., 6
Baker, T. L., 6
Ball, Joseph A., 6
Balling, L. Christian, 213
Ballot, Paul, 199
Bancroft, Bill, 183
Banister, Guy W., 6
Bannon, Barbara A., 80
Barber, Gary D., 115, 158, 166

Barger, James, 6
Barkus, G. Z. A., 213
Barnum, George A., 6
Barone, Michael, 202
Barra, Allen, 183
Barrett, Bob, 7
Barringer, Floyd S., 140
Barson, Philip, 7
Bart, Peter, 183
Bartholomew, Richard, 136
Bashour, Fouad A., 7
Baskin, Bob, 7
Batchelor, Charles, 7
Bates, John, 7
Baxter, Charles R., 7
Bealle, Morris A., 213
Beck, Melinda, 80, 100
Bedford, Sybille, 100
Beers, Ira J., 7
Beeson, Peter G., 7
Behn, Gerald, 7
Belfrage, Cedric, 115, 158
Belin, David W., 7, 111, 115, 158,
   178, 183
Bell, Audrey, 8
Bell, Jack, 8
Bellah, S., 8
Belli, Melvin M., 8, 99
Benavides, Dominigo, 8
Bennett, Glen A., 8
Bennett, Liz, 167
Benson, Michael, 223
Bentley, Paul, 8
Berendt, John, 203
Berger, Andrew, 8
Berger, Kurt Martin, 203
Bergonzi, Bernard, 216
Bergquist, Laura, 199, 203
Berkeley, Edmund C., 140, 158
Berlow, Alan, 178
Berman, Paul, 80
Bernabei, Richard, 158
Bernau, George, 213
Bernt, H. H., 115–16, 140, 159,
   167
Berolzheimer, Hobart F., 216

Berry, Wendell, 199
Bertrand, Clay, 8
Bethell, Tom, 183
Bethesda Naval Hospital, 8
Bettiza, Enzo, 203
Betzner, Hugh, 8
Bickel, Alexander, 116, 140
Billings, Richard N., 9, 153
Billson, Anne, 184
Bird, Samuel R., 9
Bishop, David, 215
Bishop, Jim, 9
Bishop, Maurice, 9
Black Dog Man, 9
Blake, Patricia, 80
Blakey, G. Robert, 9, 153, 177
Bloomgarden, Henry S., 136
Blum, Andrew, 80
Blumenthal, Sid, 153
Blyth, Myrna, 80
Blythe, Will, 80
Bodine, Larry, 80
Bodovitz, Sandra, 184
Boeth, Richard, 140
Boggs, Hale, 9
Bonazzi, Robert, 116
Bonner, Judy Whitson, 136
Bonventre, Peter, 140
Booker, Simeon, 203
Bookhout, James, 9
Boone, Eugene, 9
Boorstin, Daniel J., 203
Booth, Wayne C., 216
Boothby, Paul, 167
Borch, Herbert von, 203
Boring, Floyd, 10
Boroson, Warren, 100
Boswell, J. Thornton, 10, 142
Bosworth, Patricia, 203
Bourjaily, Vance, 213
Bowers, Faubion, 167
Bowers, Lee Jr., 10
Bowron, Diana H., 10
Bradlee, Benjamin, 199
Bradley, Richard M., 227
Brady, Martin A., 167

Brandon, Henry, 116
Braverman, Shelley, 140
Brazil, Martin, 223
Brehm, Charles, 10
Brener, Milton E., 165
Brennan, Howard, 10, 196
Breo, Dennis L., 140, 184
Breslin, Jimmy, 140
Brewer, E. D., 10
Brewer, Johnny, 10
Bringuier, Carlos, 10, 153
Bromberg, Walter, 100
Bronson, Charles, 11
Brossmann, Brent Gene, 227
Brown, Joe B., 11
Brown, Madeleine, 11
Brown, Ray, 153
Brown, Robert S., 227
Brown, Walt, 11, 111, 153, 213,
   223
Bruning, Fred, 184, 203
Buchanan, Coke, 11, 196
Buchanan, Thomas G., 11, 153
Buckley, Priscilla L., 100
Buckley, William F., Jr., 213
Bundy, Vernon, 11
Bunton, Lucius D., 80
Burke, Yvonne B., 11
Burkley, George, 11
Burleson, Phil, 11
Burr, Ty, 183
Burroughs, Henry, 11
Burroughs, Warren, 12
Butterfield, Roger, 116

C

Cabell, Earle, 13
Calder, Michael, 153
Callahan, Bob, 153
Callahan, John W., 100
Campbell, Alex, 116
Campbell, Judith, 13
Camper, Frank, 154
Canada, Robert O., 13
Cancellare, Frank, 13
Canfield, Michael, 13, 154

Carleton, William G., 203
Carlson, Michael, 81
Carmichael, Dan, 81
Carnes, William H., 13
Carousel Club, 13
Carr, Waggoner, 13
Carrico, Charles J., 13
Carroll, Bob K., 13
Carroll, Ginny, 183
Carroll, Mary, 216
Carroll, Maurice C., 99
Carter, B. Thomas, 13
Carter, Cliff, 14
Carter, Manfred A., 203
Cartwright, Gary, 101, 159
Cartwright, H. L., 101
Casey, Kathryn, 81
Castellano, Lillian, 81
Castle, 14
Castro, Fidel, 14
Catchpole, Terry, 159
Cato, 116
Catton, Bruce, 109
Chamberlin, Anne, 203
Chambliss, Sanford, 101
Champagne, Donald E., 14
Chaney, James M., 14
Chaplin, J. P., 81
Chapman, Ann, 77
Chapman, Gil, 77
Cheek, Timothy, 14
Cheramie, Rose, 14
Cherryholmes, Edward J., 196
Chetta, Nicholas, 14
Chin, Sylvia Fung, 167
Church Committee, 14
Ciccone, Craig, 223
Cirello, Joseph. *See* Civello,
   Joseph
Citizen's Commission Of Inquiry,
   14
Citizens For Truth About The
   Kennedy Assassination, 14
Civello, Joseph, 15
Clapperton, Jane, 81
Clark Panel, 15

Clark, Bob, 15
Clark, Hubert, 15
Clark, William K., 15
Clarke, Gerald, 204
Clemmons, Acquilla, 15
Clemons, Walter, 216
Clifford, G., 204
Clifton, Chester, 15
Cline, R. A., 117
Coalition On Political
  Assassinations, 15
Cockburn, Alexander, 81, 117,
  184
Coe, John I., 15
Cohen, Jacob, 81, 117, 141, 184
Cohen, Jeff, 159
Cohn, Henry S., 81
Cole, Alwyn, 141
Coleman, William T., 16
Collier, Peter, 184
Collins, Max Allan, 213
Collom, Mark, 157
Committee to Investigate
  Assassinations, 223
Conant, Jennet, 184
Condon, Richard A., 213
Connally, Idanell, 16, 197
Connally, John, 16, 196, 197
Conners, Leila, 186
Conroy, Edward A., 16
Conzelman, James, 16
Cook, Fred J., 117, 141
Cook, I., 167
Cooper, John Sherman, 16
Cope, Virginia, 193–94
Corliss, Richard, 184
Corn, David, 184, 194
Cornwell, Gary, 16, 177
Costello, George, 81
Costner, Kevin, 16
Couch, Malcolm, 16
Cournos, John, 199
Courson, J. W., 17
Cousins, Norman, 204
Coyne, J. R., 167
Craig, John R., 154

Craig, Roger, 17
Craven, Thomas J., 17
Crawford, Allan, 159
Crawford, Curtis, 111
Crawford, Kenneth, 117
Crenshaw, Charles A., 17, 141,
  196
Crinklaw, Don, 216
Crinkley, R., 117
Crist, Judith, 184
Cronkite, Walter, 17
Crowdus, Gary, 185
Crown, James Tracy, 223
Cuff, Sergeant, 81, 101, 167
Cummins, Ken, 185
Cunningham, Elmo L., 17
Cunningham, Valentine, 216
Curriden, Mark, 139
Currie, Gordon, 99
Curry, Jesse, 17, 196
Curtis, C. Michael, 82
Curtis, Don T., 17
Curtis, Gregory, 82
Cushing, Richard Cardinal, 17
Cushman, Robert F., 117
Custer, Jerrol F., 17
Cutler, Robert Bradley, 17, 136

D

d' Apollonia, L., 202
Dagger, 18
Dale, Bobby Joe, 18
Dallas Trade Mart, 18
Daly, Steve, 185
Dandy, 18
Dark Complected Man, 18
Darnell, Jimmy, 18
Dasher, 18
David, Dennis, 18
David, Jay, 111
Davies, Col, 154
Davis, John H., 18, 154
Davis, Joseph H., 18
Davis, Marc, 111
Davis, William H., 165
Davison, Jean, 18, 77

Davy, William, 165
Day, Carl, 19
Daylight, 19
Dazzle, 19
Deacon, 19
Dealey Plaza Tramps, 19
Dealey Plaza, 19
Dean, Ruth, 19
Debut, 19
Decker, Bill, 19
Del Valle, Eladio, 19
Delgado, Nelson, 19
Delillo, Dan, 213
Dellinger, Dave, 117
DeLoria, Robin T., 136
Demaris, Ovid, 20, 100, 104
Demohrenschildt, George, 20
Dempsey, David, 117
Denby, David, 185
Denson, R. B., 99
Denton, Tommy, 185
Devine, Samuel L., 20
Devlin, Patrick, 82, 118
DiEugenio, James, 20, 165
Digest, 20
Dillard, Thomas C., 20
DiMaio, Vincent J. M., 86
Dimona, Joseph, 214
Dirix, Bob, 159
Dodd, Christopher, 20
Dole, Grace Fuller, 82
Domino, 20
Donadio, Stephen, 217
Donahue, Howard C., 20, 141
Donahugh, Robert H., 217
Donhoff, Marion, 204
Dowell, Pat, 185
Downey, Durbin H., 154
Downing, Thomas N., 20
Dox, Ida, 20
Doyle, Harold, 20
Dresser, 20
Drinnon, Richard, 118
Drummer, 21
Dudman, Richard, 197
Duffy, James, 21

Duffy, James P., 223
Dugger, Ronnie, 101
Duheme, Jacqueline, 199
Duke, James, 21
Dulaney, Richard B., 21
Dulles, Allen, 21
Duncan, Richard, 136
Duncan, Susana, 82
Dunn, Cyril, 82
Dunn, Robert, 217
Dunshee, Tom, 136
Duplex, 21
Dusty, 21
Dyson, Paul H., 82

E

Ebersole, John H., 22
Eddowes, Michael, 22, 154
Edgar, Robert W., 22
Egginton, Joyce, 82
Eisenberg, Melvin A., 22
Elaine Shannon, 178
Elfin, Mel, 204
Ellis, Starvis, 22
Ellis, W., 118
Ely, John H., 22
Emerson, William A., 141
Endt, Frisco, 204
Ephron, Nora, 185
Epstein, Edward Jay, 22, 77, 82,
    111, 118, 165, 168, 185
Erlebacher, Albert, 118
Evans, M. Stanton, 82, 118, 159
Evica, George M., 22, 154, 185
Ewell, Jim, 22
Ewing, Michael, 22
Exner, Judith Campbell, 22

F

Fain, John, 23
Fair Play For Cuba Committee, 23
Faulkner, Jack, 23
Fauntroy, Walter E., 23
Fein, Arnold L., 82, 118
Felberbaum, A., 185
Felder, James L., 23

Feldman, Harold, 82, 159, 168, 196, 198
Fensterwald, Bernard, Jr., 23, 118, 159, 168
Fenton, Cliff, 23
Ferguson, Andrew, 204
Ferlinghetti, Lawrence, 204
Ferrell, Mary M., 23
Ferrell, Thomas H., 83
Ferrie, David W., 24
Fetherling, Douglas, 83
Fetzer, James H., 136
Fiddick, Thomas C., 101
Field, Maggie, 168
Fife, Darlene, 168
Finck, Pierre A., 24
Fine, William M., 199
Fisher, Bob, 185
Fisher, Russell, 24
Fithian, Floyd J., 24
Fixx, James F., 118
Flammonde, Paris, 24, 165
Fleming, Charles, 185–86
Fonzi, Gaeton, 24, 118, 177, 178
Forbes, Malcolm S., 204
Ford, Gerald R., 24, 111, 118
Ford, Harold E., 24
Foreman, Percy, 24
Forman, Robert, 141
Forslund, Morris A., 101
Foster, Robert, 24
Fox, Sylvan, 24, 112, 119
Fox, Victor, 214
Fraker, Susan, 159, 178
Fraley, Oscar, 214
Frankel, Haskel, 168
Frazier, Buell Wesley, 25
Frazier, Robert A., 25
Freed, Donald, 159, 214
Freedman, Lawrence Z., 83
Freedman, Nancy, 214
Freeman, H. D., 25
Freeman, Lucy, 77
Freeman, Peter B., 89
Freese, Paul L., 119
Freund, Hugo, 204

Frewin, Anthony, 168, 214, 224
Friedman, Rick, 119
Friedrich, Ron, 196
Fritz, Will, 25
Frook, John Evan, 186
Furiati, Claudia, 25, 154

G

Galanor, Stewart, 136
Galloway, Calvin, 26
Gandolfo, Ted, 177
Gappert, Gary, 204
Gardels, Nathan, 186
Gardner, Francis V., 199
Gardune, Joseph A., 199
Garrick, J. B., 26
Garrison, Jim, 26, 165, 214
Gates, David, 159
Gaudreau, Richard E., 26
Gearhart, Ira D., 26
Gedney, John, 26
Gelman, David, 83, 178
Georgakas, Dan, 186
Gerard, Jeremy, 186
Gershman, Bennett L., 168
Gerson, Jack, 214
Gertz, Elmer, 99, 100, 101
Gest, Ted, 119
Giampietro, Wayne B., 101
Giancana, Sam, 26
Giesceke, Adolph H., 26
Giglio, James N., 186, 224
Giquel, Bernard, 168
Gitlin, Todd, 186
Givens, Ron, 204
Glenn A. Vasbinder, 225
Glikes, Edwin A., 199
Glynn, Lenny, 217
Gold, Victor, 205
Goldberg, Alfred, 26
Goldman, Alex J., 199
Goldman, Peter, 178, 205
Gonzalez, Henry B., 27
Goodhart, Arthur L., 119
Goodman, Bob, 154
Gordon, Bruce, 155

Gotte, Fritz, 205
Graham, Hugh Davis, 141
Grandmaison, Ann M., 217
Grant, David B., 27
Grant, Donald C., 27
Grassy Knoll, 27
Graves, A. C., 27
Graves, Florence, 141
Gray, L. E., 27
Gray, Paul, 217
Gray, Simon, 217
Graziani, Gilbert, 119
Green, Philip, 186
Green, Stephen, 186
Greenfield, Marjorie, 83
Greenfield, Meg, 205
Greer, William R., 27
Gregory, Charles F., 27
Grenier, Richard, 186
Grichot, Jack, 141
Griffin, Burt W., 27
Griffin, Leland M., 83
Griffin, Sean, 186
Groden, Robert J., 27, 77, 137, 141
Grogan, David, 207
Gronouski, John S., 199
Gross, Alfred A., 119
Gross, Ken, 186
Grundmann, Roy, 186
Grunwald, Lisa, 187
Guinyard, Sam, 28
Guiochet, Joel Charles, 224
Gun, Nerin E., 83, 155, 168
Guth, Delloyd J., 28, 224

H

Habe, Hans, 119
Hacker, Andrew, 83, 160
Hager, Barry, 179
Hager, Steven, 169
Haggerty, Edward A., 29
Halberstam, David, 205
Hale, Hazel, 224
Halfback, 29
Hall, C. Ray, 29

Hall, Kermit L., 29, 194
Hamill, Pete, 205
Hamilton, James W., 83
Hampton, Wilborn, 196
Hamsher, J. Herbert, 119
Hancock, Larry, 214
Handlin, Oscar, 119–20, 141
Hansen, Mark, 83
Hanson, William H., 137
Hardin, Michael, 29
Hargis, Bobby, 29
Harkness, D. V., 29
Harper Bone Fragment. *See*
    Harper, William
Harper, William, 29
Harrelson, Charles, 29
Harrington, William, 214
Harris, Larry R., 29, 138
Harris, Ruth, 214
Harrison, Barbara Grizzuti, 205
Harrity, Richard, 83
Hart, L., 205
Hartogs, Renatus, 30, 77
Havemann, Ernest, 101
Hawkins, Ray, 30
Haygood, Clyde, 30
Hayward, E. B., 217
Heath, Peter, 214
Hegyi, Karoly, 101
Helicher, Karl, 160
Helms, Richard, 30
Hemenway, Phillip, 155
Hemming, Gerry P., 30
Henchliffe, Margaret M., 30
Hendrix, Ruth, 30
Henley, Arthur, 90
Hepburn, James, 155
Hermann, Kai, 120
Hernandez, Debra Gersh, 194
Herskowitz, Mickey, 197
Hessel, Dieter, 205
Hetter, Katia, 202
Heymann, Stefan, 83
Hickey, George, 30
Hicks, Granville, 83, 217
Hidell, Alek J., 30

Hill, Clint, 30
Hill, Gerald L., 30
Hill, Jean, 31
Hill, William, 217
Himmelfarb, Gertrude, 84
Hinckle, Warren, 31, 155
Hlavach, Laura, 196
Hobbs, Richard, 137
Hoch, Paul L., 31, 87, 113
Hoefen, John, 31
Hoffa, James R., 31
Hoffman, Ed, 31, 196
Holland, Max, 120
Holland, S. M., 31
Holmes, Harry D., 31
Holt, Chauncie, 31
Holz, Denice, 224
Holzhauer, Jean, 84
Hoover, J. Edgar, 31
Hosty, James P., 32, 77
House Select Committee On
    Assassinations, 32
Houts, Marshall, 137, 142
Howard, Clyde W., 142
Howard, Jane, 205
Howard, Larry, 32
Howard, Tom, 32
Hoyle, Jeffrey P., 137
Huber, Oscar, 32
Hubert, Leon D., 32
Hughes, Robert, 32
Hughes, Sarah T., 32, 198
Humes, James J., 32, 142
Hunt, Conover, 200
Hunt, E. Howard, 32
Hunt, George P., 84
Hunt, Jackie H., 33
Hunter, Diana, 99
Hurt, Henry, 33, 155
Hutson, T. A., 33
Hutton, Patricia, 33

I

Irwin, T. H., 224
Ivon, Lou, 34

J

Jacks, Hurchel, 35
Jackson, Donald, 84, 169
Jackson, Douglas L., 35
Jackson, John J., 169
Jackson, Katherine Gauss, 84, 218
Jackson, Robert H., 35
Jacobson, Dan, 120
James, Patricia L., 142
James, Rosemary, 165
Jamieson, John, 118
Jarman, James, 35
Jarvis, Jeff, 187
Jaworski, Leon, 35
Jenkins, Gareth, 120
Jenkins, James, 35
Jenkins, Marion T., 35
Jenner, Albert E., 35
Joesten, Joachim, 35, 77, 84, 99,
    112, 120, 137, 142, 165, 169,
    205, 224
Johns, Thomas L., 36
Johnsen, Richard E., 36
Johnson, Brian D., 187
Johnson, Clemon Earl, 36
Johnson, James P., 84
Johnson, Lyndon B., 36, 196
Johnson, Marion M., 224
Johnson, Priscilla, 84
Johnston, David L., 36
Joling, Robert J., 142
Jones, Kirby, 160
Jones, Mervyn, 84
Jones, Penn, Jr., 36, 112, 168
Jones, Ronald C., 36
Jones, Wyman, 198
Joyce, William, 36
Judge, John, 36

K

Kaiser, David E., 205
Kantor, Seth, 37, 99
Kaplan, David A., 120
Kaplan, John, 99, 120
Karel, Thomas A., 160
Karp, Irwin, 120

Kartsonis, Louis P., 142
Kates, Don B., 84
Kathchik, Keith, 84
Katz, Bob, 37
Katz, Joseph, 84
Kauffman, Stanley, 187
Kazan, Molly, 200
Keisler, J. R., 120
Keisling, Phil, 160
Keith, Jim, 155
Keller, James R., 187
Kellerman, Roy, 37
Kelley, Daniel Otis, 101
Kellner, Abraham, 200
Kellogg, Mary Alice, 187
Kelly, Frank, 120
Kempton, Murray, 84, 101–2, 121,
    205
Kendall, Bruce, 201
Kennedy, Jacqueline Bouvier, 37
Kennedy, John F., 37
Kennedy, Robert F., 37, 85
Kenney, Edward, 37
Kerby, Phil, 121, 169
Khrushchev, Nikita, 37
Kidder, Tracy, 179
Kilduff, Malcolm, 37
Kilgallen, Dorthy, 38
King, Peter, 206
Kinney, Samuel, 38
Kirkwood, James, 38, 166, 169
Kister, Kenneth F., 160, 218
Kitching, Jessie, 121
Kivett, Jerry D., 38
Klawans, Stuart, 187
Klein, Harry T., 200
Klein, Kenneth D., 38
Klein, Valerie J., 84
Knabb, Wayne M., 169
Knebl, Fletcher, 121
Knight, Marianna I., 207
Koch, Thilo, 206
Kopkind, Andrew, 187, 206
Krebs, A. V., 121, 142
Krippendorff, Ekkehart, 206
Kritzberg, Constance, 214

Kuntz, Phil, 194
Kurnoth, Rudolf, 206
Kurtz, Michael, 38, 85, 121, 137

L

La Fountaine, George, 214
La Manna, Roger, 78
Lace, 39
LaFontaine, Mary, 77
LaFontaine, Ray, 77
Lancer, 39
Land, Barbara, 87
Land, Myrick, 87
Landis, Paul E., 39
Lane, Mark, 39, 85, 102, 112, 121,
    155, 169, 214
Lardner, George, Jr., 179
Lark, 39
LaSalle, Peter, 218
Lasseter, Don, 153
Latham, Aaron, 85
Lattimer, Gary, 142, 143
Lattimer, John K., 39, 137, 142–
    43
Lattimer, Jon, 142, 143
Laulicht, Murray J., 39
Lauzon, A., 85
Lawrence, Lincoln, 155
Lawrence, Perdue W., 39
Lawson, Winston G., 39
Lazar, Emily, 85
Leavelle, James R., 39
Lee, O. H., 39
Lemann, Nicholas, 169
Leo, John, 187
Leonard, John, 218
Lesar, James H., 40
Lesher, Stephan, 178
Levi, Barbara G., 143
Levin, Bernard, 206
Levy, Clifford V., 200
Lewis, Anthony, 110
Lewis, David F., 40
Lewis, L. J., 40
Lewis, Richard Warren, 102, 112
Lewis, Ron, 40, 77

Lewis, Roy E., 40
Liebeler, Wesley J., 40, 187
Lifton, David, 40, 137
Lincoln, Evelyn, 40, 196
Linklater, Andro, 218
Linn, Edward, 102
Lister, W., 116
Liu, Melinda, 80
Livernash, Bob, 179–80
Livingston, R. W., 41
Livingstone, Harrison Edward, 40, 137–38
Loebs, Bruce, 187
Logan, Andy, 206
Lohmar, Ulrich, 206
Lopez, Edwin, 41
Loquvam, George S., 41
Love Field, 41
Love, Ruth L., 227
Lovelady, William Nolan, 41
Lowe, Jacques, 200, 206
Lowney, Douglas, 169
Lucia, Cynthia, 186
Luckinbill, Lawrence, 187
Ludwig, Jack, 85
Lumpkin, George L., 41
Lumpkin, W. G., 41
Lundberg, George D., 143
Luther, Daniel W., 102
Lutz, Monty C., 41
Lynd, Staughton, 144, 160
Lyric, 41

M

Macdonald, Dwight, 85, 121
Macdonald, Neil, 121, 169
MacFarlane, Ian Colin A., 155
Mack, Gary, 42
MacKenzie, John P., 188
MacKenzie, N., 122
Maclean, Don, 113
MacNeil, Robert, 42, 196, 200
Maddox, Henry, 169
Magic Bullet, 16, 42
Magnuson, Ed, 143, 160

Mailer, Norman, 42, 77, 85, 102, 188
Malzberg, Barry N., 214
Manchester, William, 42, 200, 206
Manly, Howard, 159
Mannlicher-Carcano Rifle, 42
Mano, D. Keith, 85
Mansfield, Michael J., 201
Mantik, D. W., 143
Marcello, Carlos, 42
Marchetti, Victor, 43
Marcus, Raymond, 138
Marek, Richard, 85
Market, 43
Markham, Helen Louise, 43
Marks, Stanley, 155
Marmor, Arthur K., 43
Marquand, David, 160
Marrs, Jim, 43, 156
Marshall, Alex, 188
Marten, Paul, 201
Martin, B. J., 43
Martin, Jack S., 43
Martin, William C., 86
Mathews, Jim, 111
Matthews, James P., 201
Maxfield, Marietta, 197
Mayer, Martin, 102
Mayer, Milton, 206
Mayfield, Douglas, 43
Mayhew, Aubrey, 201
McBirnie, William Stewart, 78
McBride, G. C., 43
McCaffrey, Raymond Aloysius, 227
McCarry, Charles, 215
McClain, H. B., 43
McClelland, Robert N., 43
McCloy, John J., 43
McCue, Howard, 102
McDonald, Hugh C., 44, 156
McDonald, M. N., 44
McHugh, Godfrey, 44
McIntyre, William T., 44
McKinney, Bruce C., 227
McKinney, Stewart B., 44

McKinven, Mary Jane, 160
McLaughlin, M., 206
McMillan, Priscilla Johnson, 44,
 78, 86
McNaspy, C. J., 207
McReynolds, R. Michael, 144
McWatters, Cecil J., 44
McWilliams, Carey, 144
McWillie, Lewis, 44
Meagher, Sylvia, 44, 86, 113, 122,
 144, 168, 170, 224
Medved, Michael, 207
Meek, Jeff, 156
Melanson, Philip H., 45, 78
Mellen, Joan, 188
Menninger, Bonar, 45, 138
Mercer, Julia Ann, 45
Meredith, Lynn, 45
Merritt, H. Houston, 143
Meunier, Robert F., 113
Meyer, Karl E., 86, 122
Michalak, Thomas J., 122
Michaud, Charles, 86
Micozzi, Marc S., 144
Midgett, William, 45
Miller, Tom, 225
Miller, Warren, 218
Miller, William Thomas, 144
Mills, Andrew, 122
Milteer, Joseph A., 45
Minnis, Jack, 144
Montague, Ivor, 122
Montgomery, Leslie D., 45
Moore, Jim, 45, 138
Moore, T. E., 45
Moore, Thomas, 207
Moorman, Mary, 45
Morgan, Russell, 45
Morganthau, Tom, 180
Moriarty, Jack, 46
Morris, Wright, 215
Morrow, Lance, 86, 188, 207
Morrow, Robert D., 46, 156
Mortiz, Alan, 46
Moscovit, Andrei, 156
Mosk, Richard M., 46, 86, 88, 122

Moss, Armand, 113
Moynihan, Daniel Patrick, 207
Muchmore, Maria, 46
Muggeridge, Malcolm, 86, 122,
 207
Muhlen, Norbert, 123
Murray, Hugh, 160
Murray, Norbert, 201
Murret, Charles, 46
Murret, Lillian, 46
Myers, Dale K., 78

N

Nagell, Richard Case, 47
Names, Larry D., 215
Nash, George, 123
Nash, Harry C., 113
Nash, Patricia, 123
National Commission On The
 Causes And Prevention Of
 Violence, 47
Nechiporenko, Oleg M., 47, 78
Nelson, Anna Kasten, 47
Nelson, Doris Mae, 47
Newcomb, Fred T., 144, 156
Newcomb, Joan I., 225
Newman, Albert H., 47, 113
Newman, Gayle, 47
Newman, John, 47, 78, 188
Newman, William J., 47
Newquist, Andrew M., 48
Nichols, John, 144
Nivaggi, Gary, 138
Nix, Orville O., 48
Nizer, Louis, 109
Norman, Harold, 48
North, Mark, 48, 156
Northcott, Kaye, 123
Norton, Linda E., 86
Nosenko, Yuri, 48
Novak, Ralph, 188
Noyes, Peter, 156

O

O'Brien, Conor Cruise, 87, 123,
 207

O'Brien, John J., 49
O'Brien, Larry, 49
O'Connor, Paul, 49
Odio, Sylvia, 49
O'Donnell, Ken, 49
O'Donnell, M. K., 215
Oglesby, Carl, 49, 156, 188
Olds, Greg, 123, 170
O'Leary, John J., 49
Oliver, Beverly, 6, 49, 196
Olson, Don, 144
Oneal, Vernon B., 49
O'Neill, Francis X., 50
O'Reilly, Kenneth, 87
Orr, Leonard, 218
Osbaine, Cecil, 207
Oser, Alvin, 50
Osterburg, James W., 123
O'Sullivan, John, 188
Osvald, Frank, 123
Oswald, June, 50
Oswald, Lee Harvey, 50, 87
Oswald, Marguerite C., 50, 78, 123
Oswald, Marina, 50
Oswald, Rachel, 50
Oswald, Robert L., 50, 78, 87
Oswald, Robert Lee, Sr., 50
O'Toole, George, 50, 87
Ottenberg, Miriam, 109
Oxford, J. L., 50

P

Pabst, Ralph M., 99
Packer, Herbert L., 123
Paine, Ruth H., 51
Palmara, Vincent M., 197
Parkland Memorial Hospital, 51
Parshall, Gerald, 87
Payne, Darwin, 196
Perry, Malcolm O., 51
Peters, Paul C., 51
Peterson, Roger S., 194
Petras, James, 188
Petty, Charles, 51, 144
Peyer, Tom, 207

Phelan, James, 170
Phillips, David, 51
Phillips, Robert A., 225
Pic, John Edward, Jr., 51
Pickard, Roy, 188
Pietrusza, David, 102
Pilger, John, 188
Piper, Michael Collins, 157
Pitzer, William B., 51
Plastrik, Stanley, 87
Plummer, William, 102, 207
Podhoretz, Norman, 123
Policoff, Jerry, 123
Pollak, Stuart R., 51
Pond, Steve, 189
Popa, Stefan, 103
Popkin, Richard H., 51, 78, 170
Posner, Gerald, 52, 78, 87
Posner, Michael, 144
Possony, Stefan T., 123, 160
Postal, Julia, 52
Pottecher, Frederic, 99–100
Pouillon, Jean, 207
Powers, Dave, 52
Powledge, Fred, 170
Poznanska, A., 103
President John F. Kennedy Assassination Records Collection Act, 52
President's Commission On The Assassination Of President Kennedy, 52
Preston, Gregor A., 87, 103, 160
Preyer, Richardson, 52
Price, J. C., 52
Progoff, Ira, 87
Prouty, L. Fletcher, 52, 157
Prusakova, Marina Nikolaevna, 52
Puterbaugh, Jack, 53

Q

Queen Mary, 54
Quigley, John, 54

R

Radin, Victoria, 218

Rafferty, Terrence, 218
Ragan, Charles A., 145
Ragano, Frank, 55
Ralston, Ross F., 78
Randall, Teri, 145
Randle, Linnie Mae, 55
Rankin, J. Lee, 55
Raskin, Marcus, 189
Rather, Dan, 197
Ready, John D., 55
Redlich, Norman, 55
Reed, Edward, 55
Reeves, Richard., 207
Reid, Elizabeth, 55
Relation, A. Joseph, 161
Remus, Bernhard, 208
Rendulic, Lothar, 208
Reston, James, Jr., 87
Revere, Guy, 103
Reynolds, Warren, 55
Ricci, Vincent L., 223
Rice, William R., 225
Rich, Joe Henry, 55
Richard, Paul, 87
Richler, Mordecai, 218
Rickerby, Arthur, 56
Riebe, Floyd, 55
Rieland, Randy, 189
Rifkind, Shepard, 88
Rike, Aubrey, 56
Ringgold, Gene, 78
Ritchie, Raymond E., 225
Rivera, Geraldo, 56
Robach, M., 189
Roberts, Charles, 56, 113, 198
Roberts, Craig, 157, 225
Roberts, Delphine, 56
Roberts, Earlene, 56
Roberts, Emory, 56
Rockefeller Commission, 56
Roddy, Joseph, 208
Rodman, Peter, 88
Roffman, Howard, 56, 79
Rogers, Philip A., 154
Rogers, Warren, 170
Rogin, Michael, 189

Rohe, Terry Flettrich, 170
Romanowski, William D., 189
Rose, Earl, 56
Rose, Guy F., 56
Rose, Jerry, 56
Roselli, Johnny, 57
Rosen, Sol Z., 123
Rosenbaum, Ron, 161, 189
Rosenberg, Maurice, 124
Rosenstone, Robert A., 189
Rothstein, David A., 88
Rowley, James J., 57
Rubenstein, Jacob, 57
Ruby, Earl, 57
Ruby, Jack, 57, 103
Rudnicki, Jan Gail, 57
Ruge, Gerd, 170
Russell, Bertrand, 124
Russell, Brian, 138
Russell, Dick, 57, 157, 161
Russell, Francis, 124
Russell, Richard, 57
Russo, Perry R., 57

S

Sable, Martin H., 225
Salandria, Vincent J., 145, 161
Salerno, Ralph, 58
Salholz, Eloise, 161
Salinger, Pierre, 201, 208
Salisbury, Harrison E., 109
Salyer, Kenneth E., 58
Sample, Glen, 157
Sanders, Charles J., 194
Sarti, Lucien, 58
Sauvage, Leo, 58, 88, 113, 124,
    161, 168
Savage, Gary, 138
Sawa, James P., 225
Sawyer, Harold S., 58
Sawyer, J. Herbert, 58
Saylor, V. Louise, 218
Scally, Christopher, 177
Scheim, David E., 58, 157
Schiller, Herbert, 189
Schlesinger, Arthur M., Jr., 208

Schlesinger, Edward B., 143
Schmidt, Bernadette, 201
Schneider, Joseph, 88
Schoenman, Ralph, 58
Schoenmann, Ralph, 124
Schonfeld, Maurice W., 145
Schorr, Daniel, 189
Schubert, Gregory Kent, 227
Schulz, Donald E., 161
Schwaber, Paul, 199
Schwartz, Benjamin L., 145
Schwartz, Jay, 124
Schweiker Committee, 59
Schweisheimer, W., 145
Schwelien, Joachim, 170
Sckolnick, Lewis B., 79
Scobey, Alfredda, 59, 124
Scoggins, William W., 59
Scott, Liz, 170
Scott, Peter Dale, 59, 79, 113, 157, 161
Seal, Mark, 189
Seely, Hart, 207
Seelye, John, 145
Segal, Jeff, 180
Seigenthaler, John, 166
Selesnick, Herbert Lawrence, 227
Sellier, Charles, 138
Sevilla, Charles M., 124
Shadow, 59
Shaffer, Charles N., Jr., 59
Shahn, Ben, 199
Shaneyfelt, Lyndal L., 59
Shanklin, Gordon, 59
Shannon, Elaine, 83, 178
Shannon, William V., 125
Shapiro, Jonathan S., 88
Shapiro, Joseph P., 119
Shapiro, Stanley, 215
Sharrett, Christopher, 189–90
Shaw, Clay, 59
Shaw, J. Gary, 60, 138
Shaw, Robert R., 60
Shearer, Russ, 225
Sheed, Wilfrid, 206
Shires, George T., 60

Shiverick, David, 79
Shiverick, Kathleen, 79
Shrear, Arnold, 215
Sibert, James, 60
Sidey, Hugh, 198, 208
Silver, Isidore, 88, 145
Simon, Art, 183, 190
Simon, Arthur, 227
Simpson, Alan W. B., 125
Singer, Loren, 215
Sinkle, Billy, 60
Sites, Paul, 79
Sitzman, Marilyn, 60
Sixth Floor Museum, 60
Skelton, Royce G., 60
Sklar, Zachary, 183, 190
Skow, John, 218
Slawson, W. David, 60, 88
Sloan, Bill, 60, 197, 215
Sloan, Jane E., 190
Smart, R., 61
Smilgis, Martha, 188
Smith, Jack A., 88, 125–26, 161
Smith, Matthew, 157
Smith, Merriman, 61, 197, 198
Smith, Robert P., 147
Smith, Wayne S., 146
Smolla, Rodney A., 190
Sneed, Larry, 197
Snider, Arthur J., 146
Snyder, LeMoyne, 88
Sokolov, Raymond, 89
Sorrels, Forrest V., 61
Sparrow, John Hanbury Angus, 113
Specter, Arlen, 61, 89
Spencer, B. Z., 89
Spitz, Werner U., 61
Sprague, Richard A., 61
Sprague, Richard E., 61, 89, 146, 161, 170
Sproesser, Louis, 166
Stafford, Jean, 61, 79, 89
Stahl, Walter, 208
Stanglin, Douglas, 208
Steck, Henry, 146, 161–62

Steel, Ronald, 190
Steiner, Stan, 126
Stern, R., 100
Stern, Samuel A., 61
Stetler, Russell, 113
Stevens, James, 215
Stewart, Charles J., 201
Stiles, John R., 61, 111
Stokes, Louis, 61
Stolley, Richard B., 62, 146
Stone, Nancy, 228
Stone, Oliver, 62, 126, 183, 190
Stoughton, Cecil W., 62
Stout, Stewart G., 62
Stover, John, 62
Stringer, John, 62
Strior, Murray, 201
Strout, Richard L., 209
Stuckey, William, 62
Studebaker, Robert Lee, 62
Sturgis, Frank, 62
Styron, William, 209
Summers, Anthony, 62, 157
Swindal, James, 62
Szasz, Thomas S., 103
Szulc, Tad, 126

T

Tagg, Carl Francis, 228
Tague, James, 63
Tamana, Tetsuo, 116
Tannenbaum, Robert K., 63, 215
Taylor, Gilbert, 89, 170
Taylor, Warren, 63
Telford, V. Q., 146
Texas School Book Depository,
  63
Texas Theater, 63
Theis, William H., 171
Thomas, D. M., 215
Thomas, Evan, 146, 162, 194
Thomas, J., 209
Thomas, Ralph D., 138–39
Thompson, Josiah, 63, 126, 139,
  146
Thompson, Robert E., 215

Thompson, Thomas, 89
Thompson, William Clifton, 225
Thomson, George C., 114
Thone, Charles, 63
Thornley, Kerry W., 63, 79, 215
Thurston, Wesley S., 215
Tiger, 63
Tillinger, Eugene, 126
Tippit, J. D., 64
Todd, Glenda, 89
Tomlinson, Darrell C., 64
Tonahill, Joe, 64
Toney, John, 64
Tooley, Jo Ann, 146
Toplin, Robert Brent, 190
Towner, James M., 64
Towner, Tina, 198
Trafficante, Santos, 64
Trask, Richard B., 64, 139
Tretick, Stanley, 199
Trevor-Roper, Hugh, 112
Trillin, Calvin, 126
Truels, William P., 157
Truly, Roy S., 64
Tschappat, R., 209
Tuchler, Maier I., 126
Tunheim, John, 64
Tupa, Stefan, 103
Turner, F. M., 64
Turner, Nigel, 64
Turner, Ralph F., 144
Turner, William W., 65, 155, 171
Tuteur, Werner, 103
Tyrrell, R. Emmett, 190

U

Ulam, Adam B., 209
Umbrella Man, 66
Underhill, Gary, 66
Underwood, Anne, 100
Underwood, James R., 66
Ungar, Sanford J., 180
Ushakov, G., 103

V

Van Bemmelen, J. M., 89

Van Buren, Alice, 89
Van Der Karr, Richard, 228
Vanocur, Sander, 201
Varsity, 67
Vaughn, Roy E., 67
Veciana, Antonio, 67
Victoria, 67
Vilnis, Aija, 202
Vinson, Donald E., 89
Viorst, Milton, 162
Vollmann, William T., 89
Volunteer, 67

W

Wade, Henry, 68
Waggoner, Jeffrey, 158
Wainwright, Loudon, 103
Walker, C. T., 68
Walker, Edwin A., 68
Walker, Timothy, 103
Wall, James M., 190
Wallechinsky, David, 207
Walsh, William G., 202
Walther, Carolyn, 68
Walthers, Eddy, 68
Waltz, Jon R., 99
Wand, 68
Ward, Geoffrey C., 90
Ward, Nathan, 171
Wardlaw, Jack, 165
Warner, Ken, 146
Warren Commission, 68
Warren, David M., 215
Warren, Earl, 68
Warrior, 69
Watchman, 69
Waters, Harry F., 191
Watson, Allan C., 126
Webb, Lucas, 216
Weberman, Alan J., 69, 154
Webster, Vanessa L., 195
Wecht, Benjamin, 139
Wecht, Cyril, 69, 139, 147, 162
Wegmann, Edward, 69
Wegmann, William, 69
Wehle, Philip C., 69

Weinreb, Lloyd L., 69
Weisberg, Harold, 69, 114, 139, 158, 166
Weisman, John, 209
Weiss, Mark, 69
Weitzman, Seymour, 69
Wells, Jeffrey, 191
Wells, Thomas, 69
Welsh, David, 103, 162
West, Jessamyn., 90
West, John R., 114
Westbrook, W. R., 70
Weston, James, 70
Whalen, Richard J., 126
Whaley, William W., 70
Wharton, Dennis, 191
Wheeler, Keith, 147
Whitaker, Charles, 180
White, Anthony, 147
White, Jack, 70
White, Ricky, 70
White, Roscoe, 70
White, Stephen, 114
Whitmore, Reed, 209
Wice, Brian, 104
Wicker, Tom, 177, 197
Wiegman, David, 70
Wilber, Charles G., 70, 139, 147
Willens, Howard P., 70
Williams, Bonnie Ray, 70
Williams, Otis, 70
Williamson, Chilton, 126
Willis, Philip L., 71
Willow, 71
Wills, Garry, 71, 100, 104
Wilson, Arthur J., 148
Wing, 71
Wise, Dan, 197
Witt, Louis S., 71
Wolanin, Thomas R., 126
Wolk, Robert L., 90
Woodfield, William Read, 103
Woodward, Mary E., 71
Woolley, Bryan, 216
Worsnop, Richard L., 162
Worthington, Peter, 104

Wright, Frank, 71
Wright, O. P., 71
Wrone, David R., 71, 90, 148,
  224, 226

X

X-100, 72

Y

Yarborough, Ralph W., 73
Yazijian, Harvey, 73, 153
Yefimov, Igor, 158
Young, Roger, 171

Youngblood, Rufus W., 73, 197

Z

Zaid, Mark S., 194
Zaller, Robert, 191
Zapruder Film, 74
Zapruder, Abraham, 74
Zelizer, Barbie, 228
Zimmerman, Paul D., 191
Zirbel, Craig I., 74, 158
Zoglin, Richard, 90, 191

About The Author

WILLIAM E. SCOTT, a history and government teacher at St. Joseph's Preparatory School in Philadelphia, received a B.A. From West Chester University and an M.A. From Villanova University. A member of Phi Alpha Theta, he was honored with the National Broadcasting Company's Teacher of the Year Award in 1989 and the Freedoms Foundation's Teachers Medal in 1991. *November 22, 1963* is his first published work. He currently resides in Clifton Heights, Pennsylvania with his wife Diane.